FRANK LLOYD WRIGHT

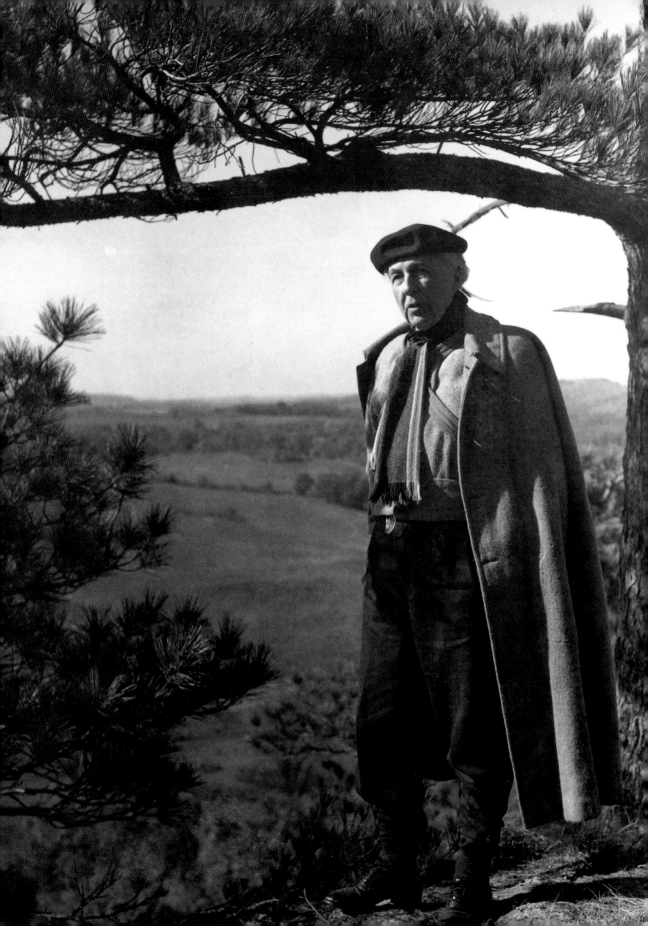

FRANK LLOYD WRIGHT

Text by Bruce Brooks Pfeiffer

Edited by Peter Gössel and Gabriele Leuthäuser

TASCHEN

KÖLN LONDON LOS ANGELES MADRID PARIS TOKYO

FRONT COVER · UMSCHLAGVORDERSEITE · COUVERTURE
Solomon R. Guggenheim Museum in New York
Photo: Ezra Stoller © Esto.
R. Guggenheim Foundation, New York

BACK COVER · UMSCHLAGRÜCKSEITE · DOS
Sketch for the Yahara Boathouse for the University of
Wisconsin Boat Club, Madison, Wisconsin, 1905 (project)

PAGE 2
Frank Lloyd Wright in Taliesin, Spring Green, Wisconsin, 1939

© 2002 TASCHEN GmbH
Hohenzollernring 53, D–50672 Köln
www.taschen.com

Original edition: © 1991 Benedikt Taschen Verlag GmbH
© 1991 Frank Lloyd Wright Foundation, Scottsdale, Arizona

Layout: Gabriele Leuthäuser, Peter Gössel, Nuremberg
Cover design: Angelika Taschen, Claudia Frey, Cologne

German translation: Klaus Reckert, Cologne
French translation: Thérèse Chatelain-Südkamp, Lohmar

Printed in Italy
ISBN 3–8228–2030–X
ISBN 2–7434–4328–6 (Édition réservée pour Maxi-Livres)

CONTENTS

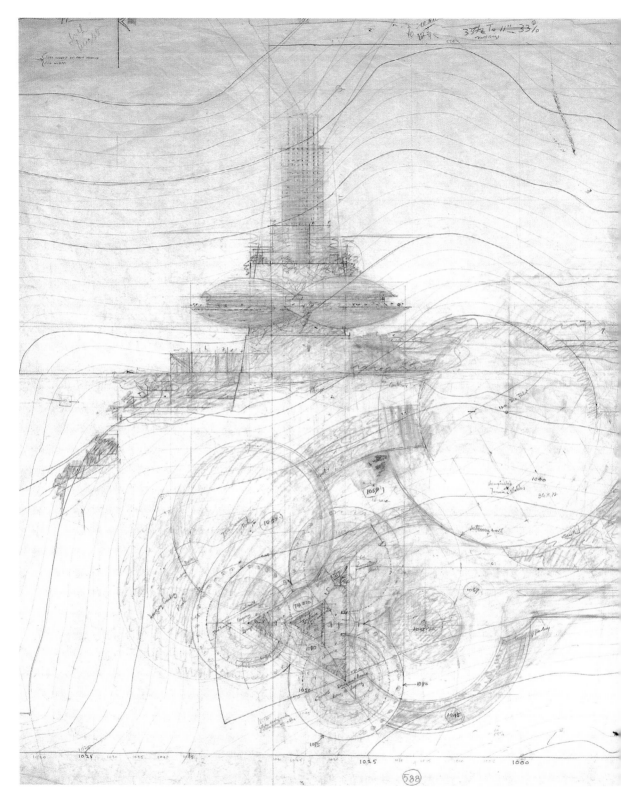

Play Resort, Hollywood, California,
1947 (project)

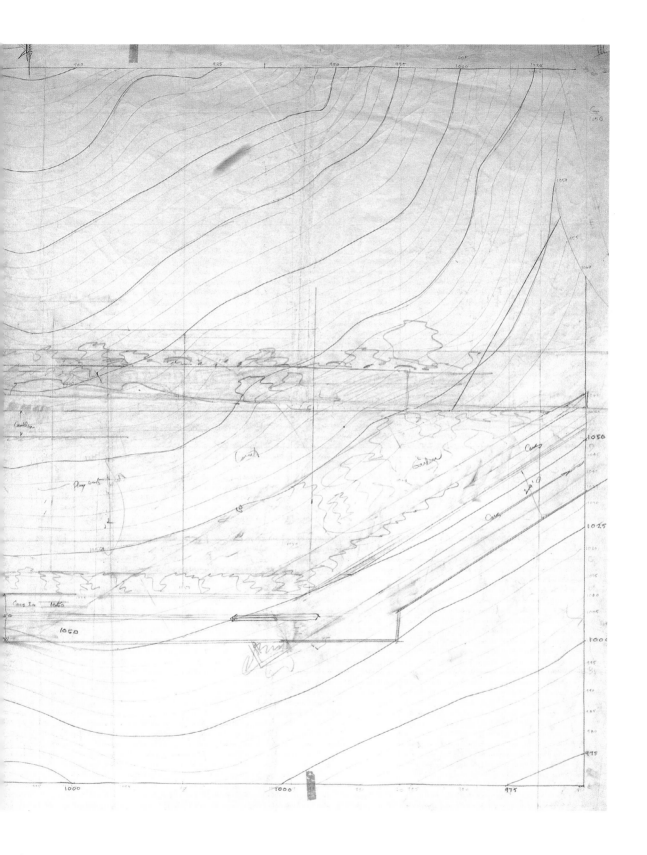

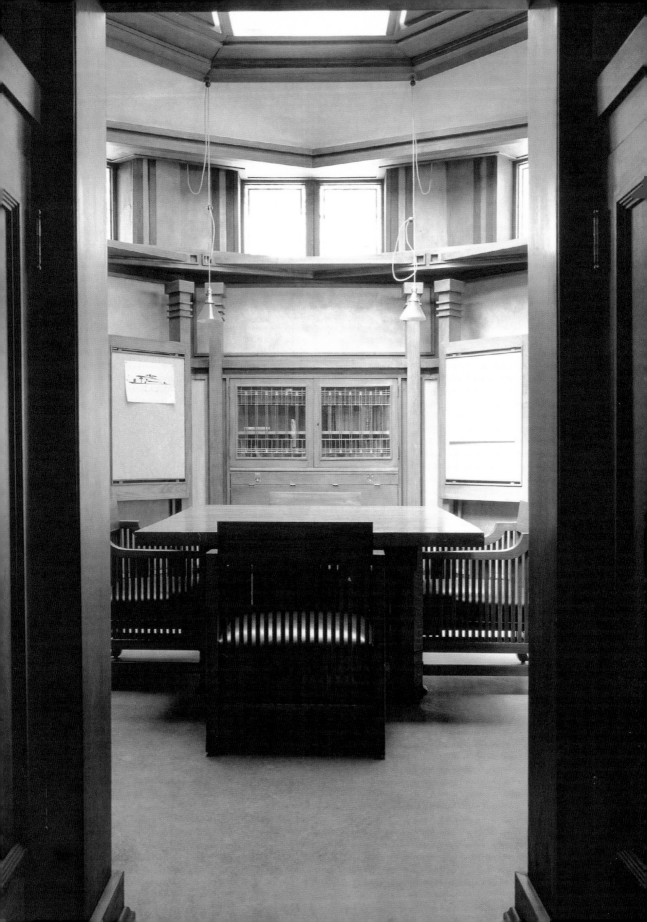

ESSAY

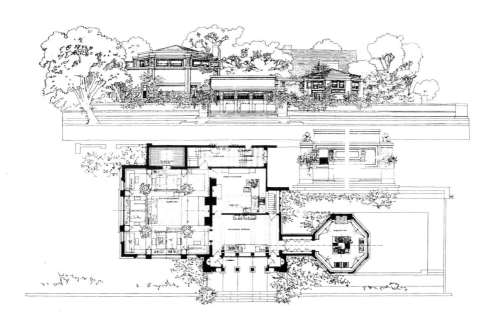

Frank Lloyd Wright Studio, Oak Park,
Illinois, 1895. Interior, presentation
drawing

In 1895, Nathan G. Moore, a prominent Chicago attorney and Oak Park neighbor of architect Frank Lloyd Wright, came into Wright's Schiller Building office and asked him to design a house. He had one important stipulation: »Now we want you to build our house, but I don't want you to give us anything like that house you did for Winslow. I don't want to go down the backstreets to my morning train to avoid being laughed at.«[1] To understand the sensation made by that one home, tucked quietly away in a sedate, wooded suburb, we must consider the architecture in the United States at that time; and in particular, the architecture of Chicago and its environs.

BACKGROUND

The architecture of the United States at the turn of the century – 1895 to 1905 – was, at best, a collection of eclectic styles, with hardly one relating in any way or sense to the ideal of the nation in which it was built. This was an era which regarded architecture as an application of fashions and styles, unrelated to structure or construction techniques. Yet it was also a time when the entire construction industry was undergoing revolutionary changes. New materials were emerging, and new methods of handling the older materials were being developed at the same time. But the architecture being designed reflected little if anything of those new methods and materials.

The Chicago Fair of 1893, the Columbian Exposition, was a supreme case in point. On the one hand, Louis Sullivan claimed that the Exposition »put American architecture behind for at least 50 years«[2]; while on the other hand, Daniel Burnham, a fashionable Chicago architect of the time, lauded the fair as an example of what the Americans would want to build. He told Wright, when urging him to go to the Beaux-Arts in Paris, »The Fair, Frank, is going to have a great nfluence in our country. The American people have seen the Classics on a grand scale for the first time.«[3] The young architect, just starting his own practice with the William Winslow house (and Burnham said of that work: »A gentleman's home, from grade to coping.«) replied, »No, there is Louis Sullivan... And if John Root were alive I don't believe he would feel that way about it. Richardson I am sure never would.« Burnham further argued, »Frank, the Fair should have shown you that Sullivan and Richardson are well enough in their way, but their way won't prevail – architecture is going the other way.«[4] And of course, it was. It is ironical to realize that the date of that architectural disaster of 1893 coincides with the date at which Frank Lloyd Wright opened his private architectural practice, after nearly seven years spent in the office of Adler and Sullivan, in Chicago.

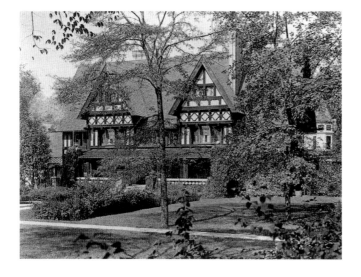

Nathan Moore House, Oak Park,
Illinois, 1895. View

Im Jahr 1895 kam Nathan G. Moore, ein prominenter Chicagoer Rechtsanwalt und Nachbar von Frank Lloyd Wright in Oak Park, in dessen Architekturbüro im Schiller-Gebäude. Er bat ihn, ein Haus zu entwerfen, hatte dabei aber eine wichtige Bedingung: »Wir möchten, daß Sie unser Haus bauen, aber ich möchte nicht, daß Sie uns etwas präsentieren, das auch nur im geringsten an Ihr Haus für Herrn Winslow erinnert. Ich würde nicht gerne morgens über Seitenstraßen zu meinem Zug schleichen müssen, damit man mich nicht auslacht.«[1] Um das Aufsehen verstehen zu können, das durch dieses versteckt in einem stillen, waldigen Vorort liegende Haus erregt wurde, müssen wir uns die Architektur der damaligen Zeit in den Vereinigten Staaten vor Augen führen, vor allem in Chicago und Umgebung.

HINTERGRUND

Um die Jahrhundertwende – die Jahre 1895 bis 1905 – war die Architektur in den Vereinigten Staaten bestenfalls eine Ansammlung eklektischer Stile, von denen kaum einer in irgendeiner Beziehung zu den Ideen und Idealen der Nation stand. Es war eine Ära, in der das Applizieren von Moden und Stilen ohne Bezug zu Bau- und Konstruktionstechniken als Architektur galt. Andererseits war es aber auch eine Zeit, in der sich in der gesamten Bauindustrie radikale Umwälzungen vollzogen. Neue Baumaterialien tauchten auf, und gleichzeitig wurden neue Verarbeitungsmethoden für die älteren Baustoffe entwickelt. Aber in der tatsächlich entworfenen Architektur jener Tage fand sich wenig oder nichts von diesen neuen Methoden und Materialien wieder.

Die große Chicagoer Ausstellung von 1893, die Columbian Exposition, war ein gutes Beispiel für diese Verhältnisse. Einerseits konnte Louis Sullivan behaupten, die Ausstellung werfe »die Architektur in Amerika um mindestens fünfzig Jahre zurück«[2]; zum anderen aber pries der Chicagoer Mode-Architekt der Zeit, Daniel Burnham, die Ausstellung als ein Beispiel dafür, was die Amerikaner gerne bauen würden. Als er Wright drängte, die Beaux-Arts in Paris zu besuchen, sagte er zu ihm: »Frank, die Messe wird großen Einfluß in unserem Land haben. Die Amerikaner haben zum ersten Mal die Klassiker in großem Maßstab gesehen.«[3] Der junge Architekt, der gerade sein eigenes Büro mit dem Auftrag für William Winslow eröffnet hatte (eine Arbeit, über die Burnham urteilte: »Das Haus eines Gentleman, vom Fundament bis zur Mauerkappe«), antwortete:»Nein, denn schließlich gibt es Louis Sullivan ... Und wenn John Root noch lebte, glaube ich nicht, daß er wie du darüber denken würde. Richardson täte es mit Sicherheit nicht.« Burnham argumentierte weiter:

En 1895, Nathan G. Moore, avocat éminent de Chicago et voisin de l'architecte Frank Lloyd Wright à Oak Park, se rendit au bureau de Wright, au Schiller Building, et lui demanda de lui établir les plans pour une maison. Il posait toutefois une condition importante: »Nous voulons que ce soit vous qui construisiez notre maison, mais je ne désire rien qui ressemble à celle de M. Winslow. Le matin, quand je vais prendre mon train, je ne veux pas être obligé de passer par les petites rues afin d'éviter les moqueries.«[1] Si l'on veut comprendre l'effet produit par cette maison, blottie tranquillement au fond d'une banlieue calme et boisée, il faut se pencher sur l'architecture des Etats-Unis à cette époque, et en particulier sur l'architecture de Chicago et de ses environs.

ORIGINES

Autour de 1900 – de 1895 à 1905 –, l'architecture des Etats-Unis était, au mieux, un assemblage de styles éclectiques, ne se rapportant sous aucun point de vue, ni en aucune façon, aux idéaux de la nation. C'était une époque qui considérait l'architecture comme une mise en pratique des idées en vogue et des styles, sans se soucier des techniques de construction. Néanmoins, c'était aussi une époque où l'industrie du bâtiment tout entière connaissait des changements révolutionnaires. De nouveaux matériaux faisaient leur apparition et, parallèlement, de nouvelles méthodes étaient mises au point afin de travailler les anciens matériaux. Toutefois, l'architecture telle qu'elle était pratiquée ne reflétait que modérément la découverte de ces nouvelles méthodes et de ces nouveaux matériaux.

L'exposition de Chicago en 1893, la Columbian Exposition, fut un cas d'espèce suprême. D'un côté, Louis Sullivan affirmait que l'exposition »faisait revenir l'architecture américaine à au moins 50 ans en arrière«[2], tandis que de l'autre côté, Daniel Burnham, architecte de Chicago en vogue à l'époque, louait l'exposition qui était l'exemple de ce que les Américains voulaient construire. Quand il encouragea Wright à aller aux Beaux-Arts de Paris, il lui dit: »L'exposition, Frank, va avoir une grande influence dans notre pays. Pour la première fois, les Américains ont vu les œuvres classiques à une grande échelle.«[3] Le jeune architecte, qui venait juste de se faire une clientèle avec la maison William Winslow (et dont Burnham disait: »Une vraie maison de gentleman, du palier au chaperon«) répondit: »Non, il y a Louis Sullivan ... Et si John Root était encore en vie, je ne crois pas qu'il penserait ainsi. Quant à Richardson, je suis sûr que cela ne sera jamais son avis.« Burnham continuait: »Frank, l'exposition a bien dû te montrer

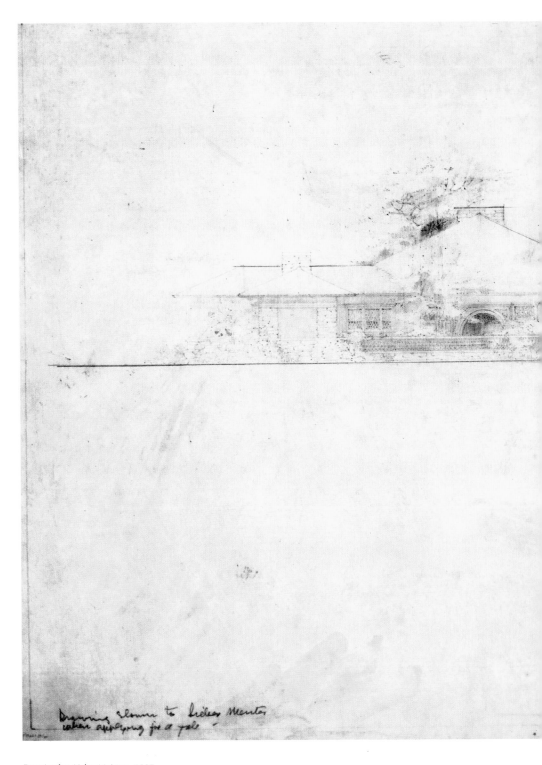

Drawing for »Lieber Meister«, 1887

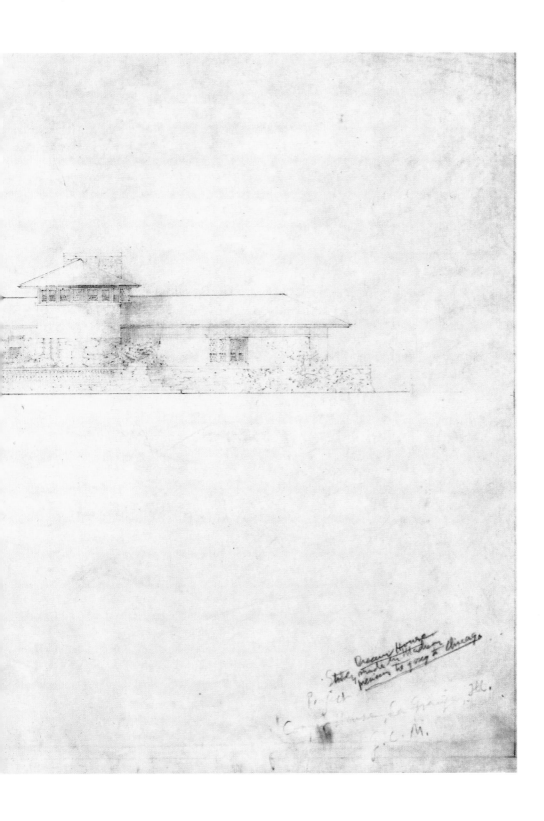

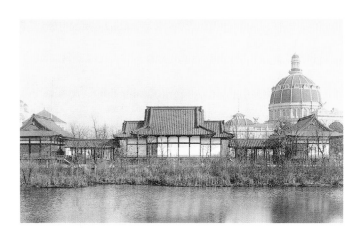

The Ho-o-den Temple at the World's Columbian Exposition, Chicago, Illinois, 1893

Richardson, Sullivan and Wright. The progression of these three architects has been cited over and over again as the progression of an American architecture from classicism towards a new ideal. Richardson was certainly steeped in a Romanesque tradition, but his work still bears a remarkably masculine, truly American, virility and strength of its own. Sullivan, the poet, the designing partner of the Chicago firm Adler and Sullivan, made the tall building truly tall, not just piling up massive masonry boxes. In his work, the tall, long, accentuated vertical line gave birth to the true aesthetic expression of the skyscraper.

Both Richardson and Sullivan were educated, urbane and highly sophisticated. Both attended school on the East coast, both went to Paris to the Ecole des Beaux-Arts. None of this was the case with Wright. His background, by contrast, was steeped in strong Unitarian, transcendental principles. He was raised in a rather poor family, his father a minister and music teacher, his mother a teacher. He spent his younger boyhood on his uncle's farm in southwestern Wisconsin. His surroundings were pastoral, educational, agricultural and strongly Welsh. On his mother's side he was descended from ministers, farmers and educators, who came to the New World in 1844 from Wales. He grew up in their ancestral valley, and it was to that valley that he returned, after leaving wife and family behind in Oak Park, to build his own home, Taliesin, at the age of 44.

Combined with this ancestral background and through the influence of his mother he was brought up on the writings and teachings of such Americans as Whitman, Thoreau and Emerson, combined with Byron, Shelley and Blake. He soon learned to read and absorb Schiller and Goethe; on the trolley to school he carried a pocket version of Shakespeare's plays and sonnets. He was steeped in music, especially Bach and Beethoven, due to the daily influence of his father, who played Bach chorales on the organ in church (the young Frank confined to pumping the bellows) and in the evening Beethoven sonatas on the piano at home. »I fell asleep night after night to strains of Beethoven sonatas all throughout my early childhood«, Wright admitted.

Now, at the same time that he was immersed in these influences of literature, poetry, philosophy and music, he was also right in the middle of the Industrial Revolution. This should have fostered in him irreconcilable conflicts both in purpose and in ethics, but it did not. In fact, it was this combination that made him the person he was and the architect he became. The Industrial Revolution gave him the tools he needed to build the buildings his fertile imagination created; the transcendental background posited in him an abiding

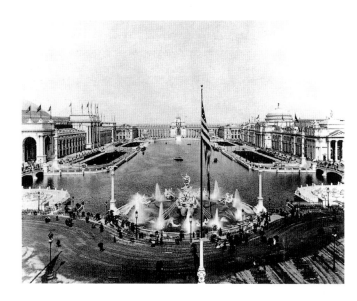

General view of the World's Columbian Exposition, 1893

»Frank, die Messe hätte dir zeigen sollen, daß Sullivan und Richardson zwar ganz gut in ihrer Art sind, daß sich aber ihr Weg nicht durchsetzen wird – die Architektur entwickelt sich in die andere Richtung.«[4] Und natürlich tat sie genau das. Es liegt eine Ironie darin, daß das Datum dieses architektonischen Desasters von 1893 mit dem Datum zusammenfällt, an dem Frank Lloyd Wright nach fast sieben Jahren im Büro von Adler und Sullivan sein eigenes Architekturbüro in Chicago eröffnete.

Richardson, Sullivan und Wright: die Entwicklung dieser drei Architekten ist immer wieder als die Entwicklung der amerikanischen Architektur vom Klassizismus zu einem neuen Ideal angeführt worden. Richardson war sicherlich zutiefst von der romantischen Tradition beeinflußt, doch seine Arbeiten lassen dennoch eine ganz eigene, sehr männliche und sehr amerikanische Kraft erkennen. Sullivan, der »Poet« und entwerfende Partner der Chicagoer Firma Adler und Sullivan, machte aus einem Hochhaus mehr als nur einen Stapel wuchtiger Mauerwürfel. Mit seinem schlanken, hochaufragenden, die Vertikale betonenden Entwürfen schuf er den wahren ästhetischen Gestus des Wolkenkratzers.

Sowohl Richardson wie Sullivan waren gebildet, weltmännisch und hoch kultiviert. Beide hatten Schulen an der Ostküste besucht, beide gingen nach Paris an die Ecole des Beaux-Arts. Nichts davon trifft auf Wright zu. Sein Hintergrund war, ganz im Gegenteil, von starken unitarischen, transzendentalen Prinzipien geprägt. Er wuchs in einer eher armen Familie auf. Der Vater war Pfarrer und Musiklehrer, die Mutter Lehrerin. Seine frühe Jugend verbrachte er auf der Farm seines Onkels im Südwesten von Wisconsin. Das Umfeld dort war ländlich, bäuerlich und ausgesprochen walisisch. Von mütterlicher Seite her stammte er von Geistlichen, Bauern und Lehrern ab, die 1844 aus Wales in die Neue Welt gekommen waren. Er wuchs in ihrem heimatlichen Tal auf, und es war auch dieses Tal, in das er zurückkehrte, nachdem er seine Frau und seine Familie in Oak Park zurückgelassen hatte, um mit 44 Jahren sein eigenes Haus »Taliesin« zu bauen.

Zu diesem ererbten Hintergrund wurde Wright durch den Einfluß seiner Mutter mit den Schriften und Lehren von Whitman, Thoreau und Emerson vertraut gemacht. Hinzu kamen Byron, Shelly und Blake. Bald lernte er, Schiller und Goethe zu lesen und aufzunehmen; für die Fahrt zur Schule nahm er eine Taschenbuchausgabe von Shakespeares Stücken und Sonetten mit. Durch seinen Vater, der tagsüber Bach-Choräle auf der Kirchenorgel spielte (wozu der kleine Frank die Bälge treten mußte) und abends Beethoven-Sonaten auf dem häuslichen Klavier, war er von Mu-

que Sullivan et Richardson sont certes assez bons dans leur genre, mais que celui-ci ne prédominera pas – l'architecture va prendre une autre direction.«[4] Et c'est ce qu'elle fit, bien sûr. Il est ironique de constater que la date de ce désastre architectural de 1893 coïncide avec la date à laquelle Frank Lloyd Wright ouvrit son cabinet privé d'architecture, après avoir travaillé pendant sept ans chez Adler et Sullivan à Chicago.

Richardson, Sullivan et Wright. La progression de ces trois architectes a été maintes et maintes fois citée comme la progression d'une architecture américaine, partant du Classicisme pour se diriger vers un nouvel idéal. Richardson était certainement imbibé d'une tradition romane, mais son travail présentait pourtant une virilité et une force remarquables, tout à fait américaines, qui lui étaient propres. Sullivan, le »poète«, qui était dessinateur et associé de l'agence Adler et Sullivan, faisait ses hauts immeubles vraiment hauts et ne se contentait pas d'empiler des blocs massifs de maçonnerie. C'est dans son travail que la haute ligne verticale, longue et accentuée, donna naissance à l'expression esthétique de gratte-ciel.

Richardson et Sullivan étaient tous deux instruits, courtois et avaient des goûts très raffinés. Ils avaient fait leur scolarité sur la Côte est et étaient allés à Paris pour étudier à l'Ecole des Beaux-Arts. Il n'en était pas de même pour Wright. Son milieu était imprégné des sévères principes transcendantaux de l'Unitarisme. Il grandit dans une famille plutôt pauvre, son père était pasteur et professeur de musique, sa mère enseignante. Il passa sa première jeunesse à la ferme de son oncle, dans le sud-ouest du Wisconsin. Son entourage se composait de pasteurs, d'enseignants, d'agriculteurs et de Gallois convaincus. Du côté de sa mère, il descendait en effet de pasteurs, d'agriculteurs et d'enseignants qui quittèrent en 1844 le Pays de Galles pour s'établir dans le Nouveau Monde. Il passa sa jeunesse dans la vallée de ses ancêtres. A l'âge de 44 ans, c'est là qu'il se rendit, après avoir laissé sa femme et sa famille à Oak Park, pour construire sa propre maison Taliesin.

Ses origines ancestrales ainsi que l'influence maternelle orientèrent son éducation. Il fut élevé selon les écrits et les enseignements d'Américains comme Whitman, Thoreau et Emerson et de Britanniques comme Byron, Shelley et Blake. Il apprit très tôt à lire et se plongea dans les oeuvres de Schiller et de Goethe; dans le chariot l'amenant à l'école, il portait sur lui une édition de poche des pièces et sonnets de Shakespeare. Il était saturé de musique, surtout de Bach et de Beethoven, à cause de l'influence quotidienne de son père qui jouait à l'église les chorals de Bach (le jeune Frank devait actionner la soufflerie de

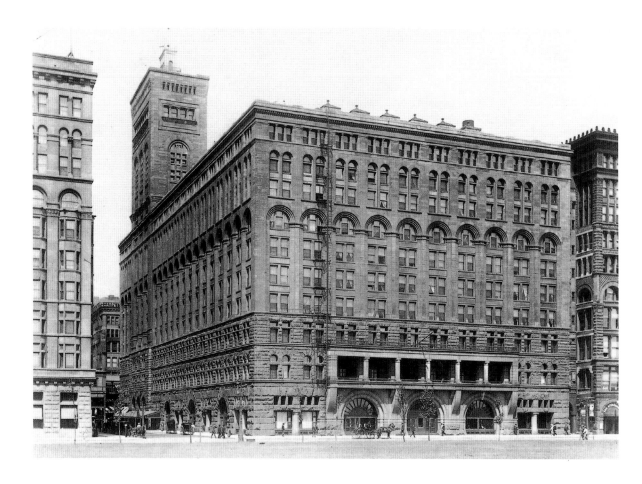

Dankmar Adler and Louis H. Sullivan,
Auditorium Building, Chicago, Illinois,
1886–1889

James Charnley House, Chicago,
Illinois, 1891–1892 (Opposite page)

sense of human values. Here we have a striking paradox: industrial tools and methods, human values and a deep love for nature. Both elements were essential to his work; he could not envision the one without the other.

He claimed that it was his mother who determined his profession, that while carrying him, she determined that the child she was to bear would be a son, who would grow to be a great architect. She nurtured his early childhood based on that conviction. She surrounded him with natural beauty, she discovered the Kindergarten Gifts of Friedrich Froebel and brought them home to her son. He took to the Gifts with a passion. When his mother realized that drawing and designing were becoming his one consuming interest, she believed it was time to introduce another, counterbalancing, factor in his early training. Consulting with her brother James Lloyd Jones, a farmer living in the family valley nearby, it was decided to send the boy to work on the farm during the summers.

A great part of his own autobiography is concerned, in the story of his early years, not with his education in school, but his education at work on the farm.

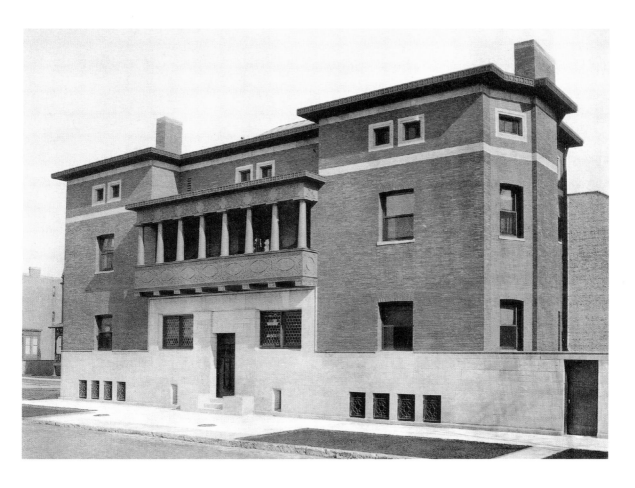

sik besonders dieser beiden Komponisten umgeben. »Meine ganze frühe Kindheit hindurch bin ich Nacht für Nacht mit den Melodien von Beethoven-Sonaten eingeschlafen«, erklärte Wright.

Während ihn nun einerseits Literatur, Dichtung, Philosophie und Musik formten, erlebte er doch gleichzeitig auch die industrielle Revolution. Dies hätte leicht zu unauflösbaren inneren Konflikten der Ideale und der Moral führen können. Aber das geschah nicht. Tatsächlich machte ihn diese Kombination zu der Persönlichkeit, die er war, und zu dem Architekten, der er wurde. Die industrielle Revolution gab ihm die nötigen Hilfsmittel, um die Gebäude zu erbauen, die seine fruchtbare Phantasie schuf; der transzendentale Hintergrund verankerte in ihm einen bleibenden Sinn für menschliche Werte. Dies ist ein auffallendes Paradoxon: industrielle Werkzeuge und Methoden, menschliche Werte und eine tiefe Liebe zur Natur. Beide Elemente waren wesentlich für sein Schaffen; er konnte sich das eine nicht ohne das andere vorstellen.

Wright behauptete, es sei seine Mutter gewesen, die seinen künftigen Beruf festgelegt habe. Während sie

l'orgue) et exécutait au piano des sonates de Beethoven, le soir à la maison. »Pendant toute ma petite enfance, je m'endormis, soir après soir, sur les accords des sonates de Beethoven« reconnut Wright.

Toutefois, à l'époque où il se plongeait dans la littérature, la poésie, la philosophie et la musique, la révolution industrielle était à son apogée. Ceci aurait pu susciter chez lui des conflits quant à la finalité et l'éthique. Ce ne fut pas le cas. En fait, ce sont ces circonstances qui firent de lui l'homme qu'il était et l'architecte qu'il devint. La révolution industrielle lui donna les outils dont il avait besoin pour construire les bâtiments conçus dans son imagination fertile; son éducation lui fournit un sens durable des valeurs humaines. Nous avons ici un paradoxe frappant: d'un côté les outils et les méthodes industrielles, de l'autre les valeurs humaines et un profond amour de la nature. Ces deux composantes étaient essentielles pour son travail; il ne pouvait pas envisager l'une sans l'autre.

Il affirmait que c'était sa mère qui avait décidé sa profession. Lors de sa grossesse, elle fut convaincue qu'elle donnerait naissance à un fils et qu'il devien-

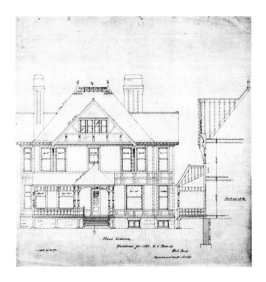

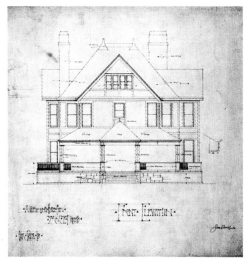

Elevations of the C.E. Roberts House, by Burnham (above) and Wright (below), 1896

Those boyhood experiences had rooted deeply values and memories of so strong a nature, sometimes so heartbreaking and backbreaking, that his own recollection, 54 years later, prompted him to regard those years as his most formative.

Hardly off the farm and past his boyhood years, he enrolled as a special student in the University of Wisconsin School of Engineering, but grew dissatisfied and after a short term ran away to Chicago to pursue a life in architecture. But before leaving Madison, Wisconsin, he witnessed the collapse of the new north wing of the old State Capitol building, then in construction. The contractor saw no fault in filling the cores of the new massive hollow piers with broken bricks and stones during construction, and the added weight proved too much: the piers gave way one summer afternoon and the structure collpsed. Workmen trapped in the building were crushed to death as floors collapsed and pinned them in. Throughout the afternoon and evening rescuers dug bodies of wounded, dying and dead out of the debris. Standing nearby was the young Wright. »The youth stayed for hours, clinging to the iron fence that surrounded the park, too heartsick to move – to go away. The horror of that scene has never entirely left his consciousness and remains to prompt him to this day«[5], he wrote.

In Chicago, after taking jobs at other architectural firms, Wright was encouraged to try for a job with Louis Sullivan, engaged at that time with the design of the Chicago Auditorium, and desperately in need of designers to assist him. With Adler and Sullivan for nearly seven years, Wright quit, following a heated disagreement with Sullivan over the terms of his contract (he was building ›boot-leg‹ houses on his own time). He set up his own practice in the Schiller Building, built by Adler and Sullivan, and into his office came his first client, William H. Winslow, of River Forest, Illinois.

THE PRAIRIE HOUSES

The »prairie house« has come to mean, in recent years, a certain type of residential design employed by Wright during the years 1900 to 1911. Wright himself did not use the term »prairie house«, rather he spoke and wrote of the type of dwelling he thought most appropriate to the Midwest prairie around Chicago and its suburbs. »We of the Middle West«, he wrote in the March 1908 issue of *Architectural Record*, »are living on the prairie. The prairie has a beauty of its own and we should recognize and accentuate this natural beauty, its quiet level. Hence, gently sloping roofs, low proportions, quiet sky lines, suppressed heavy-set chimneys and sheltering overhangs, low terraces and out-reaching walls seques-

mit ihm schwanger gewesen sei, habe sie bestimmt, das Kind werde ein Junge und später einmal ein großer Architekt. Sie prägte seine frühe Kindheit durch diese Überzeugung. Sie umgab ihn mit natürlicher Schönheit, und als sie das Kindergarten-Spielzeug von Friedrich Froebel entdeckte, kaufte sie es ihrem Sohn, der sich begeistert damit beschäftigte. Als die Mutter bemerkte, daß Zeichnen und Entwerfen die einzigen, alles andere überdeckenden Interessen ihres Kindes zu werden drohten, hielt sie es für richtig, einen ausgleichenden Faktor in seine Schulung einzuführen. In Absprache mit ihrem Bruder James Lloyd Jones, einem Farmer, der im nahe gelegenen Tal der Vorfahren wohnte, wurde beschlossen, daß der Junge während der Sommermonate dort arbeiten sollte.

Ein Großteil von Wrights Autobiographie beschäftigt sich – wenn es um die früheren Jahre geht – mit seiner Ausbildung nicht in der Schule, sondern durch die Arbeit auf der Farm. Diese Kindheitserfahrungen bildeten tief verwurzelte Einschätzungen und Erinnerungen. Sie waren so eindringlich, manchmal auch so herzzerreißend und hart, daß er sie im Rückblick 54 Jahre später noch als die Jahre seines Lebens ansah, die ihn am meisten geformt hatten.

Kaum der Farm und dem Knabenalter entwachsen, schrieb er sich als Student an der Fachhochschule für Ingenieurwissenschaften von Wisconsin ein, war aber unzufrieden und brach wenig später nach Chicago auf, um sich eine Existenz als Architekt aufzubauen. Aber bevor er Madison, Wisconsin, verließ, wurde er noch Zeuge, wie der damals gerade im Bau befindliche neue Nordflügel des altehrwürdigen State-Capitol-Gebäudes einstürzte. Der ausführende Unternehmer hielt es für vertretbar, die Hohlräume der neuen, wuchtigen Stützpfeiler während der Bauarbeiten mit zerbrochenen Ziegeln und Steinen zu füllen, doch das zusätzliche Gewicht war zuviel. An einem Sommernachmittag gaben die Pfeiler nach, und das Bauwerk stürzte ein. Im Gebäude eingeschlossene Arbeiter wurden von berstenden Zwischendecken zermalmt. Den ganzen Nachmittag und Abend lang bargen Rettungsmannschaften Verletzte, Sterbende und Tote aus den Trümmern. Dicht dabei stand der junge Frank Lloyd Wright. »Der junge Mann stand dort stundenlang an den Eisenzaun geklammert, der den Park umgab; zu betroffen, um wegzugehen. Der Schrecken dieser Szenerie hat sein Bewußtsein nie mehr ganz verlassen und bewegt ihn bis zum heutigen Tage«,[5] wie er später schrieb.

In Chicago wurde Wright dann ermutigt, sich bei Louis Sullivan um eine Stellung zu bewerben, nachdem er dort schon bei verschiedenen anderen Architekturfirmen gearbeitet hatte. Sullivan war damals

drait un grand architecte. Pendant sa première enfance, il fut élevé avec cette conviction. Elle l'entoura des beautés de la nature, elle découvrit les jeux éducatifs du jardin d'enfants de Friedrich Froebel et les amena à la maison pour son fils. Ces jeux le passionnèrent. Lorsque sa mère remarqua qu'il nourrissait un amour dévorant et exclusif pour le dessin et le design, elle pensa qu'il était temps de contrebalancer cet intérêt en introduisant un autre facteur dans son premier apprentissage. Après avoir consulté son frère James Lloyd Jones, qui possèdait tout près une ferme dans la vallée de leurs ancêtres, elle décida d'envoyer son fils travailler à la ferme pendant tous les étés.

Dans l'histoire de sa jeunesse, une grande partie de sa propre biographie est consacrée non pas à son éducation scolaire mais à ce qu'il apprit en travaillant à la ferme. Ces expériences de jeune garçon étaient des valeurs et des souvenirs profondément ancrés. Ils étaient si puissants, et parfois si déchirants et si éreintants, que, 54 ans plus tard, sa propre mémoire l'incitait à considérer ces années comme étant les plus instructives.

Lorsque les années de ferme furent écoulées et qu'il sortit de l'adolescence, il s'inscrivit comme externe à l'Ecole d'ingénieurs de l'Université du Wisconsin. De plus en plus insatisfait, il s'enfuit peu après à Chicago afin de poursuivre sa vocation d'architecte. Mais avant de quitter Madison, dans le Wisconsin, il fut témoin de l'effondrement de la nouvelle aile nord de l'ancien State Capitol, qui se trouvait alors en reconstruction. L'entrepreneur de bâtiments n'avait pas pensé à mal lorsqu'il avait fait remplir, pendant la construction, l'intérieur des piliers avec des gravats de briques et de pierres. Cette charge supplémentaire s'avéra trop lourde: un été, les piliers cédèrent et l'édifice s'écroula. Des travailleurs pris au piège dans le bâtiment moururent écrasés lorsque les étages s'effondrèrent sur eux. Pendant toute l'après-midi et toute la soirée, des sauveteurs sortirent des décombres les corps des blessés, des agonisants et des morts. Le jeune Wright se tenait à proximité. »Il resta immobile pendant des heures, s'accrochant à la grille de fer qui entourait le parc, trop bouleversé pour pouvoir bouger – pour s'en aller. L'horreur de cette scène n'a jamais complètement disparu de son esprit et elle continue à le hanter jusqu'à aujourd'hui«, écrivit-il.[5]

Après quelques emplois dans d'autres agences d'architecture à Chicago, Wright se décida à collaborer avec Louis Sullivan qui s'occupait à l'époque du projet de l'Auditorium de Chicago et cherchait désespérément des dessinateurs pour l'assister. Après presque sept ans passés chez Adler et Sullivan, Wright

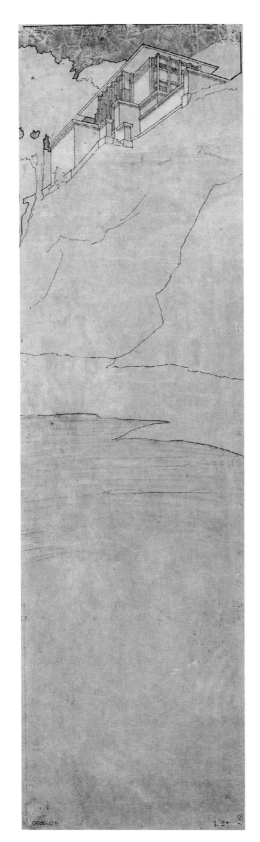

Thomas P. Hardy
House, Racine,
Wisconsin, 1905
Perspective

tering private gardens.« And later in *An Autobiography*, first published in 1932, he revealed, »I loved the prairie by instinct as great simplicity – the trees, the flowers, the sky itself, thrilling by contrast. I saw that a little of height on the prairie was enough to look like much more – every detail as to height becoming intensely significant, breadths all falling short... I had an idea that the horizontal planes in buildings belong to the ground. I began putting this idea to work.«[6]

That quality of the broad, extended horizontal line, the low proportions associated closely with the ground, the broad overhangs and gently sloping roofs are the distinctive features which characterize his early domestic architecture. But behind those exterior features a whole new language of architecture was being born. It did not happen overnight, and following the Winslow house of 1893 it took almost seven years for the ideas and forms to evolve.

The first step in this direction developed quite naturally in the plan of the home: more open spaces, screened off from one another by simple architectural devices rather than partitions and doors. This eventually came to be known as the »open plan«. The integration of the building with its natural site was another development. Those earlier houses were in suburbs, when suburbs were sparsely populated, the landscaping equally sparse. Wright believed that on this flat, extended prairie it was desirable to get up off the ground to provide a wider outlook. For that reason he raised the basement floor to ground level, letting it serve as a pedestal for the main floor above. In elevation he began to see the walls of the house more as screens, the walls rising directly from the base or water table, the second story windows a continuous band beneath the eaves. The cement stucco of the extended eaves was painted a light color, which brought reflected light into rooms that would otherwise have been dark. The open-swinging window, as opposed to the double hung or »guillotine« window let more air into the rooms, the window openings were protected against sun and wind by the overhanging eaves. In this use of materials, he advised the application of a mono-material rather than the conglomerate fashionable at the time. Cement stucco houses were cement stucco throughout, accented by wood trim. The same applied to brick masonry. If there was a combination of materials, such as brick and stucco, it was kept consistent throughout the elevation of the building, all in an attempt to achieve repose and simplicity.

The handling and developing of all these elements expanded and grew from the early houses such as Bradley, Dana and Willits to the later ones, such as

mit dem Entwurf des Chicago Auditorium beschäftigt und suchte händeringend Zeichner, die ihm assistieren konnten. Sieben Jahren bei Adler und Sullilvan, kündigte Wright nach einem hitzigen Streit über die Konditionen seines Arbeitsvertrages (er baute in seiner Freizeit auf eigene Rechnung) und eröffnete ein eigenes Büro im von Adler und Sullivan gebauten Schiller-Gebäude. Mit William H. Winslow aus River Forrest, Illinois, hatte er schon bald seinen ersten Kunden.

DIE PRÄRIEHÄUSER

Mit »Prāriehaus« bezeichnet man inzwischen einen bestimmten Haustyp, den Wright zwischen 1900 und 1911 entwickelte. Wright selbst benutzte den Begriff »Prāriehaus« nicht, er sprach und schrieb vielmehr über die Art des Wohnens, die er für die Prärie des Mittelwestens um Chicago und seine Vororte als am passendsten ansah. »Wir im Mittleren Westen«, schrieb er im Märzheft der Zeitschrift Architectural Record 1908, »leben in der Prärie. Die Prärie hat eine ganz eigene Schönheit. Wir sollten diese natürliche Schönheit, die ruhige Weite erkennen und betonen. Daher die flach geneigten Dächer, die niedrigen Proportionen, die ruhigen Silhouetten, die gedrungenen, massigen Kamine und schützenden Überstände, die niedrig gesetzten Terrassen und die vorgezogenen Mauern, die kleine Gärten abgrenzen.« Und später, in seiner 1932 erstmals veröffentlichten Autobiographie, offenbarte er: »Ich liebte die Prärie in ihrer großartigen Schlichtheit instinktiv – die Bäume, die Blumen, der Himmel selbst, ein erregender Kontrast. Ich sah, daß schon eine geringe Höhe in der Prärie sehr groß erscheint – jedes aufragende Bauteil eine enorme Bedeutung erhielt und die Breite weniger wichtig wurde ... Ich hatte die Vorstellung, daß die horizontalen Flächen der Häuser zum Erdboden gehören. Ich begann, diese Idee umzusetzen.«[6] Die langgestreckte, breit gelagerte Horizontale, die niedrigen, eng mit dem Boden verbundenen Volumen, die weiten Überstände und flach geneigten Dächer sind die herausragenden Merkmale, die Wrights frühe Hausentwürfe charakterisieren. Aber hinter diesen äußerlichen Merkmalen war eine gänzlich neue Architektursprache im Entstehen. Das geschah nicht über Nacht, und nach dem Haus Winslow 1893 dauerte es noch fast sieben Jahre, bis diese Ideen und Formen vollständig entfaltet waren.

Der erste Schritt in diese Richtung entwickelte sich völlig natürlich aus dem Grundriß des Hauses: offene Räume, eher durch einfache architektonische Kunstgriffe als durch Zwischenwände und Türen voneinander getrennt. Dies wurde in der Folge als »offener Grundriß« bekannt. Die Integration des Gebäudes in

donna sa démission à la suite d'un différend avec Sullivan portant sur les termes de son contrat (il construisait des maisons »clandestines« pendant ses heures de libre). Il ouvrit son propre cabinet dans le Schiller Building, immeuble construit par Adler et Sullivan, et son premier client fut William H. Winslow, de River Forest, Illinois.

LES »PRAIRIE HOUSES«

Depuis quelques temps, la »Prairie House« désigne l'architecture d'habitation réalisée par Wright de 1900 à 1911. Wright lui-même n'employait pas ce terme. Il parlait plutôt du type d'habitation qui semblait convenir le mieux à la Prairie du Midwest, qui s'étend autour de Chicago et de sa banlieue. En mars 1908, il écrivait dans un numéro du Architectural Record: »Nous, les habitants du Middle West, nous vivons dans la Prairie. La Prairie possède une beauté qui lui est propre. Nous devons reconnaître et accentuer cette beauté naturelle, son étendue tranquille. A l'aide de toits à douce inclinaison, de constructions basses, de silhouettes calmes, de cheminées larges et massives et de saillies, à l'aide de terrasses basses, de murs en prolongation des maisons et entourant les jardins individuels.« Dans Une Autobiographie, publiée pour la première fois en 1932, il révélait: »J'aimais la Prairie d'instinct, pour sa grande simplicité – les arbres, les fleurs, le ciel lui-même, formaient un contraste saisissant. Je m'aperçus qu'une petite hauteur était suffisante pour que les choses paraissent tout de suite plus grandes – chaque détail devenait plus important, tout devenait moins large. J'eus l'idée que les plans horizontaux dans les bâtiments appartenaient au sol. Je commençais à concrétiser cette idée.«[6]

Cette silhouette large et prolongée, les proportions basses étroitement associées au sol, les larges saillies et les toits à pente douce sont les traits distinctifs qui caractérisent sa première architecture d'habitation. Toutefois, derrière ces traits extérieurs, un tout nouveau langage d'architecture faisait son apparition. Cela ne se fit pas du jour au lendemain et après la construction de la maison Winslow en 1893, il fallut attendre presque sept ans pour que idées et formes se développent pleinement.

Le premier pas dans cette direction se fit au niveau du plan de la maison: des espaces ouverts délimités les uns des autres par de simples artifices architecturaux, plutôt que séparés par des murs et des portes. Ceci fut connu par la suite sous le nom de »plan ouvert«. Un autre développement consista à intégrer le bâtiment à son site naturel. Ces premières maisons étaient situées dans la banlieue, à une époque où celle-ci était peu peuplée et où le paysage était pauvrement amé-

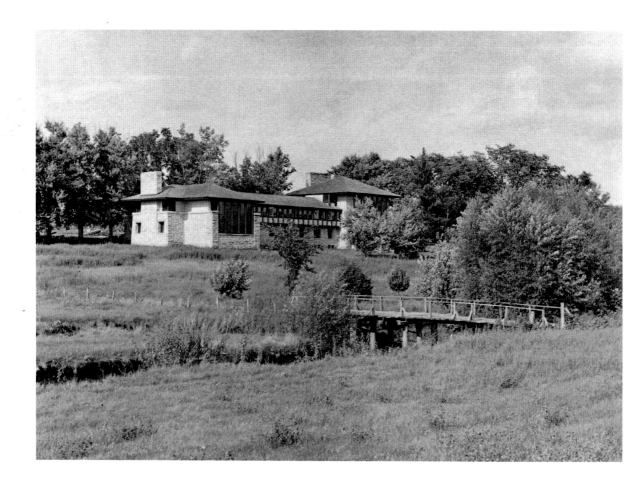

Hillside Home School, Spring Green,
Wisconsin, 1902

Frank Lloyd Wright in his workroom at
Taliesin East, 1956

Martin, Coonley and Robie. But from first to last, they
were all conceived as homes for the prairie, and
although they fall into different design types, this one
common denominator – the Midwest prairie – groups
them together despite their individual differences.

THE SPACE WITHIN

All along, in the »prairie houses«, Wright's concept
of interior space was becoming more and more the
significiant feature of the building. It grew slowly,
and he pointed out the living room of the Hillside
Home School, 1902, as a significant step in that
direction. The four large stone columns that carry the
balcony around the living room are placed in from
the window edge, the balcony itself is also in from the
tall windows that run unimpeded from sill to soffit
above. In this Hillside living room it is evident that the
window walls are non-supporting screens, supports
for the structure being placed in from the edge. The
designs for the Larkin Building, in Buffalo, New York,
and Unity Temple, in Oak Park, Illinois, soon followed. While Wright was at work on the Larkin commission, a plaster model of the building was made

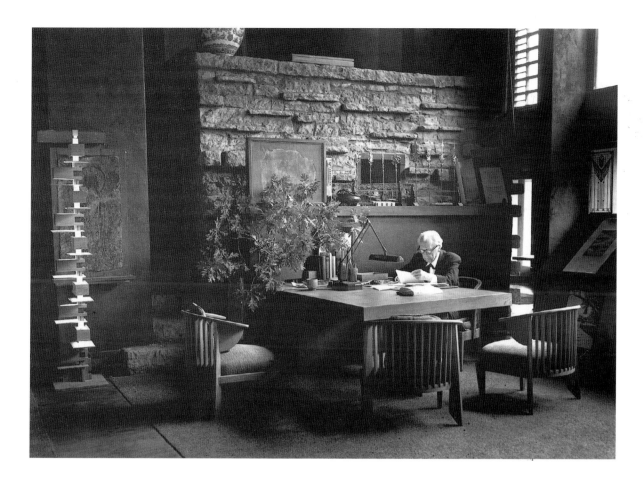

das Gelände war eine weitere Entwicklung. Wrights frühe Häuser entstanden in Vororten, zu einer Zeit, als diese noch spärlich bewohnt waren und auch die Landschaft noch nicht so stark zersiedelt war. Er war überzeugt, daß es in dieser ebenen, weiten Prärielandschaft erstrebenswert sei, vom Erdboden »wegzukommen«, um so eine bessere Sicht zu erzielen. Deshalb hob er das Kellergeschoß auf das Niveau des Erdgeschosses, um es als Sockel für die Hauptetage zu nutzen. Darüber begann er nun, die Außenmauern mehr als Wandschirme zu sehen, die Mauern erheben sich unmittelbar von der Basis oder dem »Wasserspiegel«. Die Fenster im zweiten Stock bilden ein durchgehendes Band unterhalb der Traufe. Der Zementverputz der weit vorgezogenen Überstände wurde in einem hellen Farbton gestrichen, was reflektiertes Licht in die Räume brachte, die sonst recht dunkel geblieben wären. Aufschwingende Fenster – anstatt der waagerecht geteilten, hintereinander gehängten »Guillotine«-Schiebefenster – ließen mehr Luft in die Zimmer, wobei die Fensteröffnungen durch die breiten Dachüberstände vor Sonne und Wind geschützt wurden. Beim Umgang mit den Ma-

nagé. Wright pensait qu'il était souhaitable, sur cette Prairie longue et plate, de s'élever du sol afin d'avoir une meilleure vue. Pour cette raison, il réhaussa le sous-sol au niveau du sol, qui servait ainsi de socle à l'étage principal supérieur. Au niveau supérieur, il commençait à voir les murs de la maison comme des cloisons, les murs s'élevaient directement des soubassements ou du »niveau des eaux souterraines«, les fenêtres du deuxième étage s'alignaient en une rangée continue sous les avant-toits. Le crépi en ciment des avant-toits était peint d'une couleur claire, reflétant ainsi la lumière dans les pièces qui sinon auraient été plongées dans l'obscurité. Par opposition à la fenêtre à guillotine, la fenêtre à double battant faisait entrer plus d'air dans les pièces. Les ouvertures des fenêtres étaient protégées du vent et du soleil grâce aux avant-toits en saillie. En ce qui concerne les matériaux, il conseillait l'emploi d'un seul plutôt que le mélange de plusieurs, alors en vogue à l'époque. Le crépi en ciment des maisons était partout en ciment, accentué par une moulure en bois. Il en était de même pour les constructions en brique. S'il lui arrivait d'associer quand même différents matériaux,

and delivered to his Oak Park Studio. He recalled, »Suddenly, the model was standing on the studio table in the center. I came in and saw what was the matter. I took those four corners and I pulled them away from the building, made them individual features, planted them. And there began the thing that I was trying to do... I got features instead of walls. I followed that up with Unity Temple where there were no walls of any kind, only features, and the features were screens grouped about interior space. The thing that had come to me by instinct in the Larkin Building began to come consciously in Unity Temple. When I finished Unity Temple, I had it. I was conscious of the idea. I knew I had the beginning of a great thing, a great truth in architecture. And now architecture could be free.«[7]

What he had achieved in Unity Temple was, in his own words, the »destruction of the box« in architecture. Exterior walls were no longer the support of the overhead, be it slab or sloped roof. Cantilever construction placed the supports in from the outside edge, much like the extended arm of the branches of a tree. The walls outside now became non-supporting elements which he termed »screens«, either opaque – concrete, masonry or wood –, or transparent – glass windows and glass doors. The interior space took on a new freedom and at the same time a closer relationship to the landscape of nature outside. That once so limited distinction between exterior and interior vanished, and a new flow from one to the other became possible and wholly desirable. All of this act, this freeing of the interior to the exterior, gave meaning to the phrase »the space within became the reality of the building«, not the walls or ceilings.

MATERIALS

In his very first work, Frank Lloyd Wright manifested a careful knowledge and diligent respect for natural materials. He saw the general lack of such respect in the work of other architects of his era, as well as previous eras. Stone, brick and wood – those basic architectural materials – had long been covered, painted, plastered and altered to suit any particular fashion or taste. His work in these materials always adhered to what he perceived as most natural to them, letting the masses of stone become the feature of the building, or the rich earth-tones of the brick, product of the kiln, rise in masses and forms that glorified the brick. And wood he considered the most loved of all materials, saying »Wood is universally beautiful to man. Man loves his association with it; likes to feel it under his hand, sympathetic to his touch and to his eye.«[8]

Not only were the natural materials ignored in most

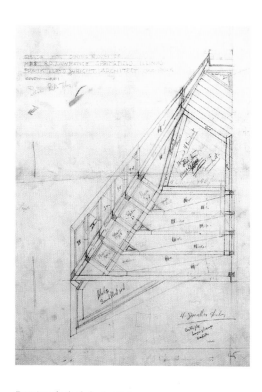

Drawing of a shade for the Dining Room of the Mrs. Lawrence Dana House, Springfield, Illinois, 1900

terialien riet er eher zur Einheitlichkeit als zu dem Konglomerat von Baustoffen, das damals in Mode war. Häuser mit Zementverputz waren bei ihm eben komplett verputzt und mit Holz akzentuiert. Dasselbe galt für Ziegelhäuser. Wenn Materialien kombiniert wurden, wie etwa Ziegel und Putz, dann geschah dies konsequent am ganzen Gebäude, um eine ruhige Schlichtheit zu erreichen.

Die Ausarbeitung und Handhabung all dieser Elemente erweiterte und entwickelte sich von den frühen Häusern, wie Bradley, Dana und Willits, bis zu den späteren, wie Martin, Coonley und Robie. Aber vom ersten bis zum letzten wurden sie alle als Wohnhäuser für die Prärie erdacht, und dies ist, auch wenn sie im Entwurf verschieden sind, der gemeinsame Nenner, auf den sie sich trotz aller individuellen Unterschiede bringen lassen.

DER UMSCHLOSSENE RAUM

In den »Präriehäusern« wurde Wrights Konzept für den Innenraum immer deutlicher zum prägenden Merkmal des Gebäudes. Es entstand allmählich, und er bezeichnete den Wohnraum der Hillside-Home-Schule von 1902 als wichtigen Schritt in diese Richtung. Die vier großen Steinsäulen, die den Balkon vor dem Raum tragen, sind hinter die Fensterecke zurückgenommen; auch der Balkon selbst springt hinter die hohen Fenster zurück, die ohne Teilung von der Brüstung bis zum Sturz aufsteigen. Damit wird offensichtlich, daß die Fensterwände in diesem Wohnraum in Hillside nicht tragend sind, da die Stützen der Konstruktion deutlich dahinter stehen. Bald folgten die Entwürfe für das Larkin-Gebäude in Buffalo, New York, und die Unity-Kirche in Oak Park, Illinois. Während Wright am Larkin-Auftrag arbeitete, wurde ein Gipsmodell des Gebäudes gefertigt und in sein Studio in Oak Park geliefert. »Plötzlich stand das Modell mitten im Raum auf dem Studiotisch«, erinnerte er sich. »Ich kam herein und sah, was zu tun war. Ich nahm die vier Ecken und zog sie vom Gebäude weg, machte sie zu eigenständigen Elementen, postierte sie. Und damit begann das, was ich erreichen wollte ... Ich hatte nun Charakteristika anstatt Mauern. Ich verfolgte das bei der Unity-Kirche weiter, wo es überhaupt keine eigentlichen Mauern mehr gab, sondern nur noch determinierende Elemente, nämlich zum Innenraum geordnete Wandschirme. Was beim Larkin-Gebäude noch instinktiv geschah, war jetzt bewußt. Als ich die Unity-Kirche fertigstellte, hatte ich es. Ich war mir der Idee bewußt. Ich wußte, daß ich den Anfang zu einer wirklich großen Sache gefunden hatte, einer großen Wahrheit in der Architektur. Und von jetzt an konnte die Architektur frei sein.«[7]

comme la brique et le crépi, il le faisait d'une façon uniforme dans tout le bâtiment afin d'obtenir une impression de tranquillité et de simplicité.

Tous ces éléments se développèrent et prirent de l'envergure entre les premières maisons, comme les maisons Bradley, Dana et Willits, et celles qui furent réalisées plus tard, comme les maisons Martin, Coonley et Robie. Cependant, toutes ces maisons furent conçues pour la Prairie et bien qu'elles aient différents types de plans, elles ont toutes un dénominateur commun qui les regroupe: la Prairie du Midwest.

ESPACE INTERIEUR

Dans ces »Prairies Houses«, le concept de Wright pour l'espace intérieur devint de plus en plus le trait caractéristique du bâtiment. Il se développa lentement. Wright indiqua la salle des fêtes de l'école privée de Hillside, en 1902, comme étant un pas important dans cette direction. Les quatre larges colonnes de pierre, qui supportent le balcon tout autour de la salle des fêtes, sont situées à l'intérieur, et le balcon lui-même est en retrait des hautes fenêtres qui, sans être entravées, s'élèvent du rebord de fenêtre jusqu'au linteau. Dans cette salle des fêtes, il est clair que les murs-fenêtres ne sont pas des murs de soutènement, les supports de la structure sont situés vers l'intérieur. Les plans pour le bâtiment administratif de la société Larkin, à Buffalo, New York et pour le temple de l'Unité à Oak Park ne devaient pas tarder à suivre. Alors que Wright travaillait à la commande Larkin, une maquette en plâtre du bâtiment fut réalisée et déposée à son atelier de Oak Park. »Tout à coup, la maquette fut là, sur la table, au milieu. J'entrais et vis ce qui n'allait pas. J'ôtais du bâtiment les quatre angles, les transformait en caractéristiques individuelles et les replaçait. J'avais alors des caractéristiques qui accrochaient le regard et non plus des murs. J'employais le même procédé avec le temple de l'Unité où je ne construisis aucun mur traditionnel, mais seulement ces caractéristiques. Et celles-ci étaient des cloisons regroupées dans l'espace intérieur. Ce que j'avais fait par instinct avec le bâtiment Larkin, je le fis peu à peu consciemment avec le temple de l'Unité. Lorsque le temple fut achevé, j'en étais tout à fait conscient. Je savais que je me trouvais au commencement d'une grande chose, d'une grande vérité dans l'architecture. L'architecture pouvait maintenant être libre.«[7]

Ce qu'il avait réalisé dans le temple de l'Unité, c'était, en reprenant ses propres mots, »la destruction des blocs« dans l'architecture. Les murs extérieurs ne soutenaient plus la partie supérieure, qu'ils s'agisse de dalles ou de toit en pente. Avec les encorbellements, les supports étaient placés en retrait du bord

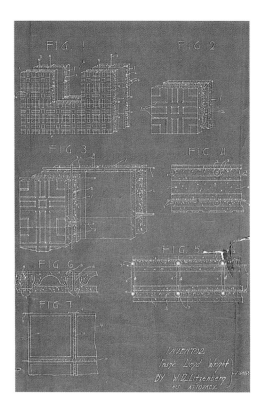

Block System construction scheme,
1921

nineteenth century architecture, but even the newer materials, concrete, steel, sheet metal and glass, were used in out-dated ways. He perceived these new materials and the methods of using them as a wonderful »tool box« for the architect of the twentieth century. Steel combined with concrete – reinforced concrete – was the great liberating element that could produce an entirely new architecture for the twentieth century. The Johnson Wax building, Kaufmann's Fallingwater, the Johnson Wax Research Tower and H. C. Price Tower, and the Guggenheim Museum are all examples of the use of reinforced concrete cantilever construction.

Realizing early on in the twentieth century that handicraft work was becoming more and more costly, thus less and less desirable for general architectural design, Frank Lloyd Wright turned to the machine and machine methods. The idea of prefabrication in housing appealed to him as well, and in 1915 he began work along that line in the American Ready-Cut System Houses. But the concept and the scheme proved too far in advance of what industry, housing, and construction financing would permit at that time. The four concrete block houses in Los Angeles are a splendid example of what Wright meant when he said the »machine should be a tool in the hand of the artist.« In this case, the »machine« was the form, or mold, into which the concrete was poured in order to form the block. Up until this time concrete block was the »gutter-child« of the building trade. Wright saw that the block, if treated as a decorative as well as structural element, could rise into the air and sunlight as a beautiful product.

Other facets of the building industry he treated the same way: sheet metal, too, could be turned by machine from simple, unadorned sheets of steel, copper and aluminum into patterned surfaces to adorn the edifice.

NATURE

Like all the transcendentalists, Frank Lloyd Wright regarded nature in almost mystical terms. He deeply believed that the closer man associated himself with nature, the greater his personal, spiritual and even physical well-being grew and expanded as a direct result of that association. Wright liked to refer to his way of thinking of nature as »Nature spelled with a capital ›N‹ the way you spell God with a capital ›G‹«, and he further maintained that »Nature is all the body of God we will ever know.«[9]

From this point of view, from his reverence and subsequently his respect for nature, his buildings, where placed in the landscape, had this one aim in common: to let the human being experience and partici-

Was er mit dem Entwurf der Unity-Kirche erreicht hatte, war in seinen eigenen Worten »die Zerstörung der Kiste« in der Architektur. Außenwände waren nicht länger die Stütze des darüber liegenden Daches, sei es nun flach oder geneigt. Kragkonstruktionen, einem ausgestreckten Arm oder den Zweigen eines Baumes ähnlich, erlaubten es, die Stützen hinter die Fassadenfläche zu legen. Die äußeren Wände wurden nun zu nichttragenden Elementen, die er »Schirme« nannte; entweder undurchsichtig – aus Beton, Mauerwerk oder Holz – oder transparent – mit Glasfenstern und -türen. Der Innenraum gewann so eine neue Freiheit und gleichzeitig eine engere Beziehung zu der natürlichen Landschaft außerhalb. Die früher so strikte Trennung zwischen außen und innen verschwand, und ein ungewohnter Fluß vom einen zum anderen wurde möglich und auch ausdrücklich gewünscht. Dies alles zusammen, diese Befreiung des Inneren vom Äußeren, steht hinter dem Satz »der umschlossene Raum wurde zur Realität des Gebäudes«, nicht die Mauern oder Decken.

MATERIALIEN

Bereits in seinen ersten Arbeiten zeigte Frank Lloyd Wright Wissen, Sorgfalt und Respekt im Umgang mit natürlichen Baumaterialien. Er sah den generellen Mangel an solchem Respekt in den Werken anderer Architekten seiner eigenen wie auch vorangegangener Zeiten. Stein, Ziegel und Holz – diese architektonischen Grundmaterialien waren lange versteckt, überstrichen, verputzt und verändert worden, um jeder beliebigen Mode- oder Geschmacksrichtung zu entsprechen. Er aber benutzte sie in seinen Arbeiten in einer Weise, die er hinsichtlich ihrer Natur für am angemessensten hielt, indem er etwa die Masse des Steins zum dominanten Element eines Hauses werden ließ oder die vollen Erdtöne des Ziegels, dieses Produkts des Brennofens, in Volumen und Formen arrangierte, die den Ziegel verherrlichten. Holz war für ihn das meistgeliebte aller Materialien, und er meinte dazu: »Holz ist ganz generell schön für den Menschen. Der Mensch liebt die enge Verbindung mit ihm, liebt es, mit der Hand darüberzustreichen. Es ist angenehm beim Berühren und für das Auge.«[8]
Nicht nur die natürlichen Baustoffe wurden in der Architektur des neunzehnten Jahrhunderts weitgehend vernachlässigt, auch die neuen Materialien wie Beton, Stahl, Metallplatten und Glas wurden auf veraltete Weise eingesetzt. Wright aber entdeckte diese neuen Werkstoffe und die Methoden, sie zu benutzen, als einen wundervollen »Werkzeugkasten« für den Architekten des zwanzigsten Jahrhunderts. Stahl, verbunden mit Beton – Stahlbeton –, war das großartige Element, das eine völlig neue Architektur für das

extérieur et ressemblaient à un bras étendu ou aux branches d'un arbre. Les murs extérieurs devinrent des éléments sans fonction de support qu'il nomma »parois«, soit opaques – en ciment, en pierre ou en bois – soit transparentes – fenêtres et portes en verre. L'espace intérieur acquit une nouvelle liberté et, en même temps, une relation plus étroite avec le paysage naturel extérieur. Cette distinction si étroite de jadis entre extérieur et intérieur disparaissait, et un passage de l'un à l'autre devenait possible et tout à fait souhaitable. C'est ce passage libre de l'intérieur vers l'extérieur qui donna un sens à cette phrase »l'espace intérieur devint la réalité du bâtiment« et non pas les murs, ni les plafonds.

MATERIAUX

Dans ses premiers travaux, Frank Lloyd Wright manifesta une connaissance approfondie et un respect constant envers les matériaux naturels. Il remarquait qu'un tel respect faisait défaut aux architectes de son époque, et des époques précédentes. La pierre, la brique et le bois – matériaux de base – étaient depuis longtemps recouverts, peints, enduits ou modifiés afin de répondre aux exigences d'une mode ou d'un goût particulier. Il utilisa toujours ces matériaux de la manière qui lui semblait la plus conforme à leur nature, laissant les masses de pierre devenir la caractéristique de l'immeuble ou employant les riches couleurs de terre de la brique, sortie du four, dans des formes qui la glorifient. Quant au bois, son matériau préféré, il en disait: »Pour l'Homme, le bois est universellement beau. On aime s'associer à lui, le sentir sous la main. Il est agréable à l'œil et au toucher.«[8]
Dans la plus grande partie de l'architecture du 19ème siècle, non seulement les matériaux naturels étaient dédaignés, mais les matériaux plus nouveaux, comme le béton, l'acier, les plaques de métal et les feuilles de verre, étaient employés de façon démodée. Wright pressentit que ces nouveaux matériaux ainsi que les nouvelles méthodes de les utiliser seraient une merveilleuse »boîte à outils« pour l'architecte du 20ème siècle. L'acier associé au béton – le béton armé – était le grand élément libérateur qui produirait une toute nouvelle architecture pour le 20ème siècle. Le bâtiment Johnson Wax, la maison Kaufmann »Fallingwater«, la tour des laboratoires Johnson Wax et la tour H.C. Price ainsi que le musée Guggenheim sont tous des exemples de constructions aux encorbellements à béton armé.
S'apercevant très vite que pendant le 20ème siècle, le travail manuel deviendrait de plus en plus onéreux et donc de moins en moins désirable pour l'architecture en général, Frank Lloyd Wright se tourna vers les machines. L'idée d'éléments préfabriqués le sédui-

pate in the joys and wonderment of natural beauty. Today we call it site planning, environmental design and all manner of sophisticated terms that really mean the same thing: respect for the earth. Without that respect the earth, as we know it, is destined to become a dead planet, covered by an equally dead sky. Civilization today is faced with that perilous fear and now for the first time begins to take grasp of the fear and act as a result of that fear. Nearly 100 years ago, Wright offered solutions in the form of architecture, showing how to live in harmony with the environment, not out of fear (a mere animal instinct, basically) but out of a deeply-rooted love for natural beauty. It was his conviction that mankind, if exposed to and set into the fabric of Nature, would respond affirmatively and grow spiritually.

His eloquence in the manner in which he wrote and spoke of nature is surpassed only by the buildings he set on earth.

THE FLOW OF WORK

With these aforementioned ideas and principles – interior space, thus exterior form, materials and methods, nature and environment – at his disposal like pencils in his hand, Frank Lloyd Wright continued to draw the designs and buildings that would change the face of architecture in the world. He elected to call his buildings »organic architecture«, a phrase that was initiated by his »Lieber Meister«, Louis Sullivan. But he went far beyond Sullivan in his work and in his interpretation of that definition. Wright sometimes referred to organic architecture as one in which all the parts were related to the whole, as the whole was related to the parts: continuity and integrity. But in an even broader, and deeper sense, he said that an organic building, wherever it stood in time, was appropriate to time, appropriate to place, and appropriate to man. Using that lexicon as a guideline, one can trace all the great buildings down through all the great epochs of time, and conversely one can eliminate a great many other ventures into the art of architecture as mere fashion or sham.

Wright's work progressed as his own ever-creative mind expanded. From the massive, sculptural office building for the Larkin Company, he made, 30 years later, the fluid, plastic, curvilinear, light and airy office building for the S. C. Johnson & Son Company. From the formal »sphinx-like« plan of the Imperial Hotel and Midway Gardens, evolved the ultimate concept of a fluid space flow, again 30 years later, in the Guggenheim Museum. From the simple house of Mrs. Thomas Gale on a simple lot on the Midwest prairie, Oak Park, 1909, he progressed to the concrete and stone terraces projecting out and over a

Frank Lloyd Wright on a visit in Ocotillo, 1928

zwanzigste Jahrhundert hervorbringen konnte. Das Johnson-Wax-Gebäude, Kaufmanns »Fallingwater«, der Johnson-Wax-Forschungsturm und der H.C.-Price-Turm sowie das Guggenheim-Museum sind sämtlich Beispiele für den Einsatz von Stahlbeton-Kragkonstruktionen.

Frank Lloyd Wright hatte schon früh in diesem Jahrhundert erkannt, daß manuelle Arbeit immer teurer und darum immer unattraktiver für die Architektur wurde. Darum wandte er sich verstärkt der Maschine und maschinellen Verfahren zu. Die Idee, das Konzept der Vorfertigung auch auf Häuser zu übertragen, reizte ihn, und so begann er schon 1915 mit dem »American Ready-Cut«-System in dieser Richtung zu arbeiten. Doch es erwies sich, daß Konzept und Pläne im Hinblick auf die technischen Möglichkeiten, das Wohnen und die Baufinanzierung ihrer Zeit zu weit voraus waren.

Die vier Betonblockstein-Häuser in Los Angeles sind ein großartiges Beispiel dafür, was Wright meinte, als er sagte: »Die Maschine sollte ein Werkzeug in der Hand des Künstlers sein.« Die »Maschine« war dabei die Gußform, in der der Betonstein hergestellt wurde. Bis dahin war der Betonblockstein das Stiefkind des Baugewerbes gewesen. Wright aber sah, daß er sich, wenn er sowohl als dekoratives als auch strukturierendes Element verwendet wurde, durchaus sehen lassen konnte.

Andere Materialien behandelte er ähnlich: So konnten Maschinen aus unscheinbaren Stahl-, Kupfer- und Aluminiumblechen gemusterte Oberflächen herstellen, die das Gebäude schmückten.

NATUR

Wie fast alle Transzendentalisten sah Frank Lloyd Wright die Natur fast mystisch. Er war zutiefst davon überzeugt, daß das persönliche, spirituelle und auch körperliche Wohlergehen eines Menschen in dem Maße zunehme, in dem er sich mit der Natur assoziiere. Wright bezog sich in seiner Denkungsweise gerne auf »Natur, mit großem ›N‹ geschrieben, so wie man im Englischen auch Gott mit großem ›G‹ schreibt.« Natur war für ihn »alles vom Körper Gottes, das wir je kennenlernen werden«[9].

Durch diese Sichtweise, seine Verehrung und seinen Respekt vor der Natur, haben Wrights Gebäude alle ein Ziel gemeinsam: den Menschen ein Staunen erfahren und am Glück der natürlichen Schönheit teilhaben zu lassen. Heute bezeichnen wir so etwas mit Fachausdrücken wie standortgerechtes Bauen, die letztlich das gleiche meinen: Respekt vor der Erde. Ohne diesen Respekt ist die Erde, wie wir sie heute kennen, dazu verdammt, ein toter Planet zu werden, überwölbt von einem ebenso toten Himmel. Unsere

sait et, en 1915, il commença à travailler dans ce sens aux American Ready-Cut System Houses. Toutefois, ces conceptions et ces projets s'avérèrent bien trop en avance sur les possibilités de l'industrie, de logement et de financement de l'époque.

Les quatre maisons en blocs de béton de Los Angeles illustrent merveilleusement ce que Wright entendait lorsqu'il affirmait que »la machine devait être un outil dans la main de l'artiste«. Ici, la »machine« était le coffrage, ou le moule, dans lequel le béton était versé pour former les blocs. Jusqu'à cette époque, le bloc en béton était l'enfant pauvre des entreprises de construction. Employé comme décoration ou comme matériau de construction, le bloc était considéré par Wright comme un beau produit pouvant s'élever dans les airs et dans la lumière du soleil.

Il traita de la même façon les autres facettes de l'industrie du bâtiment: de simples plaques de métal, de cuivre et d'aluminium, sans ornement, pouvaient être transformées à l'aide d'une machine en surfaces travaillées afin de décorer l'édifice.

NATURE

Comme tous les autres adeptes du transcendantalisme, Frank Lloyd Wright considérait la nature de façon quasi mystique. Il croyait fermement que plus l'homme s'associait à la nature, plus son bien-être personnel, spirituel et même physique se développait comme conséquence directe de cette association. Wright se plaisait à évoquer sa conception de la nature dans ces termes: »Ecrire la Nature avec un ›N‹ majuscule comme l'on écrit Dieu avec un grand ›D‹« et il soutenait: »La Nature est tout ce que nous connaîtrons jamais de l'apparence de Dieu«.[9]

A partir de cette conception, de cette vénération et par conséquent de son respect de la nature, ses bâtiments, qui étaient intégrés au paysage, avaient tous un but commun: permettre à l'être humain d'éprouver et de participer aux joies et à l'émerveillement de la beauté de la nature. Aujourd'hui, nous parlons de l'aménagement du site, de l'étude de l'environnement et employons des termes compliqués qui en fait désignent la même chose: le respect de la Terre. Sans ce respect, nous savons bien qu'elle deviendra une planète morte, surplombée d'un ciel tout aussi mort. De nos jours, notre civilisation est confrontée à la peur de ce péril et, pour la première fois, elle commence à prendre conscience de sa peur et à entreprendre des actions, qui sont stimulées par la peur. Il y a presque 100 ans, Wright proposait des solutions sous forme d'architecture, montrant comment vivre en harmonie avec l'environnement, non pas par peur (qui est primairement un instinct animal), mais parce qu'il était animé d'un amour profond pour les beautés

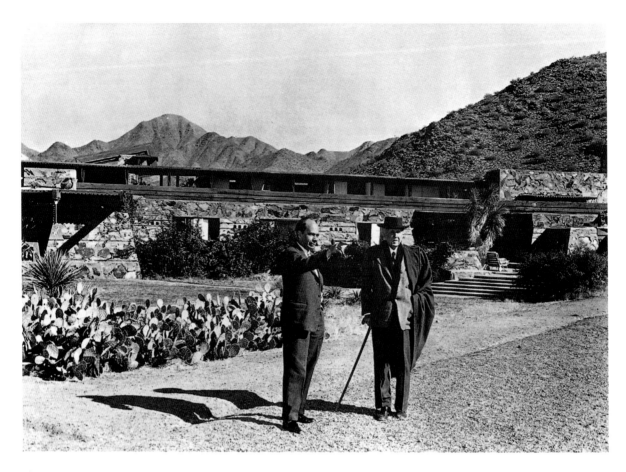

The German architect Werner Hebe-
brand visits Frank Lloyd Wright at
Taliesin West, Phoenix, Arizona, in
November 1956

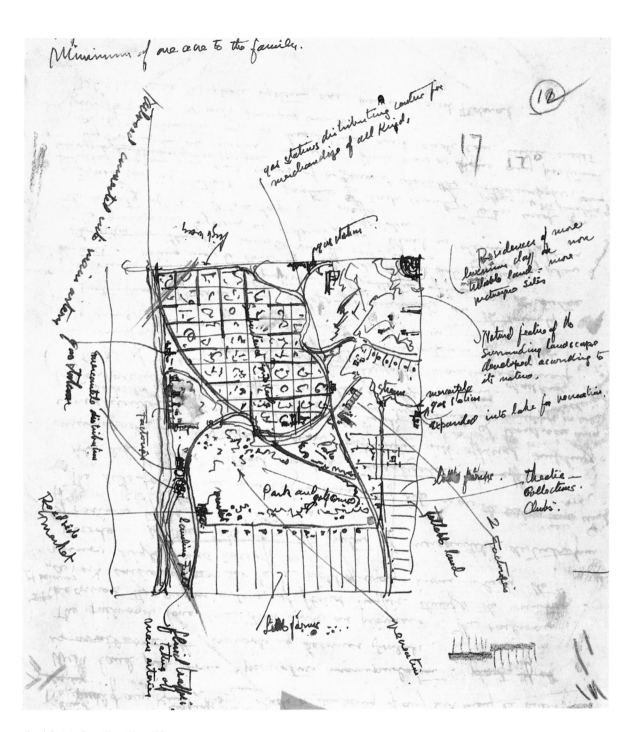

Sketch for Broadacre City project, 1934

31

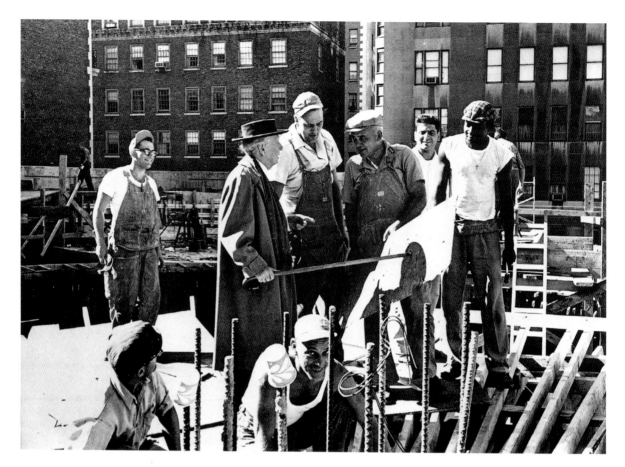

Frank Lloyd Wright inspects construction of the Guggenheim Museum in
New York, 1957

Zivilisation ist jetzt mit dieser furchtbaren Drohung konfrontiert und beginnt erstmals, aus dieser Angst heraus zu handeln. Vor fast 100 Jahren schon hat Wright in der Architektur Lösungen angeboten, die zeigen, wie man in Harmonie mit der Umwelt leben kann. Aber nicht aus Angst heraus, sondern aus tiefverwurzelter Liebe zur natürlichen Schönheit und aus der Überzeugung, daß die Menschen, wenn man sie wieder in das Gefüge der Natur einbindet, mit Zustimmung reagieren und spirituell wachsen werden.

Wrights mündliche und schriftliche Eloquenz zum Thema Natur wird nur noch von den Gebäuden, die er auf diese Erde setzte, überboten.

SCHAFFENSSTRÖME

Mit den erwähnten Ideen und Prinzipien – innerer Raum, der die äußere Form bestimmt, Materialien und Verfahren, Natur und Umgebung, die nun wie Zeichenstifte zu seiner Verfügung standen – fuhr Frank Lloyd Wright fort, Bauten zu entwerfen, die die Architektur der ganzen Welt verändern sollten. Er wählte die Bezeichnung »organische Architektur« für sein Schaffen, ein Ausdruck, der auf seinen »lieben Meister« Louis Sullivan zurückging. In seiner Interpretation und Umsetzung dieses Begriffes ging er allerdings weit über Sullivan hinaus. Wright definierte organische Architektur gelegentlich als eine Baukunst, in der die Teile ebenso auf das Ganze bezogen sind wie das Ganze auf die Teile: Kontinuität und Integrität. Aber in einem noch weiteren und tieferen Sinne erklärte er, ein organisches Haus passe, unabhängig davon, wann es gebaut worden sei, stets zur Gegenwart, zur Umgebung und zum Menschen. Nimmt man diese Definition als Leitfaden, kann man die bedeutenden Bauten aller großen Epochen ausmachen und umgekehrt etliche gewagte Abenteuer der Baukunst als bloße Modeerscheinungen oder Täuschungen entlarven.

Wrights Schaffen entfaltete sich wie seine stets kreative Persönlichkeit. Ausgehend von dem wuchtigen, skulpturalen Bürohaus für die Larkin Company, schuf er dreißig Jahre später das fließende, lichte, plastisch-gerundete Bürohaus für die S.C. Johnson & Sohn Company. Aus den formalistischen, »sphinxhaften« Anlagen des Imperial-Hotels und der »Midway Gardens« entwickelte er wiederum dreißig Jahre später das gültige Konzept für das fließende Raumkontinuum des Guggenheim-Museums. Vom einfachen Haus für Thomas Gale, 1909 auf einer kleinen Parzelle in Oak Park, Chicago, gebaut, gelangte er zu den weit auskragenden Beton- und Naturstein-Terrassen des weltweit berühmten Hauses »Fallingwater« für Edgar Kaufmann über einem Wasserfall in

naturelles. Il était convaincu que l'humanité, si on la plaçait dans le contexte de la nature, réagirait positivement et se développerait spirituellement.

Seuls les bâtiments qu'il construisit sur terre surpassèrent l'éloquence dont il faisait preuve lorsqu'il parlait de la nature.

EVOLUTION DES TRAVAUX

Avec ces idées et ces principes à sa disposition – espace intérieur et forme extérieure, matériaux et méthodes, nature et environnement – tels des crayons dans sa main, Frank Lloyd Wright continua à dessiner et concevoir les bâtiments qui changeront le visage de l'architecture dans le monde. Il avait nommé ses bâtiments »une architecture organique«, désignation qui avait été lancée par son »cher maître«, Louis Sullivan. Dans ses travaux comme dans l'interprétation de cette désignation, il alla toutefois bien plus loin que Sullivan. Quelquefois, Wright affirmait que l'architecture organique était une architecture où toutes les parties sont reliées au tout et où le tout a un rapport avec toutes les parties: continuité et totalité. Mais, dans un sens encore plus large et plus profond, il disait qu'un bâtiment organique, quelle que soit sa date de construction, convient à l'époque, convient au lieu et convient à l'homme. Si l'on se réfère à cette explication, il est possible de suivre l'évolution de toutes les grandes constructions à travers toutes les grandes époques et, inversement, on peut éliminer dans l'art de l'architecture un grand nombre d'entreprises qui ne sont que des trompe-l'œil ou des manifestations de la mode.

Les travaux de Lloyd suivaient l'évolution de sa créativité. A partir du bâtiment administratif et sculptural, exécuté pour la société Larkin, il réalisa 30 ans plus tard le bâtiment administratif aérien, fluide et curviligne pour la société S.C. Johnson et Fils. A partir des plans formels en »sphinx« de l'Hôtel Impérial et des »Midway Gardens«, il développa, également 30 ans plus tard, l'ultime concept d'un espace fluide dans le musée Guggenheim. A partir de la maison sans prétention de Thomas Gale, située sur un simple terrain de la Prairie du Midwest, à Oak Park, en 1909, il en arriva à la construction des terrasses en béton et en pierre surplombant une cascade, dans les gorges boisées de la Pennsylvanie, la très célèbre maison pour Edgar Kaufmann, »Fallingwater«. A partir du moulin Roméo et Juliette, tour en bois édifiée sur un soubassement en pierre qui était consolidé à l'aide de montants en fer, fut réalisée la tour H.C. Price, à Bartleville, Oklahoma, inaugurée soixante ans plus tard en 1956. A partir de la beauté sculpturale du temple de l'Unité, monolithe de forme carrée, où la lumière provenait des fenêtres de la nef et du plafond, il

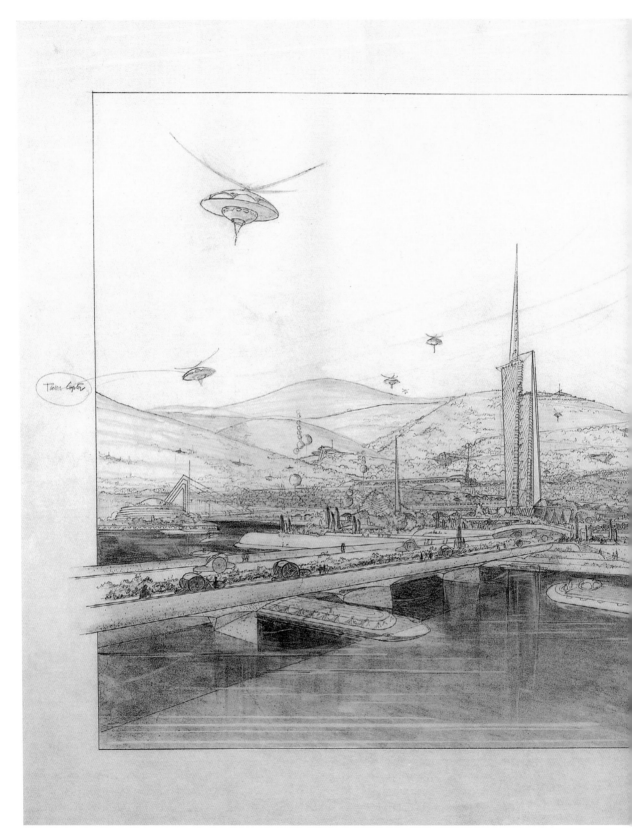

Twin Copter

34

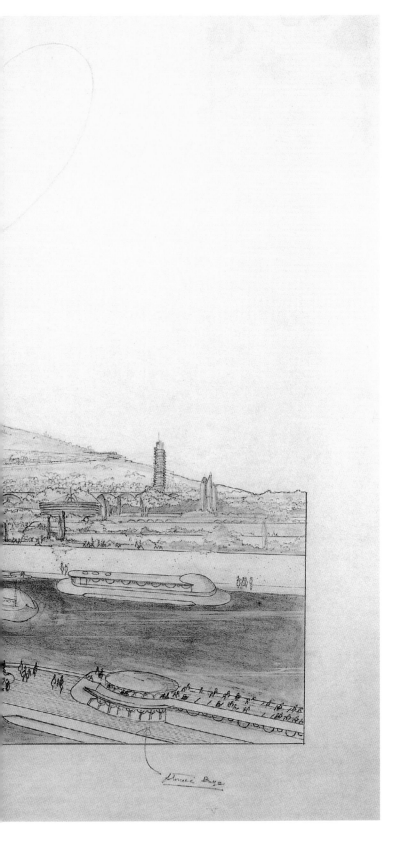

Living City project, 1958

waterfall in a wooded glen in Western Pennsylvania, the world-famous house for Edgar Kaufmann, Fallingwater. From the windmill tower Romeo and Juliet, a wooden tower set on a stone base reinforced with iron rods, sixty years passed until the opening of the H.C. Price Tower, in Bartlesville, Oklahoma in 1956. From the square-formed, monolithic, sculptural beauty of Unity Temple, where light poured in from the clerestory and ceiling above, evolved the design, almost half a century later, of the Beth Sholom Synagogue, a building that seems fabricated, embraced by, and enveloped in Light.

The forms in each of these examples are different, but the principles are consistent. It was the strict adherence to, and belief in the validity of principle that was the guiding force in all Wright's work.

HUMAN VALUES

From beginning to end, throughout all the work of Frank Lloyd Wright, one important element remains constant, prevails over all other considerations, remains, in fact, always the first consideration: human values. He often called it »Humanity«. From simple dwelling place to vast civic center, from factory to cathedral, from farm to school, wherever man is placed in relation to Wright's buildings, man is placed ostensibly in the center.

Nearing the end of his life, Wright wrote a book in 1957 called *A Testament*. It is part biographical and part explanatory, reviewing his work, how it came about, the significant principles, works and results. He summed up the forces that made his work, as he saw them, and the forms of all great Art, likewise as he saw them. In the last chapter of the book he wrote a chapter entitled »Humanity – The Light of the World«, part of which is included here:

»Constantly I have referred to a more ›humane‹ architecture, so I will try to explain what humane means to me, an architect. Like organic architecture, the quality of humanity is interior to man. As the solar system is reckoned in terms of light-years, so may the inner light be what we are calling humanity. This element, Man as light, is beyond all reckoning. Buddha was known as the light of Asia; Jesus as the light of the world. Sunlight is to nature as this interior light is to man's spirit: Manlight.

Manlight is above instinct. Human imagination by way of this interior light is born, conceives, creates: dies but to continue the light of existence only as this light lived in the man. The spirit is illumined by it and to the extent that his life is this light and it proceeds from him, it in turn illumines his kind. Affirmations of this light in human life and work are man's true happiness.

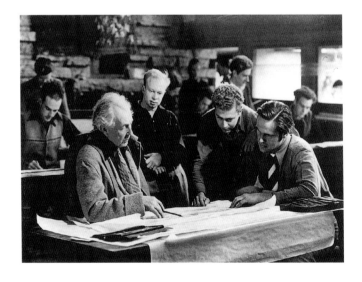

Frank Lloyd Wright and his apprentices, 1938

einer waldreichen Schlucht in Pennsylvania. Sechzig Jahre liegen zwischen dem Windmühlenturm »Romeo and Juliet«, einem Holzturm auf einem armierten Steinfundament, und der Eröffnung des H.C.-Price-Turms in Bartlesville, Oklahoma, im Jahre 1956. Von der statischen Schönheit des kubisch-monolithischen »Unity-Temple«, wo sich das Licht von hochliegenden Fensterbändern und über die Decke in den Raum ergoß, führte der Weg zu dem fast ein halbes Jahrhundert später entstandenen Entwurf für die Beth-Sholom-Synagoge, ein Gebäude, das aus Licht gemacht und von Licht umhüllt zu sein scheint. Die Formen in jedem dieser Beispiele sind unterschiedlich, aber die zugrundeliegenden Prinzipien stimmen überein. Der Glaube und das strikte Festhalten an diesen Prinzipien war die leitende Kraft in Wrights gesamtem Schaffen.

MENSCHLICHE WERTE

Von Anfang bis Ende, durch Wrights sämtliche Werke hindurch, bleibt ein wichtiges Element konstant, dominiert ein Gesichtspunkt alle anderen Erwägungen und ist stets der oberste Grundsatz: menschliche Werte. Wright sprach in diesem Zusammenhang oft von »Humanität«. Vom einfachen Wohnhaus bis zum gewaltigen Verwaltungszentrum, von der Fabrik bis zum Gotteshaus, vom Bauernhof bis zur Schule – wo immer der Mensch in Relation zu Wrights Bauten gesetzt wird, steht er deutlich erkennbar auch im Zentrum.

1957, als er sich dem Ende seines Lebens näherte, schrieb Wright ein Buch, das er *Ein Testament* nannte. Es ist zum Teil biographisch, zum Teil erläutert es sein Werk, hält Rückschau auf sein Schaffen und wie er dazu kam, behandelt die wesentlichen Prinzipien, Arbeiten und Ergebnisse. Er summiert all die Kräfte, die für sein Schaffen bestimmend waren, so wie er sie sah, und die Formen jeder großen Kunst, ebenfalls ganz, wie er sie sah. Im letzten Teil des Buches gibt es ein Kapitel mit dem Titel »Humanität – das Licht der Welt«, dessen Anfang hier wiedergegeben wird:

»Ich habe mich ständig auf eine ›humanere‹ Architektur bezogen und möchte daher versuchen zu erklären, was ich, ein Architekt, unter menschlich verstehe. Wie in der organischen Architektur liegt die Qualität der Menschlichkeit im Menschen. Wie das Sonnensystem nach Lichtjahren berechnet wird, so soll das innere Licht das sein, was wir als Menschlichkeit bezeichnen. Dieses Element, der Mensch als Licht, liegt jenseits jeder Berechnung. Buddha war als Licht Asiens bekannt; Jesus als Licht der Welt. Das Sonnenlicht verhält sich zur Natur wie jenes innere Licht zum Geiste des Menschen: Menschenlicht.

développa les plans, presqu'un demi-siècle plus tard, de la synagogue Beth Sholom, bâtiment qui semble être fait et enveloppé de Lumière.

Dans chacun de ces exemples, les formes diffèrent, mais les principes restent les mêmes. Ce furent son attachement et sa croyance en la validité de ses principes qui constituèrent la force motrice des travaux de Wright.

VALEURS HUMAINES

Du début jusqu'à la fin, dans tous les travaux de Frank Lloyd Wright, il existe un élément important qui reste constant, domine toutes les autres considérations, et constitue toujours sa première réflexion: les valeurs humaines. Cet élément, il le nommait »humanité«. Qu'il s'agisse d'une simple demeure ou d'un grand centre civique, d'une usine ou d'une cathédrale, d'une ferme ou d'une école, là où l'homme est mis en relation avec les bâtiments de Wright, il y occupe la place centrale.

Vers la fin de sa vie, Wright écrivit, en 1957, un livre intitulé *Un Testament*. En partie autobiographique, en partie explicatif, ce livre passe en revue son œuvre, ses débuts, les principes importants, les réalisations et les résultats. Il résume les forces de son œuvre ainsi que les formes du grand Art, telles qu'il les voyait. Le dernier chapitre du livre est intitulé »L'Humanité – La Lumière du Monde«. En voici des extraits:

»J'ai continuellement fait allusion à une architecture plus ›humaine‹. Je vais donc essayer d'expliquer ce que ce mot signifie pour moi, ce qu'il signifie pour l'architecte. Pareille à l'architecture organique, la qualité d'humanité est intérieure à l'homme. De même que l'on calcule le système solaire en années-lumière, il se peut que la lumière intérieure est ce que l'on nomme humanité. Cet élément, l'homme en tant que ›lumière‹, est au-dessus de toute estimation. Bouddha était appelé la lumière de l'Asie, Jésus la lumière du Monde. La lumière du soleil appartient à la nature comme la lumière intérieure appartient à l'esprit humain: la lumière humaine.

La lumière humaine est au-dessus de l'instinct. Par cette lumière humaine, l'imagination de l'homme naît, conçoit, crée, meurt certes, mais pour continuer la lumière de l'existence sous forme de cette lumière qui vivait en l'homme. L'esprit en est illuminé et dans une telle mesure que sa vie devient cette lumière, il provient de cette lumière et à son tour il illumine l'espèce. Les affirmations de cette lumière dans la vie et le travail humain sont le véritable bonheur de l'homme.

Il n'y a rien plus élevé dans la conscience humaine que les rayons de cette lumière intérieure. Nous les

There is nothing higher in human consciousness than beams of this interior light. We call them beauty. Beauty is but the shining of man's light – radiance the high romance of his manhood as we know Architecture, the Arts, Philosophy, Religion, to be romantic. All come to nourish or be nourished by this inextinguishable light within the soul of man. He can give no intellectual consideration above or beyond this inspiration. From the cradle to the grave his true being craves this reality to assure the continuation of his life as Light thereafter.

As sunlight falls around a helpless thing, revealing form and countenance, so a corresponding light, of which the sun is a symbol, shines from the inspired work of mankind. This inner light is assurance that man's Architecture, Art and Religion, are as one – its symbolic emblems. Then we may call humanity itself the light that never fails. Baser elements in man are subject to this miracle of his own light. Sunrise and sunset are appropriate symbols of Man's existence on earth.

There is no more precious element of immortality than mankind as thus humane. Heaven may be the symbol of this light of lights only insofar as heaven is thus a haven.«[10]

[1] *An Autobiography,* Frank Lloyd Wright, Longmans, Green, N.Y., 1932.
[2] *A Testament,* Frank Lloyd Wright, New York, N.Y., 1957, p. 57.
[3] Ibid., p. 124.
[4] Ibid., p. 124.
[5] Ibid.
[6] Ibid.
[7] Talk to the Taliesin Fellowship, August 13, 1952.
[8] *Architectural Record,* May, 1928.
[9] Mike Wallace Interview, September, 1957.
[10] *A Testament,* Frank Lloyd Wright, New York, N.Y., 1957.

Menschenlicht steht über dem Instinkt. Menschliche Phantasie wird durch dieses innere Licht geboren, erkennt, erschafft; stirbt, aber lebt als Lebenslicht weiter, wenn es im Menschen lebendig war. Der Geist wird von ihm erleuchtet, und zwar mit solcher Kraft, daß sein Leben selbst dieses Licht ist, von ihm ausstrahlt und seinerseits andere erleuchtet. Das stete Leuchten dieses Lichtes, welches das Menschenleben und -werk bestrahlt, ist des Menschen wahres Glück.

Es gibt nichts Höheres im menschlichen Bewußtsein als Strahlen dieses inneren Lichtes. Wir nennen sie Schönheit. Schönheit ist nur der Schein des Lichtes im Menschen – der Glanz der hohen Romantik seines Menschtums, so wie wir wissen, daß Architektur, Kunst, Philosophie und Religion romantisch sind. Sie alle nähren das unauslöschliche Licht in der Seele des Menschen oder werden von ihm genährt. Er kann keine intellektuellen Erwägungen über diese Inspiration hinaus anstellen. Von der Wiege bis zum Grab sehnt sich sein wahres Wesen nach dieser Realität, damit sein Leben nach dem Tode als Licht im Jenseits gesichert ist.

Wie das Sonnenlicht um hilflose Gegenstände spielt und ihre Form und ihr Aussehen sichtbar macht, so strömt ein entsprechendes Licht, dessen Symbol die Sonne ist, vom inspirierten Werk der Menschheit aus. Dieses innere Licht bürgt dafür, daß des Menschen Architektur, Kunst und Religion eins sind – seine Symbole. Daher können wir die Humanität selbst als Licht bezeichnen, das nie verlöscht. Niedrigere Regungen im Menschen sind dem Wunder seines eigenen Lichtes untertan. Sonnenauf- und -untergang sind angemessene Symbole für des Menschen Dasein auf Erden.

Es gibt kein kostbareres Element der Unsterblichkeit als derartig humane Menschlichkeit. Der Himmel mag das Symbol dieses Lichtes der Lichter nur insofern sein, als der Himmel in diesem Sinne zum Hafen wird.«[10]

appelons beauté. La beauté n'est rien d'autre que l'éclat de la lumière de l'homme – l'éclat du romantisme élevé de l'humanité, tout comme nous savons que l'Architecture, les Arts, la Philosophie et la Religion sont romantiques. Tout vient alimenter et est alimenté par cette lumière inextinguible dans l'âme de l'homme. Il ne peut émettre aucune considération intellectuelle qui surpasse cette inspiration. Du berceau à la tombe, son véritable moi aspire à cette réalité pour assurer la continuation de sa vie comme Lumière dans l'au-delà.

Tout comme la lumière du soleil enveloppe un objet sans défense, révélant sa forme et son expression, de même une lumière correspondante, dont le soleil est un symbole, émane du travail inspiré de l'humanité. Cette lumière intérieure est l'assurance que l'Architecture, l'Art et la Religion de l'homme ne font qu'un – ses emblèmes symboliques. Nous pouvons alors nommer l'humanité elle-même: la lumière qui ne s'éteint jamais. Les côtés vils de l'homme sont soumis au miracle de sa propre lumière. Le lever et le coucher du soleil sont les symboles appropriés de l'existence de l'homme sur terre.

Il n'existe pas d'élément d'immortalité plus précieux que l'humanité ainsi humaine. Les cieux ne peuvent être le symbole de cette lumière des lumières que dans la mesure où les cieux sont un tel hâvre.«[10]

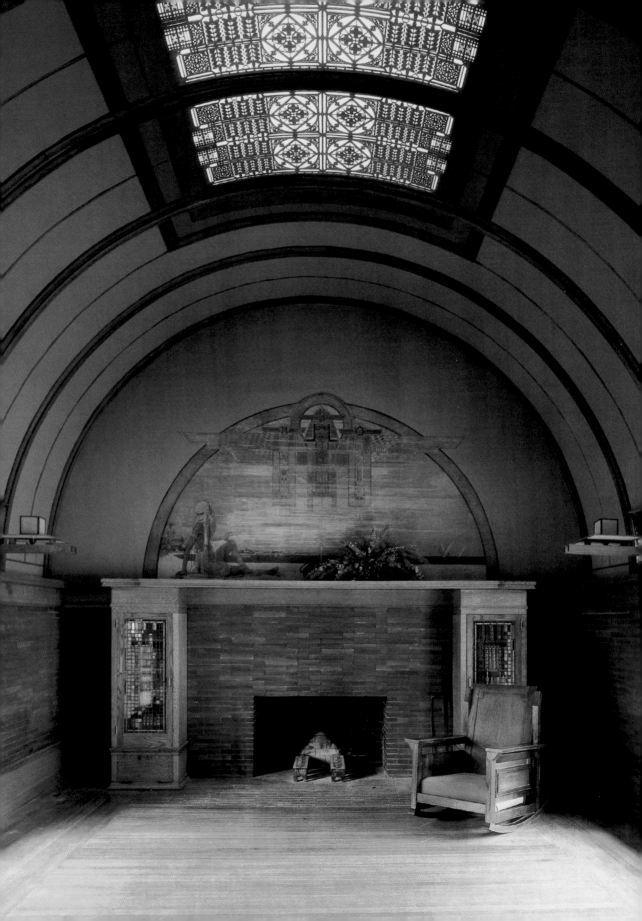

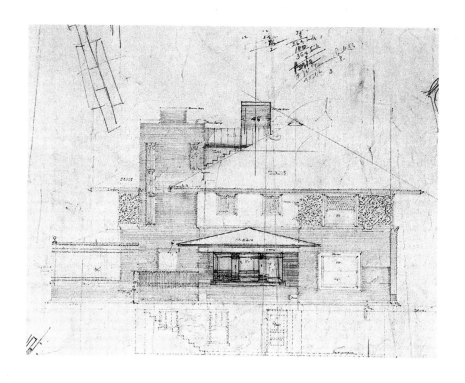

**Frank Lloyd Wright House, Oak Park,
Illinois, 1893**
Playroom

**House for William H. Winslow, River
Forest, Illinois, 1893–1894**
Elevation

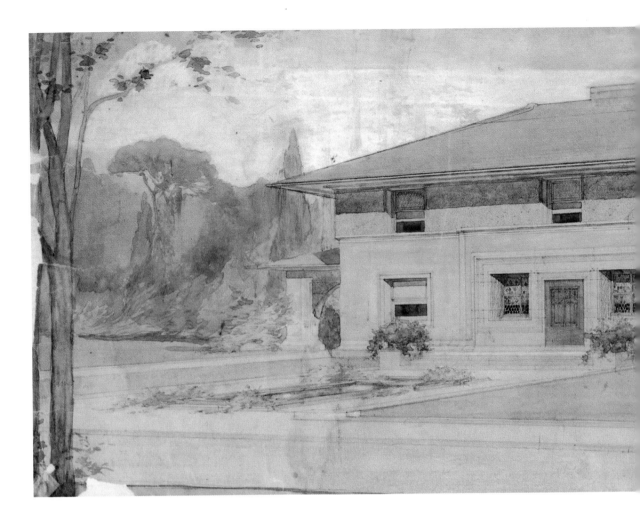

House for William H. Winslow, River Forest, Illinois, 1893–1894
Perspective drawing

By today's standards the Winslow house is simple, noble and elegant, but in 1894 was so unusual that it was the subject of neighborly ridicule. A number of features in this house are a marked departure from standards customary in 19th century residential architecture in the Midwest. The walls rise directly from a cast stone coping – which Wright termed »water-table« – and use a minimum amount of planting around the base of the building to emphasize the union of house and earth. Instead of the steeply pitched roofs pierced by tall, slim chimneys, the roof slopes gently down from a large, generous chimney mass and projects out and over the second story windows. The

windows themselves rise from sill to soffit, rather than stopping a foot or so below, and thus become openings in a screen, rather than holes in a wall. The materials are treated in a manner consistent with the nature and color of each: cast concrete is left pure, pristine white; golden Roman brick is golden Roman brick; the terracotta frieze on the second story wall surface is deep brown terracotta. This was in an era when brick was plastered, wood was painted, concrete was covered, etc. Inside, the spaces are clearly defined, but flow from one to another on the ground floor, instead of being the customary collection of boxes within boxes. The woodwork is clean, simple, and natural, a minimum of tooling and lathing replacing overwrought carving and curlicues common at the time. The whole has an understated elegant dignity previously unknown in that era of overstatement.

Aus heutiger Sicht strahlt das Haus Winslow eine schlichte, noble Eleganz aus, im Jahre 1894 jedoch war es so ungewöhnlich, daß sich die Nachbarn mokierten. Verschiedene Merkmale bezeugen eine deutliche Abkehr von der Wohnhaus-Architektur, die im neunzehnten Jahrhundert im Mittleren Westen der USA üblich war. Die Außenmauern erheben sich direkt von einem Sockel aus Betonsteinen, den Wright »Wasserspiegel« nannte. Nur wenige Pflanzen umgeben den Bau, um die Einheit von Haus und Grund zu betonen. Anstatt des üblichen steilen Daches, das von einem hohen, dünnen Kamin durchstoßen wird, fällt das Dach von einem kräftigen Kamin aus sanft ab und ragt weit über die Fenster des ersten Stocks hinaus. Die Fenster selber reichen von der Brüstung bis zur Traufhöhe, statt etwa dreißig Zentimeter tiefer zu enden, wodurch sie nicht wie Löcher in einer Mauer, sondern wie Öffnungen in einer Fläche wirken. Die Baustoffe sind ihrem jeweiligen Cha-

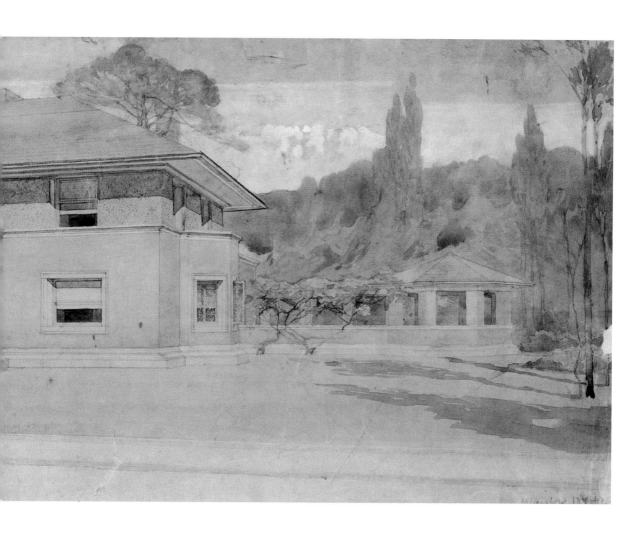

rakter entsprechend verarbeitet: Beton ist im ursprünglichen Weiß belassen, goldene römische Ziegel bleiben goldene römische Ziegel, der Terrakotta-Fries in Höhe des ersten Stocks ist tiefbraune Terrakotta, und all dies in einer Zeit, als man Ziegel verputzte, Holz bemalte, Beton versteckte usw. Im Innern des Hauses sind die Räume zwar klar definiert, fließen aber weich ineinander, statt wie üblich »Kisten in Kisten« anzuhäufen. Die Holzausstattung ist einfach und natürlich bearbeitet, nur wenig Schnitzwerk und Verkleidung finden sich im Vergleich zum üblichen Zuviel an Schnörkeln. Das Ganze verströmt eine bewußt zurückhaltende, würdevolle Eleganz, die in dieser Epoche der Übertreibungen bis dahin unbekannt gewesen war.

Pour les normes d'aujourd'hui, la maison Winslow est un bâtiment sobre, élégant, noble. En 1894 pourtant, elle était si inhabituelle qu'elle suscitait les moqueries du voisinage. Dans cette maison, un grand nombre d'éléments s'écartent des normes alors en usage dans l'architecture d'habitation du 19ème siècle. Les murs s'élèvent directement d'une corniche en pierre coffrée – que Wright nommait »le niveau des eaux souterraines«. La base de l'édifice est presque dépourvue de végétation afin d'accentuer encore l'union de la maison et de la terre. Au lieu des toits à forte pente d'où se dressent les hautes et minces cheminées, le toit s'incline doucement à partir des larges cheminées massives et s'avance en saillie, au-dessus des fenêtres du deuxième étage. Les fenêtres vont du rebord de fenêtre jusqu'au linteau, au lieu de s'arrêter une trentaine de centimètres en dessous. Elle ne sont pas percées dans un mur, mais dans une paroi. Les matériaux sont traités en fonction de leur nature et de

leur couleur: le béton garde sa couleur blanchâtre primitive; la brique romaine dorée reste une brique romaine dorée; la frise en céramique sur le mur du deuxième étage est d'un brun intense. C'était une époque où l'on recouvrait les briques de crépi, où l'on peignait le bois, où l'on revêtait le béton, etc. A l'intérieur, les espaces étaient clairement délimités, mais débouchaient l'un sur l'autre au rez-de-chaussée, au lieu de présenter l'aspect habituel de boîtes encastrées les unes dans les autres. Les parties en bois ont été travaillées proprement, simplement et garde leur aspect naturel; un minimum d'ouvrage embouti et de lattage remplace l'excès de sculptures et d'entrelacs communs à l'époque. Le tout dégage une dignité élégante et discrète qui était alors inconnue à cette époque d'exagérations.

Stables for William H. Winslow, River Forest, Illinois, 1893–1894
View

B. Harley Bradley House, Kankakee, Illinois, 1900
General view and elevation

The *Ladies' Home Journal,* Warren Hickox, and Bradley houses were built about the same time, 1900. They all exhibit features and elements that have come to define the »prairie house«. The openness and spatial flow so evident in the Hickox house is less obvious in the Bradley. But the Bradley house was certainly one of the first in which Wright exercised total control over the interior design as well as the exterior, including furnishings and carpets. He was not always able to persuade his early clients to accept his designs for furniture, other than what he planned as built-in pieces.

Die Häuser, die im *Ladies' Home Journal* vorgestellt wurden, das Warren-Hickox- und das Bradley-Haus, entstanden alle um die Jahrhundertwende. Gemeinsam sind ihnen die Grundzüge und Elemente, die das »Präriehaus« bestimmten. Die Offenheit und die fließend ineinander übergehenden Räume, die beim Haus Hickox so klar zu erkennen sind, zeigt das Haus Bradley allerdings weniger deutlich. Aber der Auftrag für Bradley war einer der ersten, bei dem Wright auch die komplette Innenausstattung übernahm, einschließlich Möbel und Teppiche. Wohl wurden seine fest installierten Einbauten auch von seinen frühen Bauherren akzeptiert, von seinen Möbelentwürfen konnte er sie jedoch nicht immer überzeugen.

Les maisons présentées dans le *Ladies' Home Journal* ainsi que les maisons Warren Hickox et Bradley furent construites à la même époque, c'est-à-dire autour de 1900. Elles offrent toutes les traits distinctifs et les éléments qui finirent par caractériser la »Prairie House«. L'espace ouvert et fluide qui est si manifeste dans la maison Hickox, apparaît de façon moins évidente dans la maison Bradley. Toutefois, celle-ci fut certainement l'une des premières maisons, où Wright put contrôler totalement aussi bien l'aspect extérieur que l'agencement intérieur, y compris mobilier et tapis. Mis à part les éléments qu'il prévoyait d'encastrer, il ne fut pas toujours capable de persuader ses premiers clients d'accepter ses projets de meubles.

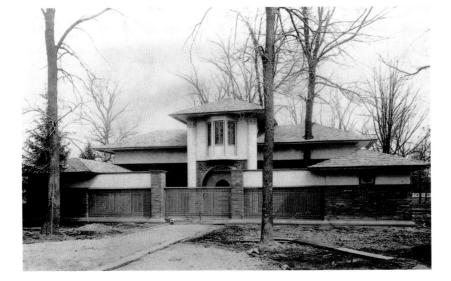

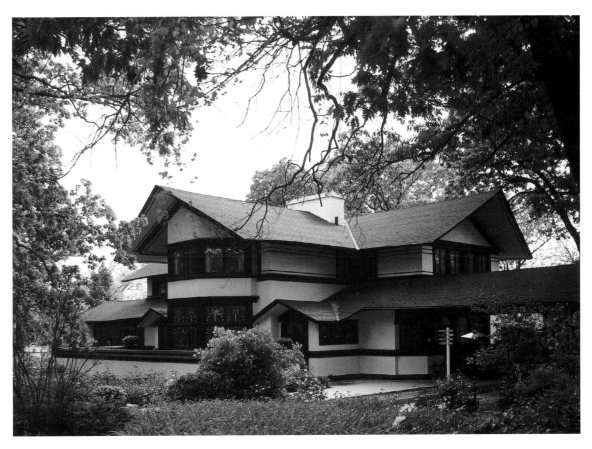

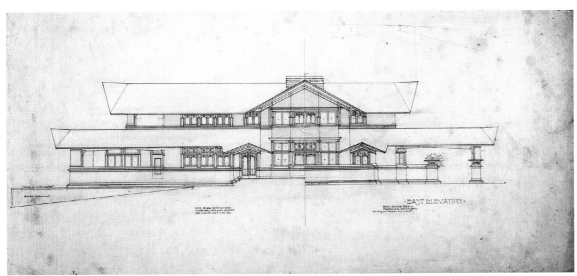

·EAST ELEVATION·

**Susan Lawrence Dana House, Spring-
field, Illinois, 1899–1900**
Street view

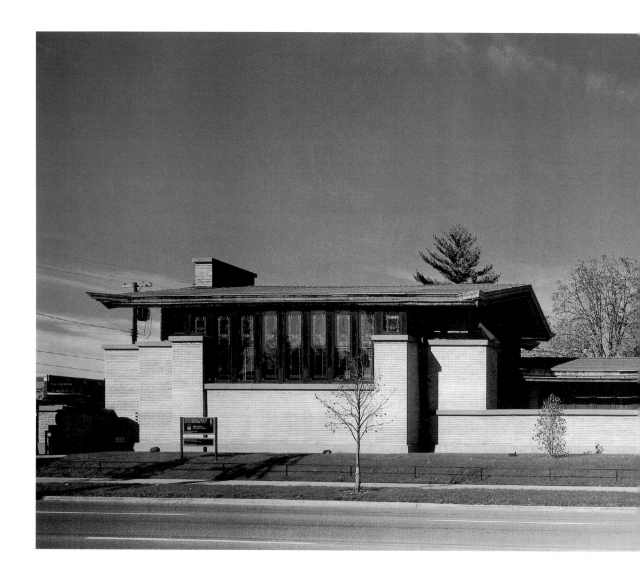

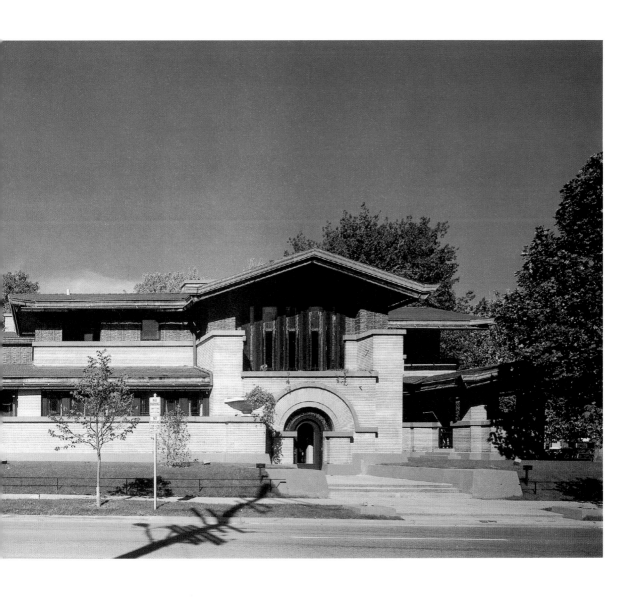

**Susan Lawrence Dana House, Spring-
field, Illinois, 1899–1900**
Elevations, sections and first floor plan

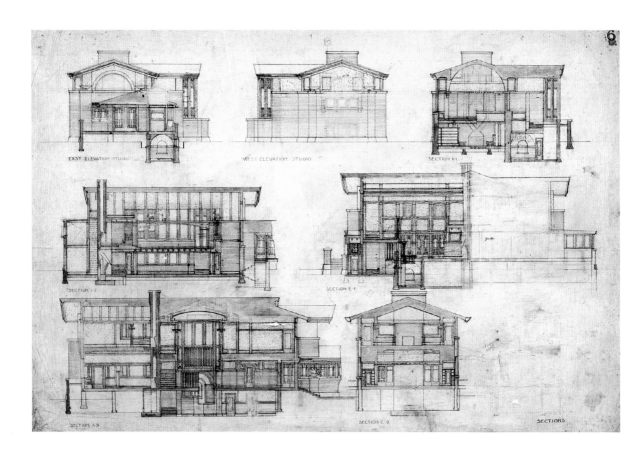

EAST ELEVATION STUDIO   WEST ELEVATION STUDIO   SECTION K L

SECTION I J   SECTION E F

SECTION A B   SECTION C D   SECTIONS

The Dana house is an example of a large, spacious home for a client who wanted a residence in which to house a fine art collection as well as allow for elaborate entertaining. This commission, built of a beautiful grey Roman brick, was one such as rarely comes to a young architect: everything in the building was designed by Wright – all the furnishings, free standing and built-in. The lighting fixtures, lamps and stained glass are notably the most lavish ever done by Wright. The use of stained glass in many ways functioned as casement draperies, of which there were none: light is allowed in, through a diffusion of delicate colors and patterns, but the passer-by is hard-pressed to see into the building. The main residence is connected to a larger studio gallery, two stories high, for parties, social events, exhibitions and gatherings.

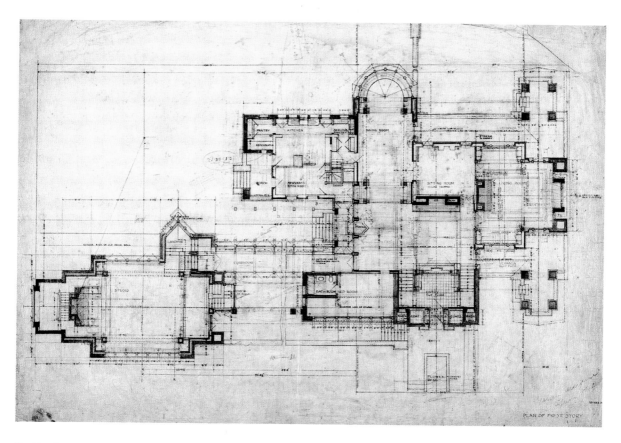

PLAN OF FIRST STORY

Das Haus Dana ist ein Beispiel für einen großen, geräumigen Wohnsitz für einen Bauherrn, der sowohl eine Kunstsammlung unterbringen wollte als auch Raum für gesellschaftliche Anlässe benötigte. Dieser Auftrag, ausgeführt in schönen römischen Ziegeln, war so, wie ihn ein junger Architekt selten erhält: Alles an und in dem Gebäude war von Wright entworfen – auch das gesamte bewegliche oder eingebaute Mobiliar. Die verschiedenen Beleuchtungskörper und die Bleiverglasung gehören zum Aufwendigsten, was Wright je entworfen hat. Das so zahlreich verwendete getönte Glas ersetzte die nicht vorhandenen Vorhänge: Das Licht dringt, gebrochen durch zarte Farben und Formen, nach innen, aber Passanten können kaum hineinschauen. Die Hauptwohnung ist mit einem größeren, zweistöckigen Studio für Parties, gesellige Anlässe, Ausstellungen und Versammlungen verbunden.

La maison Dana est l'exemple de la maison spacieuse pour un client désirant une demeure dans laquelle il peut abriter sa collection de beaux-arts et organiser de grandes réceptions. Cette maison, qui fut exécutée en belle brique grise romaine, est le genre de commande qu'un jeune architecte reçoit rarement: tout dans le bâtiment a été dessiné par Wright – tout l'ameublement, les éléments mobiles et les parties encastrées. Les éclairages muraux, les lampes et les vitraux en particulier ont été réalisés de façon particulièrement somptueuse. Le vitrail est utilisé comme rideau de fenêtre: en pénétrant à l'intérieur, la lumière passe par une dispersion de couleurs et de formes délicates; toutefois le passant ne peut que difficilement regarder à l'intérieur du bâtiment. La demeure principale est reliée à une grande galerie de deux étages où l'on peut organiser des réceptions, des réunions et des expositions.

**»A Home in a Prairie Town« for Ladies'
Home Journal, 1900 (project)**
Elevation and perspective drawing

When »A Home in a Prairie Town« was published in the April 1901 edition of *Ladies' Home Journal,* Wright supplied not only the drawings for the house but the text as well. It puts on record some of his earliest writing concerning the »prairie house«: »The exterior recognizes the influence of the prairie, is firmly and broadly associated with the site, and makes a feature of its quiet level. The low terraces and broad eaves are designed to accentuate that quiet level and complete the harmonious relationship.« In conjunction with the plans, sections and views of this house is a suggestion for its use as part of a quadruple block in which four such houses are grouped towards the center, each one facing its own corner, with privacy from the others.

Zum Beitrag »A Home in a Prairie Town«, erschienen in der Aprilnummer des *Ladies' Home Journal* von 1901, lieferte Wright nicht nur die Zeichnungen, sondern auch den Text, der einige seiner frühesten Überlegungen zum »Präriehaus« zusammenfaßte: »Das Äußere geht auf die Prärie ein, ist fest und deutlich mit der Landschaft verbunden und entspricht ihrer ruhigen, ebenen Weite. Die niedrigen Terrassen und ausgreifenden Dachüberstände betonen diese ebene Weite noch und vervollkommnen die harmonische Beziehung.« Grundrisse, Schnitte und Ansichten geben Hinweise auf eine mögliche Verwendung des »Präriehauses« in einem Viererblock, in dem die Einzelhäuser so um ein Zentrum gruppiert werden, daß jedes ein Eckgrundstück besetzt und damit von den anderen möglichst ungestört bleibt.

En avril 1901, la revue *Ladies' Home Journal* publia un numéro intitulé »A Home in a Prairie Town«. Wright avait non seulement fourni les plans de la maison, mais il avait aussi écrit le texte. Celui-ci résumait certains écrits antérieurs concernant la »Prairie house«: »Son aspect extérieur reflète l'influence de la Prairie, s'adapte au paysage et transforme en caractéristique son étendue tranquille. Les terrasses basses et les larges avant-toits servent à accentuer ce caractère et complètent ce rapport harmonieux.« Les plans, les coupes et les vues de la maison étaient accompagnés de suggestions pour son utilisation comme partie d'un bloc quadruple, dans lequel quatre maisons de ce type étaient regroupées au centre. Chacune d'entre elles était orientée vers son propre terrain et préservait ainsi l'intimité de ses habitants.

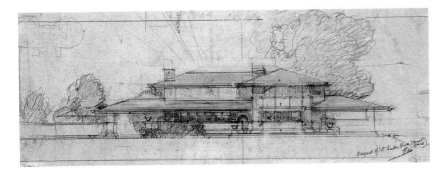

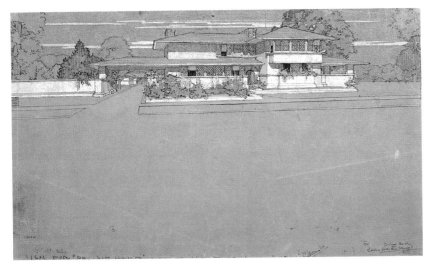

Frank Thomas House, Oak Park, Illinois, 1901
Street view

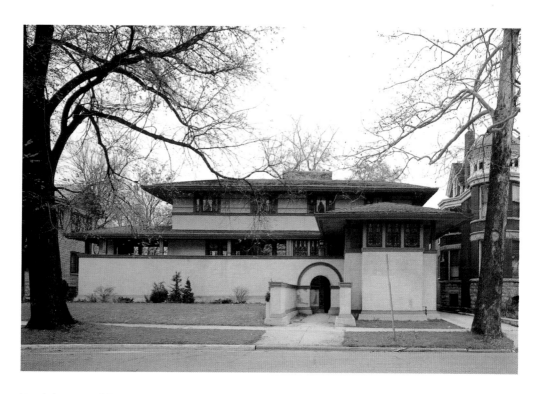

Here the basement is fully on ground level, placing the living and dining spaces up on this so-called pedestal. The entrance is intriguing: after passing through an arch in the wall, an outside staircase leads up to the long front porch that flanks the living room, and gains entry into a vestibule. The »L«-plan is far less formal than earlier axial plans and demonstrates Wright's tendency to move away from the major-minor axis type of design exemplified by the Winslow house into a plan with more plasticity, such as this one for Frank Thomas and the William Fricke house.

Hier sitzt das Kellergeschoß auf Boden-niveau, so daß die Räume zum Woh-nen und Speisen auf einer Art Sockel zu ruhen scheinen. Der Eingang ist bemer-kenswert gelöst: Nachdem man einen Mauerbogen passiert hat, führt eine au-ßenliegende Treppe zur breiten Ve-randa, die das Wohnzimmer flankiert, und von dort in eine Vorhalle. Der L-förmige Grundriß ist weit weniger for-mal als frühere axiale Pläne und zeigt Wrights Tendenz, sich von Entwürfen mit einer dominanten und einer unter-geordneten Gebäudeachse, wie etwa beim Winslow-Haus, zu entfernen. Er entwickelte nun Grundrisse mit mehr Plastizität, wie beim Frank-Thomas-Haus oder dem Haus für William Fricke.

Ici, les soubassements se trouvent com-plètement au niveau du sol, juchant ainsi la salle de séjour et la salle à man-ger sur un socle. L'entrée est de nature à intriguer: après l'arc de l'entrée, on ar-rive à un escalier extérieur. Celui-ci conduit à la grande véranda frontale, située latéralement à la salle de séjour, et débouche sur le vestibule. Le plan en »L« est bien moins formel que les plans axiaux précédents. Il témoigne de la tendance de Wright à s'éloigner du type de plans exemplifiés par la maison Winslow pour se diriger vers un plan plus flexible, que l'on retrouve aussi dans la maison William Fricke.

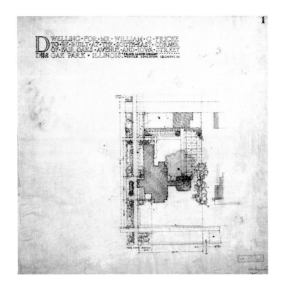

The Fricke house is a special example of a three-story house designed by Frank Lloyd Wright. The size of the lot imposed on the architect the need to go up, rather than out. The placement of the house on the lot demonstrates an important design solution: the house is set to one corner, freeing the rest for lawn and gardens, defying standards which placed the house in the center, with yards in front, at the back and on either side. Originally, a roofed-over but open pavilion was reached by a covered passage from the living room. Ideal for summer entertaining and dining, the pavilion was set in the shade, overlooking flowering gardens.

Das Haus Fricke ist das seltene Beispiel eines dreistöckigen von Frank Lloyd Wright entworfenen Wohnhauses. Die Größe des Grundstücks zwang den Architekten, mehr in die Höhe als in die Breite zu gehen, auch die Lage des Hauses auf dem Grundstück stellt eine besondere Entwurfslösung dar: Es ist ganz auf eine Straßenseite gestellt und läßt so den Rest für Rasen und Garten frei. Dies widersprach deutlich dem üblichen Vorgehen, wonach das Haus in der Mitte des Grundstückes plaziert und freie Flächen an der Front-, Rückseite und den Seiten gelassen wurden. Ursprünglich war ein überdachter, sonst aber offener Pavillon über eine geschützte Passage vom Wohnzimmer aus zu erreichen. Schattig angelegt, mit Blick auf blühende Gärten, bot er im Sommer einen idealen Platz für Abendessen und Freizeit.

La maison Fricke est un exemple particulier d'une maison à trois étages dessinée par Frank Lloyd Wright. La taille du terrain obligea l'architecte à construire en hauteur, plutôt qu'en largeur. L'emplacement de la maison propose une solution importante dans le dessin des plans: la maison est située dans un angle, libérant le reste du terrain pour la pelouse et les jardins. Elle défie les normes qui situait la maison au milieu du terrain, avec des jardins sur le devant, à l'arrière et de chaque côté. A l'origine, un passage couvert reliait la salle de séjour à un pavillon, recouvert d'un toit mais ouvert sur les côtés. Idéal pour les réceptions et les dîners en été, le pavillon était situé à l'ombre et donnait sur les jardins fleuris.

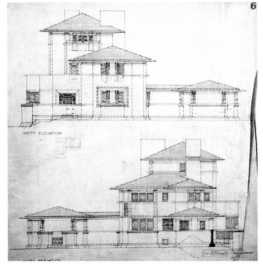

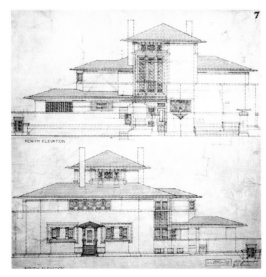

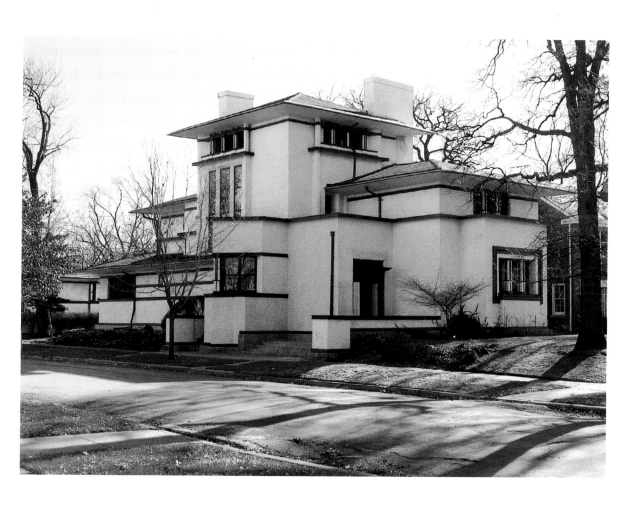

**Ward W. Willits House, Highland Park,
Illinois, 1901–1902**
Front façade and staircase

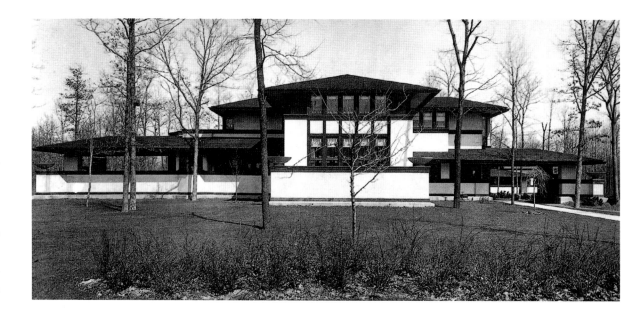

On a more spacious suburban lot is the house of Ward W. Willits. Built of cement stucco, its white surfaces are accentuated by dark stained wood trim. The plan is cruciform, the living room, dining room and reception areas separated by architectural features rather than walls and doors. As with the Dana house, the fireplace is focal to the plan, with built-in seats around it. More and more, in his early work, Wright experimented with furniture of his own design. He found, to his dismay, that when the new house was ready for the clients to move in, they brought with them the furniture of their previous dwelling. By incorporating built-in bookcases, seating, sideboards, cupboards, etc., he was certain that the basic interior, at least, would blend with his overall design. Landscaping, as well, was designed along with the building to further achieve a sense of unity in design.

Das Haus von Ward W. Willits entstand auf einem weitläufigen Vorstadtgrundstück. Die weißen Oberflächen des verputzten Baus sind mit dunkelgebeizten Holzfassungen akzentuiert. Der Grundriß ist kreuzförmig; Wohnzimmer, Eßzimmer und Eingangsbereich sind eher durch architektonische Kunstgriffe als durch Wände und Türen getrennt. Wie beim Dana-Haus bildet der offene Kamin, umgeben von fest eingebauten Sitzplätzen, den Kern. Mehr und mehr begann Wright in seinen frühen Werken mit selbstentworfenem Mobiliar zu experimentieren. Zu seinem Entsetzen stellte er nämlich fest, daß seine Bauherren, wenn das Haus fertig war, mit den Möbeln aus ihrer bisherigen Wohnung einzogen. Durch die Verwendung von fest eingebauten Bücherregalen, Sitzgelegenheiten und Schränken konnte er jedoch sicherstellen, daß sich zumindest die Grundinneneinrichtung harmonisch mit dem Gesamtkonzept verband. Auch seine Gartengestaltung strebte die Herausbildung eines einheitlichen Eindrucks im Zusammenhang mit dem Gebäude an.

La maison de Ward W. Willits est située sur un vaste terrain de banlieue. Revêtue de crépi, ses surfaces blanches sont accentuées par des ornements en bois, peints en noir. Le plan est cruciforme. La salle de séjour, la salle à manger et les halls d'entrée sont plutôt séparés par des éléments architecturaux que par des murs et des portes. Comme dans la maison Dana, l'âtre est au centre du plan, avec des siège encastrés tout autour. Dans ses premiers travaux, Wright expérimentait de plus en plus avec des meubles conçus par lui-même. A sa grande consternation, il remarquait que ses clients, lorsque la maison était terminée, y installaient le mobilier de leur ancienne demeure. En réalisant des bibliothèques, des sièges, des buffets et des placards incorporés, il était sûr qu'au moins le mobilier de base s'accorderait avec la conception générale. L'architecture des jardins était également établie en fonction du bâtiment afin d'obtenir une impression d'unité.

54

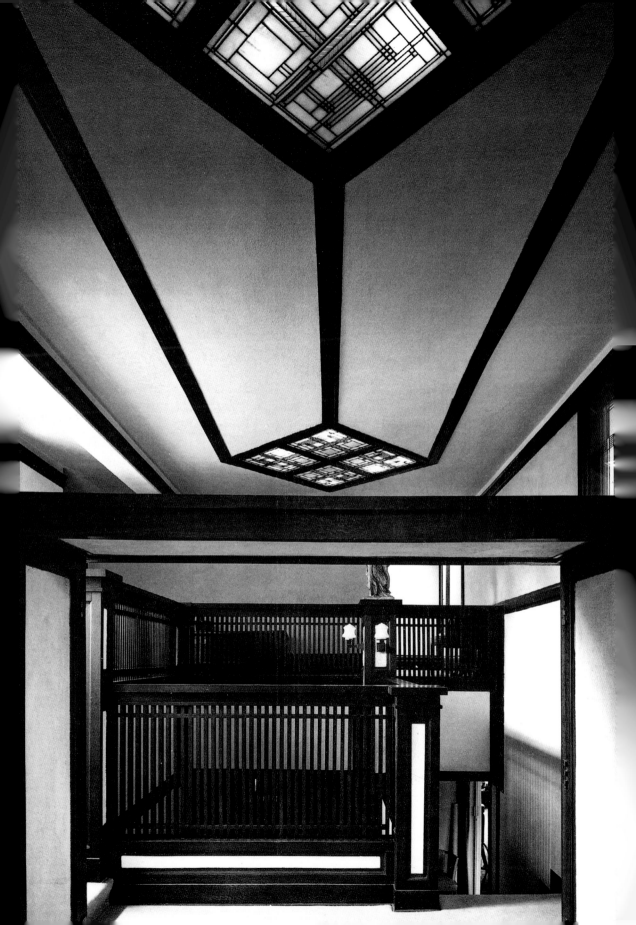

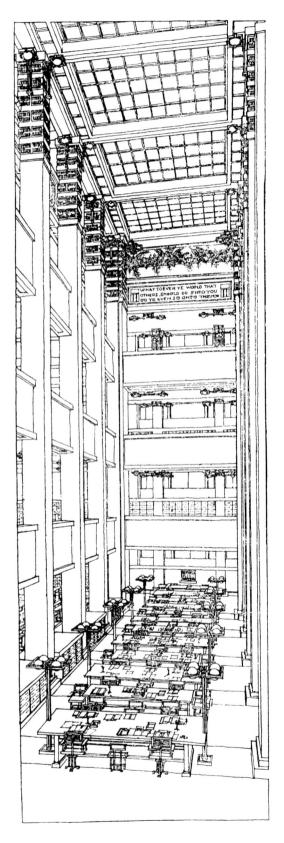

More than any other single structure in the twentieth century, the Larkin building exerted an influence that changed the face of architecture. »The building«, Wright wrote, »is a simple working out of certain utilitarian conditions, its exterior a simple cliff of brick whose only ›ornamental‹ feature is the exterior expression of the central aisle, fashioned by means of the sculptured piers at either end of the main block. The machinery of the various appurtenance systems, pipe shafts incidental thereto, the heating and ventilating air intakes, and the stairways which serve also as fire escapes, are quartered in plan and placed outside the main building at the four outer corners, so that the entire area might be free for working purposes. These stair chambers are top-lighted. The interior of the main building thus forms a single large room in which the main floors are galleries open to a large central court, which is also lighted from above. All the windows of the various stories ›galleries‹ are seven feet above the floor, the space beneath being utilized for steel filing cabinets. The window sashes are double, and the building practically sealed to dirt, odor and noise, fresh air being taken high above the ground in shafts extending above the roof surfaces.«

There were many innovative details of the building that marked it an important »first of its kind«: steel desk furniture, air-conditioning, wall-hung water closet and partitions (for ease in cleaning), glass doors set in metal frames with pintle hinges (anchored at top and bottom). The general disposition of the entire plan, working in open galleries looking into a light court, brought a sense of »family« to the corporation where all worked together without private offices or secluded spaces. This in itself was a great revolution in industrial thought in an era where the employer was usually sequestered from the employee.

Das Larkin-Gebäude hat mehr als jeder andere Bau des zwanzigsten Jahrhunderts die Vorstellungen von Architektur verändert. Für Wright war »das Gebäude die schlichte Umsetzung gewisser zweckbestimmter Bedingungen, sein Äußeres einfach ein Fels aus Ziegeln, dessen einziges ›Ornament‹ aus der äußeren Entsprechung des Mittelschiffes besteht, hervorgehoben noch

durch die herausgeformten Eckpfeiler an den beiden Seiten des Baukörpers. Die Anlagen der verschiedenen Versorgungssysteme mit ihren Rohrschächten, Heizungs- und Lüftungsöffnungen sowie die Treppen, die auch als Notausgänge dienen, sind im Grundriß abgeteilt und an den vier Außenecken plaziert, so daß die gesamte innere Fläche für Arbeitsplätze genutzt werden kann; diese Treppentürme erhalten ihr Licht von oben. Das Innere des Hauptgebäudes bildet also einen einzigen riesigen Raum, auf den die Stockwerke wie Galerien münden und sich so zu dem Lichthof hin öffnen. Alle Fenster der Stockwerke oder Galerien liegen mehr als zwei Meter über dem Fußboden, der Raum darunter wird von Aktenschränken aus Stahl eingenommen. Doppelfenster schließen das Gebäude gegen Staub, Lärm und Geruch ab, die Frischluft wird über Rohrleitungen vom Dach zugeführt.«

Der Bau hatte viele innovative Details, die hier erstmals erschienen: Möblierung mit Schreibtischen aus Stahl, Klimaanlage, Toiletten mit wassergespülten Schüsseln in Wandmontage und Raumteiler, die die Reinigung erleichterten, schließlich Glastüren in Metallrahmen, die sich um Achsen an der Ober- und Unterseite drehten. Die Anordnung des gesamten Entwurfs mit seinen offenen Galerien, die auf einen Lichthof blicken, vermittelte der Belegschaft ein »familiäres« Gefühl. Alle arbeiteten in einem Großraum, in dem es keine Privatbüros oder separierten Bereiche gab. Dies allein war schon eine Revolution in der damaligen Arbeitswelt, wo der Arbeitgeber üblicherweise von seinen Angestellten abgeschottet blieb.

Plus que toute autre construction individuelle du 20ème siècle, le bâtiment administratif de la société Larkin a exercé une influence qui a changé le visage de l'architecture. »Le bâtiment, écrivait Wright, est une simple mise au point de certaines conditions pratiques, son aspect extérieur ressemble à une falaise de briques. L'aile centrale constitue le seul ›ornement‹ avec ses piliers sculptés situés de part et d'autre de la partie principale. La machinerie des différents systèmes d'alimentation, les conduits des tuyaux qui en font partie, les conduits d'aération et de chauffage et les escaliers qui servent également de sorties de secours sont partagés en quatre sur le plan et situés en dehors du bâtiment principal, aux quatre coins extérieurs, afin que toute la surface du bâtiment puisse être utilisée comme lieu de travail. Les cages d'escaliers ont un éclairage zénithal. L'intérieur du bâtiment principal a ainsi la forme d'une grande salle unique, où les étages principaux

sont des galeries s'ouvrant sur une vaste cour centrale qui est également éclairée d'en haut. Toutes les fenêtres de ces différents étages ou ›galeries‹ sont situées à une hauteur de sept pieds au-dessus du sol, l'espace inférieur étant réservé aux armoires à dossiers en métal. Les fenêtres à guillotine sont doubles, et le bâtiment est pratiquement hermétique à la poussière, aux odeurs et au bruit. L'air frais provient de conduits situés à hauteur et se prolongeant au-dessus des toits.«

L'importance du bâtiment, considéré comme »le premier dans son genre«, réside dans ses nombreux détails innovateurs: meubles de bureau en acier, air conditionné, toilettes et cloisons fixées au mur (pour faciliter le nettoyage du sol), portes en verre entourées de cadres en métal avec des charnières à cheville (fixées en haut et en bas). La disposition générale du plan, incorporant des galeries ouvertes donnant sur une cour éclairée, apportait aux employés le sentiment d'être une »famille«. Ils travaillaient tous ensemble, sans bureaux individuels, ni pièces à l'écart. Ceci était une grande révolution dans la mentalité de cette époque, où le patron s'isolait habituellement de ses employés.

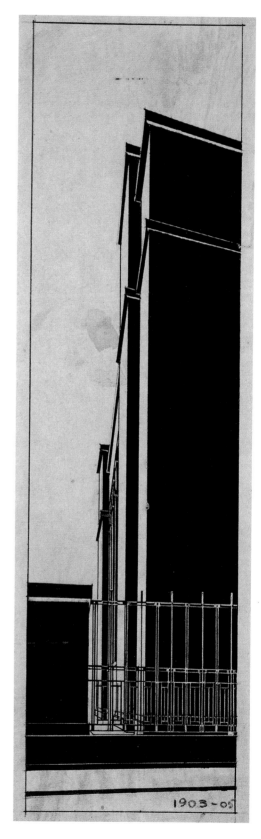

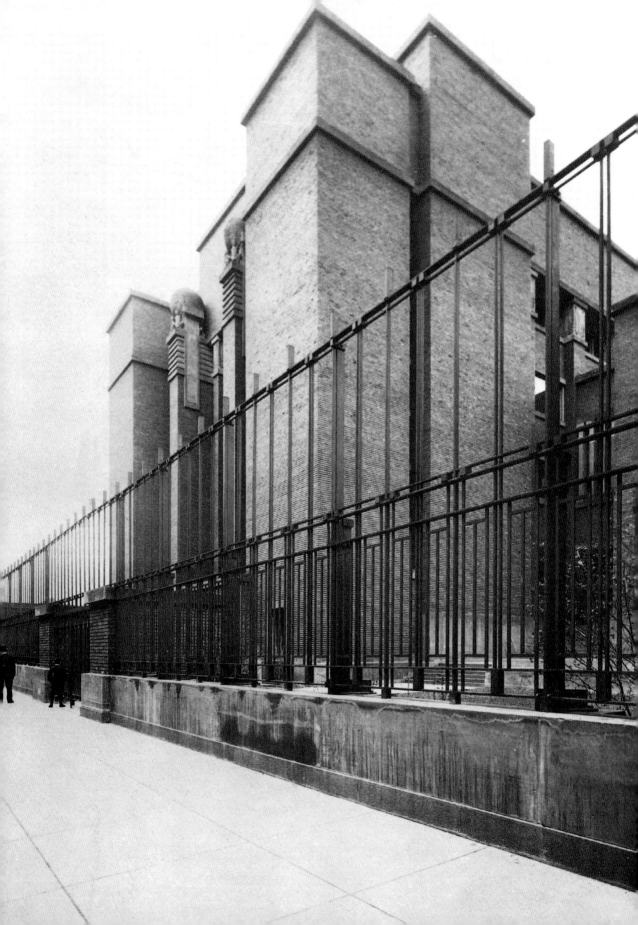

**Larkin Company Administration Build-
ing, Buffalo, New York, 1903–1905**
Street view, sketches for reception desk

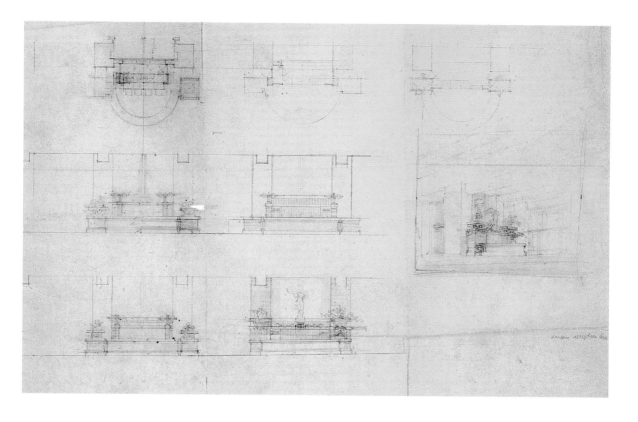

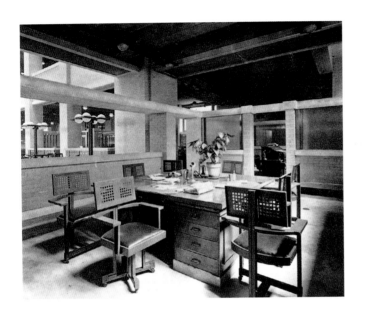

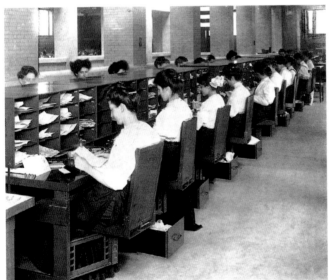

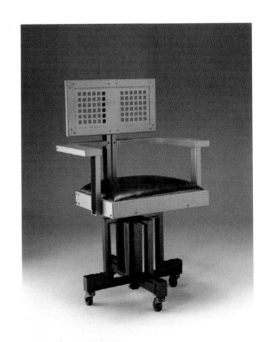

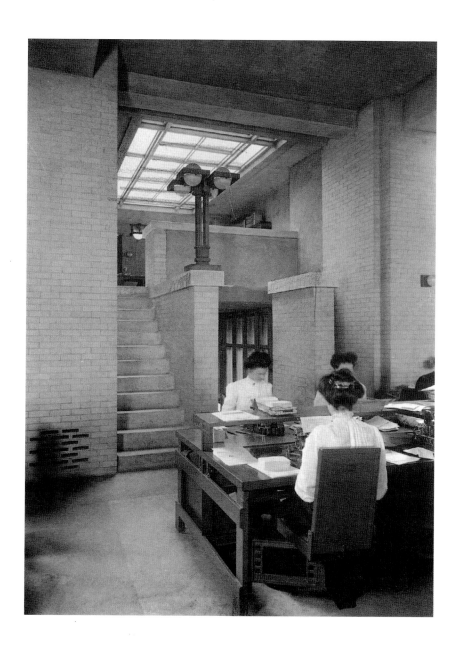

Larkin Company Administration Building, Buffalo, New York, 1903–1905
Office chair and vintage interior shots of director's office (opposite page) and office space on the ground level

**Unity Temple, Oak Park, Illinois,
1904–1907**
Interior

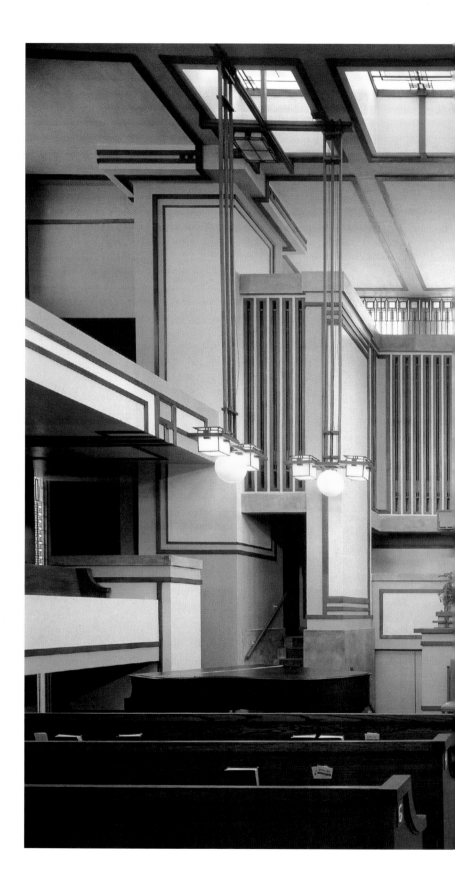

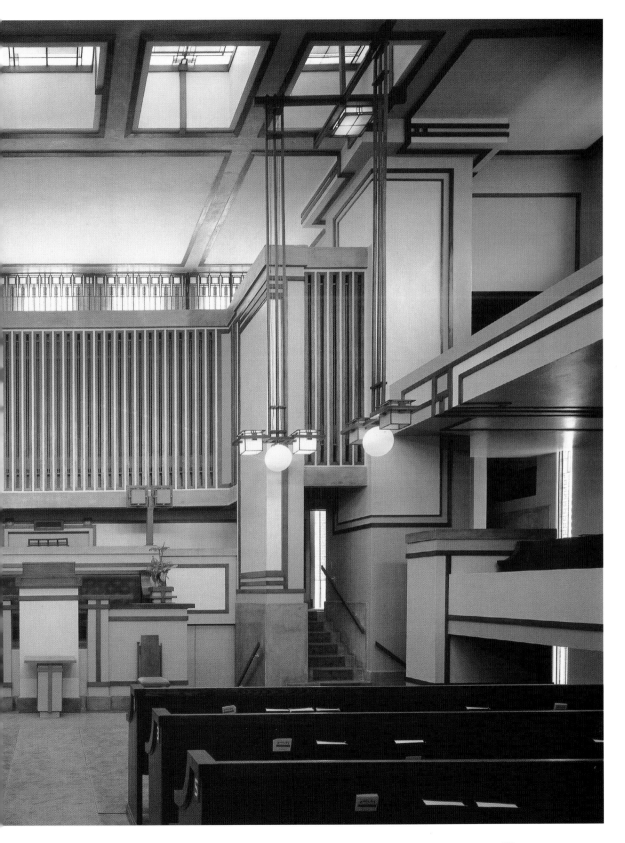

**Unity Temple, Oak Park, Illinois,
1904–1907**
Plans of ground and upper floor, perspective

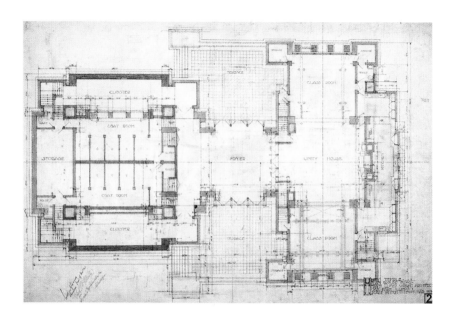

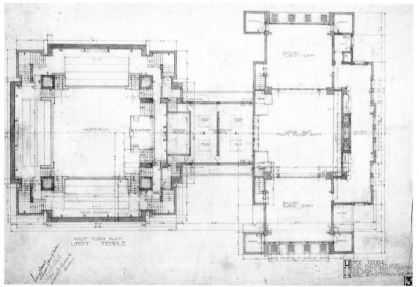

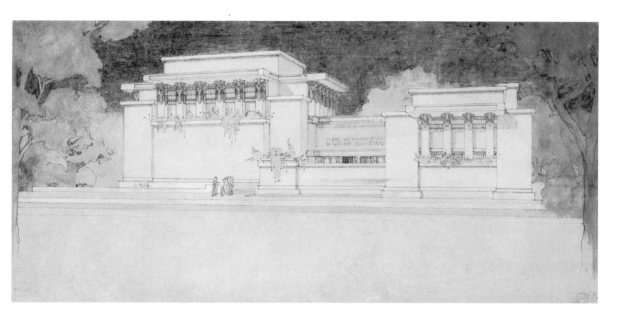

Like the Larkin Building before it, Unity Temple bears a certain fortress-like quality when seen from the outside. Two basic cubes of concrete – the larger one for the church proper, the smaller one for its secular activities, are separated by an entrance foyer. The sense of the space reveals itself inside, where four great columns, set in from the outside walls, carry the overhead roof slab. This flat roof is pierced by square skylights, and the exterior walls rise up to the second story, windowless, to provide protection in the sanctuary from the street noises outside. On the upper level, these walls become screens of glass that rise to meet the skylight above. Thus, from the inside, there appears to be no restriction of enclosed space: the outside light pours in from the top and all sides. On one of his interior drawings of this building, Wright wrote, »The unlimited overhead. Interior space enclosed by screen-features only. Idea later used in Johnson Building, Racine, Wisconsin.«

Wie das Larkin-Gebäude hat auch die Unity-Kirche etwas von einer Festung, wenn man sie von außen betrachtet. Im Prinzip sind zwei Betonwürfel durch ein Eingangsfoyer verbunden, der größere für die eigentliche Kirche und der kleinere für die Aufgaben der Gemeinde. Das Gefühl für den Raum kommt im Inneren zum Vorschein, wo vier große, von den Außenwänden eingerückte Pfeiler die von quadratischen Oberlichtern durchbrochene Dachplatte tragen. Die Außenwände steigen ohne jedes Fenster bis zum ersten Stock auf, um den Altarbereich vor Straßenlärm zu bewahren. Unter der Decke werden diese Wände zu gläsernen Schirmen, die bis zu den Oberlichtern reichen. Daher scheint es, von innen betrachtet, keine harte Begrenzung des Raums zu geben: Das Außenlicht fließt von oben und von allen Seiten herein. Auf einer seiner Entwurfszeichnungen des Innenraums notierte Wright: »Nach oben unbegrenzt. Innenraum nur wie von Wandschirmen umschlossen. Idee später für Johnson-Gebäude, Racine, Wisconsin, verwendet.«

Tout comme les bureaux Larkin, le temple de l'Unité ressemble quelque peu à une forteresse, quand on le regarde de l'extérieur. Il est constitué de deux cubes en béton – le plus grand pour l'église proprement dite, l'autre pour les activités laïques – qui sont séparés par un hall d'entrée. La sensation d'espace se manifeste à l'intérieur, où quatre grandes colonnes, placées en retrait des murs extérieurs, soutiennent le plafond. Dans ce plafond plat, des ouvertures carrées sont percées. Les murs qui s'élèvent jusqu'au second étage sont dépourvus de fenêtres afin que le sanctuaire soit protégé des bruits de la rue. Au niveau supérieur, les murs deviennent des parois de verre qui rejoignent les ouvertures du toit. Ainsi, de l'intérieur, l'espace semble illimité: la lumière extérieure qui se répand dans le bâtiment vient d'en haut et de tous les côtés. Sur l'un des plans de l'intérieur, Wright notait »Espace supérieur illimité. Espace intérieur encadré seulement par des cloisons. Idée reprise plus tard dans le bâtiment Johnson, Racine, Wisconsin.«

Yahara Boathouse for the University of Wisconsin Boat Club, Madison, Wisconsin, 1905 (project)

Wright originally designed this simple structure of wood frame and cement stucco to store the long, narrow racing shells of the University of Wisconsin crew team. Twenty five years later he asked draftsman Heinrich Klumb to make sepia drawings of several monolithic buildings: the Larkin Building, Unity Temple, the Richard Bock Studio, the Winslow House, the Robie house and the Yahara Boathouse. These six drawings were central to the touring exhibition of Frank Lloyd Wright's work of 1930. Long considered a project of 1902, the recent discovery of correspondence now places the Yahara Boathouse in 1905.

Wright entwarf diesen einfachen Bau, in dem die langen, schmalen Rennboote der Mannschaft von der Universität von Wisconsin untergebracht werden sollten, ursprünglich als verputzte Holzrahmenkonstruktion. Fünfundzwanzig Jahre später bat er den Zeichner Heinrich Klumb, Sepiazeichnungen von einigen monolithischen Gebäuden anzufertigen: vom Larkin-Gebäude, der Unity-Kirche, dem Richard-Bock-Studio, den Häusern Winslow und Robie sowie dem Yahara-Bootshaus. Diese sechs Zeichnungen waren zentrale Exponate der Frank-Lloyd-Wright-Ausstellung 1930. Lange als Projekt von 1902 vermutet, muß nach der kürzlichen Entdeckung der Korrespondenz das Yahara-Bootshaus auf das Jahr 1905 datiert werden.

A l'origine, cette simple construction, à la charpente en bois et recouverte de crépi en ciment, devait abriter les canots de course, longs et fuselés, de l'équipe de l'Université du Wisconsin. Vingt-cinq ans plus tard, Wright demanda au dessinateur Heinrich Klumb de réaliser des sépias de plusieurs bâtiments monolithiques: le bâtiment Larkin, le temple de l'Unité, le studio Richard Bock, la maison Winslow, la maison Robie et le club nautique Yahara. Ces six dessins occupèrent une place centrale dans l'exposition itinérante de 1930 qui présenta les travaux de Frank Lloyd Wright. Pendant longtemps, le club nautique Yahara fut considéré comme un projet datant de 1902. Des lettres découvertes récemment permettent de situer maintenant son édification en 1905.

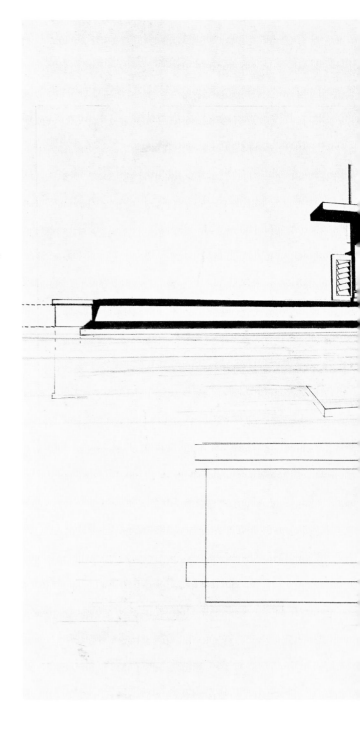

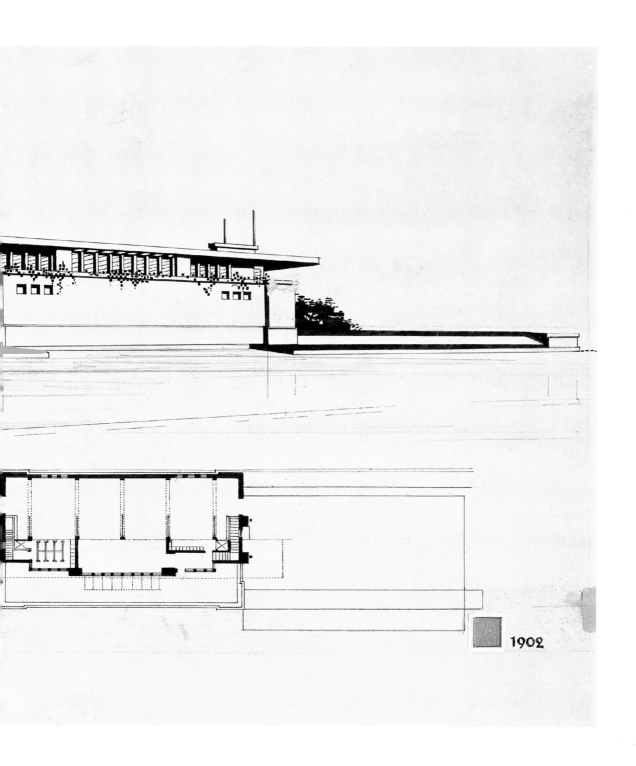

1902

Darwin D. Martin House, Buffalo, New York, 1904–1905
Site plan, street view, living room

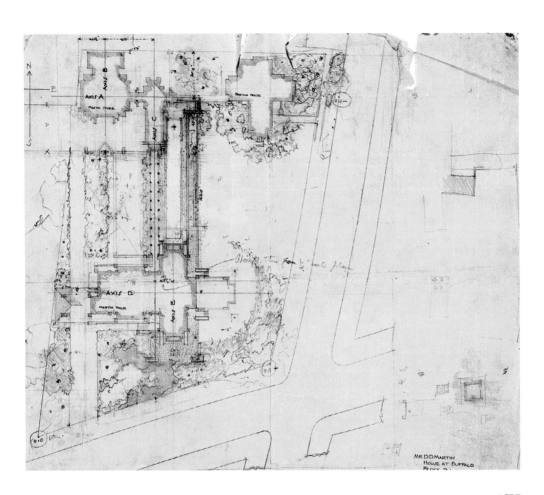

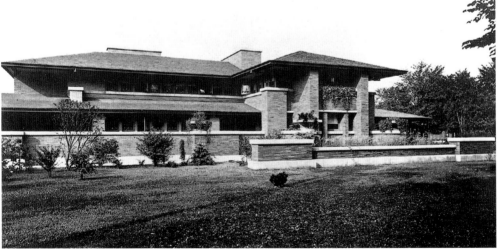

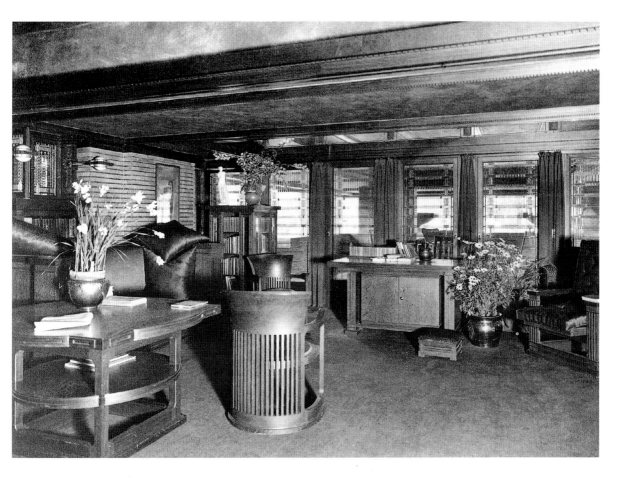

Darwin D. Martin was the chief executive officer of the Larkin Company, and responsible for Wright getting the commission for their building. At the same time, he commissioned Wright to design his own home. The plan is essentially cruciform, dining room, living room and library along one axis, the other housing reception room, kitchen, and covered porch. The gallery leading off the dining room passes through two flower gardens until it reaches the conservatory at the other end of the property, with garage, stable and greenhouses. The brickwork is of exceedingly beautiful quality, matched only by the equally fine craftsmanship on the woodwork throughout. These materials, so sensitively handled, are complemented by the fine art glass and the special furniture Wright designed for the home.

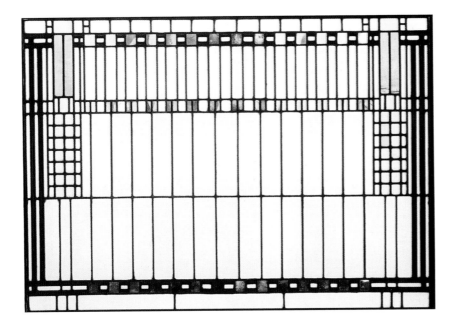

Darwin D. Martin, Vorstandsvorsitzender der Larkin Company, war ausschlaggebend dafür gewesen, daß Wright den Auftrag für das neue Verwaltungsgebäude bekommen hatte. Zur gleichen Zeit bat er Wright, für ihn ein privates Anwesen zu planen. Der Grundriß ist im wesentlichen kreuzförmig; entlang der einen Achse sind Eß und Wohnzimmer sowie die Bibliothek, entlang der anderen ein Empfangssalon, die Küche und eine überdachte Veranda angeordnet. Eine vom Eßzimmer ausgehende offene Galerie führt vorbei an zwei Blumenanlagen zum Wintergarten am anderen Ende der Besitzung, wo neben Treibhäusern auch die Garage und Stallungen untergebracht sind. Die Ziegelarbeit ist von außerordentlicher Qualität und wird nur noch von der ebenso bestechenden Kunstfertigkeit sämtlicher Holzarbeiten übertroffen. Diese so feinfühlig gehandhabten Materialien werden ergänzt durch die herrlichen Glasarbeiten und das speziell für dieses Heim entworfene Mobiliar.

Darwin D. Martin était le directeur général de la société Larkin et avait été responsable de la commande de leur bâtiment. Par la même occasion, il chargea Wright de lui construire sa propre maison. Le plan est essentiellement cruciforme; la salle à manger, la salle de séjour et la bibliothèque sont situées sur un axe, le hall d'entrée, la cuisine et une véranda couverte, sur l'autre axe. La galerie commence par la salle à manger, passe à travers deux jardins fleuris et mène au jardin d'hiver, qui se trouve, avec le garage, l'écurie et la serre, à l'autre extrémité de la propriété. Les travaux en brique sont de toute beauté et n'ont d'égal que les ouvrages de menuiserie qui reflètent une dextérité manuelle particulière. A ces matériaux, si bien travaillés, s'ajoutent les ouvrages artistiques en verre et le mobilier spécial dessiné par Wright.

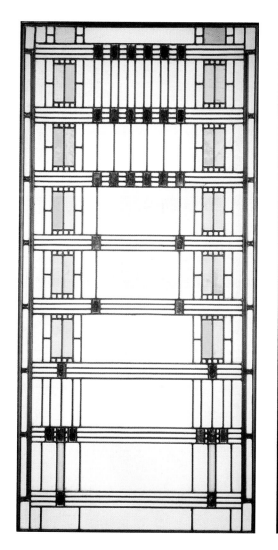
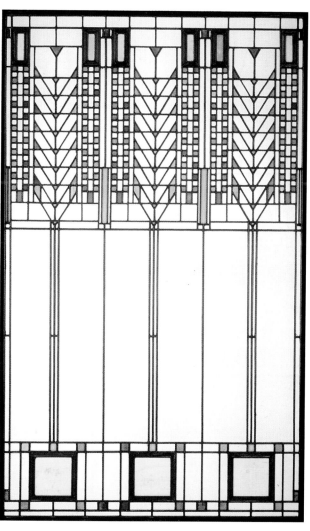

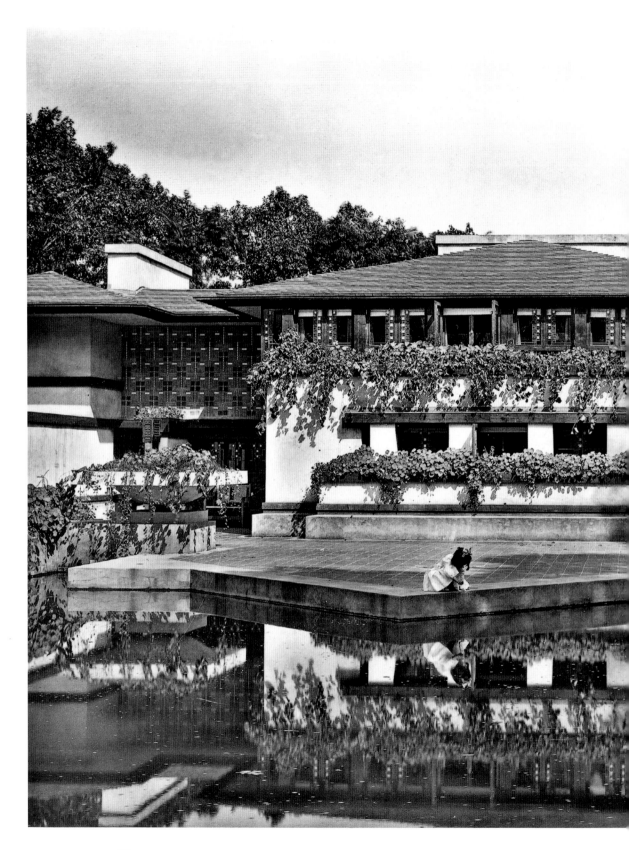

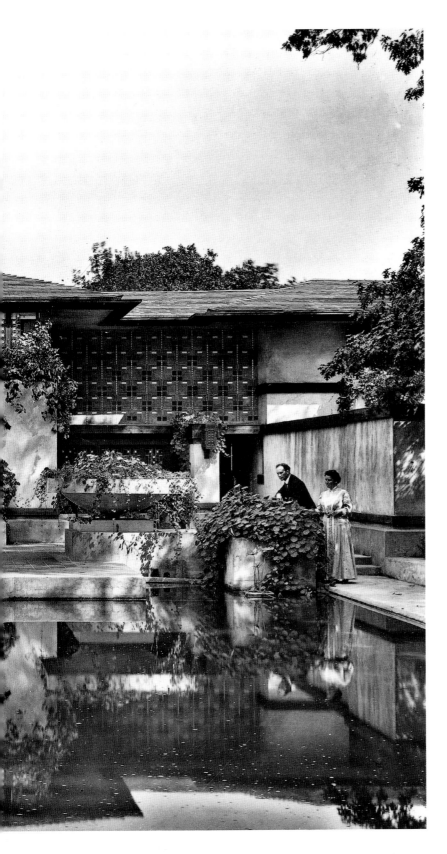

**Avery Coonley House, Riverside,
Illionis, 1907–1908**
First floor plan, design of wall pattern
and living room (opposite page)

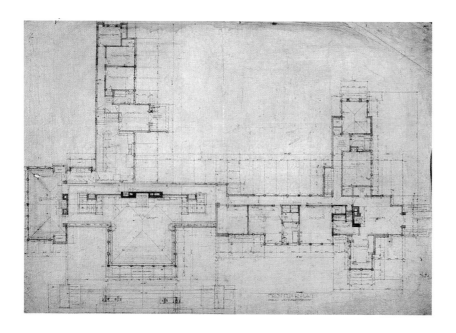

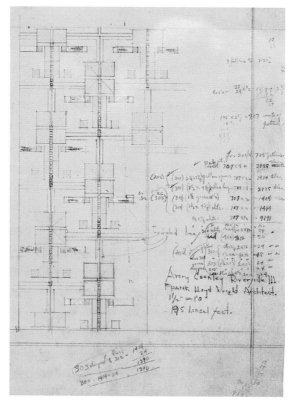

When the Coonleys came into Wright's office and asked him to design their home the architect asked what prompted them to choose him. Mrs. Coonley replied that as they saw his other houses they saw in his work »the countenances of principle.« Writing about that commission, he said, »This was to me a great and sincere compliment. So I put my best into the Coonley House.« The Coonleys had ample space on a wooded flat lot in which to place a house that could spread out. The plan was one that Wright called »zoned« because of the separation of the different functions: living, dining in one wing, bedrooms stretching out in another, and a third for kitchen and servants, crossing over the entrance drive and reaching into gardens beyond.

Als die Coonleys Wrights Büro aufsuchten und ihn baten, ein Haus für sie zu entwerfen, fragte er, warum sie gerade ihn ausgewählt hätten. Mrs. Coonley antwortete, bei der Besichtigung seiner anderen Arbeiten sei ihnen die »prinziporientierte Haltung« aufgefallen. Später schrieb Wright über diesen Auftrag: »Dies war ein großes und aufrichtiges Kompliment für mich. Also gab ich mein Bestes für das Coonley-Haus.« Die Coonleys hatten reichlich Raum auf einem flachen, waldigen Grundstück zur Verfügung, auf dem sich ihr Haus ausbreiten konnte. Den Entwurf bezeichnete Wright als »in Zonen aufgeteilt«, da die verschiedenen Wohnfunktionen getrennt wurden: Essen und Wohnen in einem Flügel, Schlafen in einem anderen, und in einem dritten Flügel, der sich quer zur Auffahrt bis zu den hinteren Gartenanlagen erstreckt, Küche und Personalräume.

Lorsque les Coonley se rendirent au cabinet de Wright et le prièrent de faire les plans de leur maison, l'architecte leur demanda pourquoi ils l'avaient choisi lui plutôt qu'un autre. Mme Coonley répondit qu'ils avaient remarqué dans son ouvrage »l'expression d'un principe«. En évoquant cette commande, Wright écrivait: »Ce compliment sincère me flatta beaucoup. J'investis tout mon talent dans la maison Coonley«. Les Coonley possédaient un vaste terrain, plat et boisé, sur lequel la maison pouvait s'étendre. Wright appelait son plan un plan »partagé«, en raison de la séparation des différentes fonctions: salle de séjour et salle à manger étaient situées dans une aile, les chambres débouchaient les unes sur les autres dans une deuxième aile, la cuisine et les chambres des domestiques se trouvaient dans une troisième qui traversait l'allée pour les voitures et s'étendait jusqu'aux jardins.

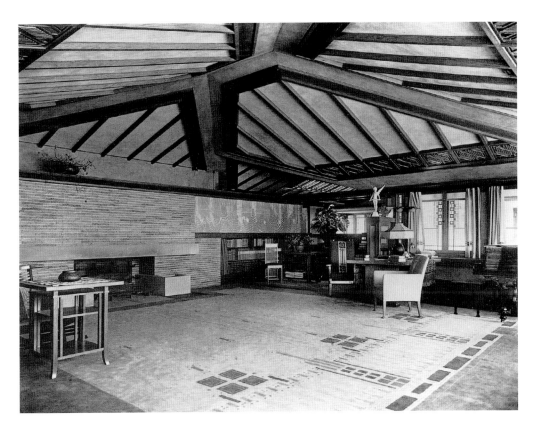

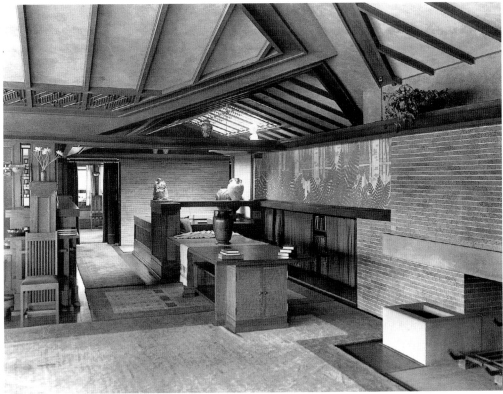

**Avery Coonley House, Riverside,
Illinois, 1907–1908**
Stained glass windows and view
of the rear side

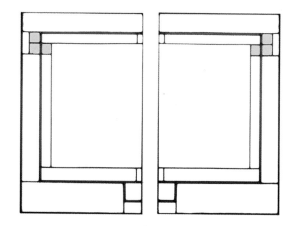

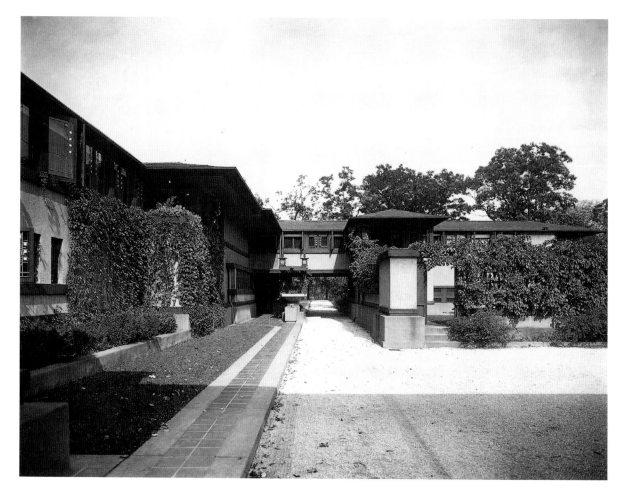

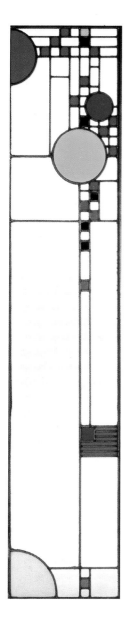

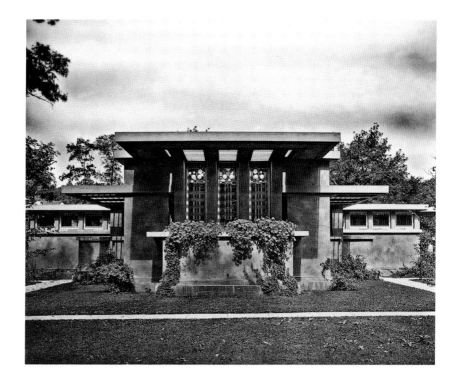

Mr. and Mrs. Coonley were intensely concerned with education. The special school and playhouse was the answer. The straight-line, streamline-masses, flatroof overhangs, perforated trellises and general design composition predate such works as Midway Gardens, the Emil Bach house, and the Imperial Hotel. An especially delightful feature of the playhouse are the brightly colored windows, called »Balloons and Confetti«.

Das Ehepaar Coonley beschäftigte sich intensiv mit Erziehungsfragen. Das »Playhouse« war Wrights Antwort. Die geradlinig-gestrafften Körper, die flachen Dachüberstände, die durchbrochenen Spaliergitter – die ganze architektonische Komposition nimmt Arbeiten wie Midway Gardens, das Emil-Bach-Haus und das Imperial Hotel vorweg. Ein besonders schönes Detail sind die leuchtend gefärbten Fenster mit dem Namen »Ballons und Konfetti«.

M. et Mme Coonley s'occupaient intensivement d'éducation. L'école privée fut la réponse de l'architecte. Les lignes droites, les formes fuselées, les toits plats en saillie, les treillis perforés et la composition générale du plan préfigurent des travaux comme les Midway Gardens, la maison Emil Bach et l'Hôtel Impérial. Les vitres aux tons vifs forment une caractéristique particulièrement ravissante, intitulées »Ballons et Confettis«.

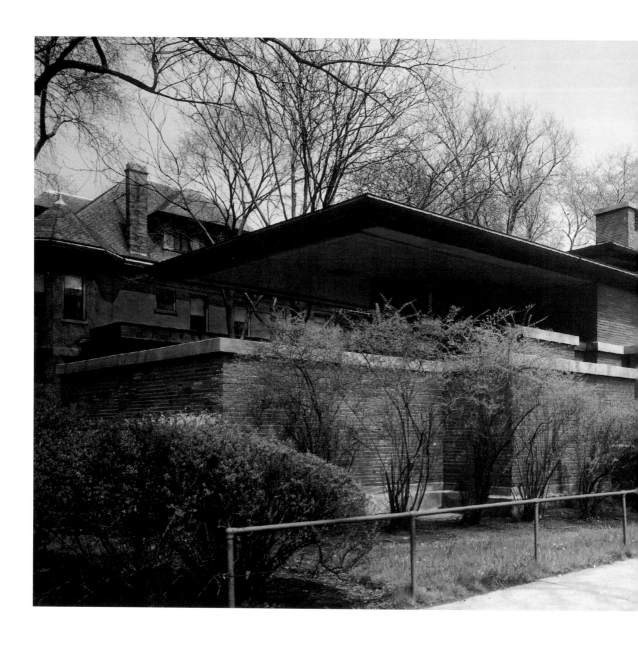

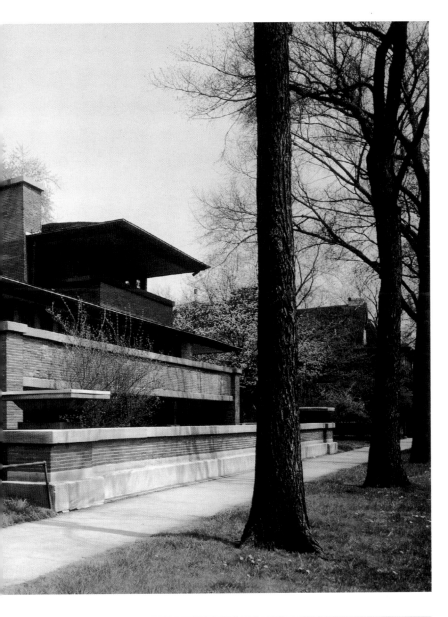

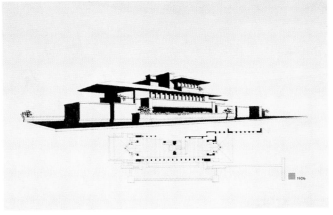

**Frederick C. Robie House, Chicago,
Illinois, 1906–1909**
Drawing for gate, living room

One of the reasons the Robie house was such a successful work were the explicit requirements on the part of the client. He wanted a house that was fireproof, that did not have boxed up spaces, that had none of the usual »decorator« items such as draperies, storebought carpets, etc. He was an engineer by training and desired a home that worked as well as any fine machine. The corner lot location of the Robie house explains many of its design factors: the ground floor, like so many of the prairie houses, contains playroom, billiard room, heating, laundry and storage. Access to the house is on this level, set on the side of the plan, with stairs to the main floor. This is basically one long space, with a fireplace in the center, which divides the living room at one end from the dining room at the other. On the third level are the bedrooms, rising in their own tower-like belvedere.
The furniture for the house was all designed by Wright; the dining room table and chairs are especially famous. The table places four stands at the four corners, containing stained glass lamps and shelves for flower arrangements. There was a definite idea behind this design: most flower arrangements, with candlesticks and candles, run down the center of the table as a visual barrier between host, hostess and guests. Here, however, all decoration and lighting is safely placed at the corners to let the center remain free and open.

Einer der Gründe für den enormen Erfolg des Hauses lag schon in den expliziten Vorstellungen des Auftraggebers Frederick Robie. Er wünschte sich ein feuerfestes Haus ohne aufgereihte, geschlossene Zimmer und ohne die üblichen »Dekorateur-Stücke« wie Vorhänge oder fertig gekaufte Teppiche. Als Ingenieur wünschte er sich zudem ein Haus, das genauso wie eine gute Maschine funktionieren sollte. Die Lage direkt an der Straße erklärt viele der Entwurfsmomente: Wie bei anderen Präriehäusern beherbergt das Erdgeschoß Spiel- und Billardzimmer, Heizung, Waschküche und Vorratsraum. Von hier aus führt auch der Zugang – an der Rückseite des Grundrisses – über Treppen in das Wohngeschoß. Es ist im Prinzip nur ein langgezogener Raum mit einem Kamin in der Mitte, der als Raumteiler Wohn- und Speisezimmer trennt. Im zweiten Stock befinden sich die Schlafzimmer in einem turmähnlichen Ausguck.
Das gesamte Mobiliar wurde von Wright entworfen, besonders bekannt geworden sind Tisch und Stühle aus dem Eßzimmer. Der Tisch trägt an den vier Ecken Aufbauten mit Lampen aus getöntem Glas und Schalen für Blumen-

arrangements. Die Idee bei diesem Entwurf war, daß Blumenschmuck und Kerzenleuchter nicht – wie üblich – in der Mitte plaziert und dort als Sichtbarriere zwischen den Sitzenden wirken sollten. Hier befinden sich nun Beleuchtung und Dekoration an den Ecken, und die Mitte des Tisches bleibt völlig frei.

L'une des raisons du succès de la maison réside dans les exigences exprès formulées par le client. Il voulait une maison qui soit protégée contre les incendies, dont les espaces ne soient pas en forme de boîtes, et qui ne contienne aucun des éléments »décoratifs« habituels, comme des rideaux, des tapis vendus en magasin, etc. L'emplacement en coin du terrain de la maison Robie explique en grande partie sa forme: comme dans beaucoup de maisons de la Prairie, la salle de jeux, la salle de billard, la chaufferie, la buanderie et les caves sont au rez-de-chaussée. L'entrée de la maison se trouve à ce niveau et est située latéralement. Des escaliers conduisent au niveau principal. Ce niveau est constitué d'une grande pièce, coupée en son milieu par la cheminée qui sépare la salle à manger de la salle de séjour. Les chambres se trouvent au troisième niveau et dominent la maison comme des belvédères. Tous les meubles de la maison ont été conçus par Wright; la table et les chaises de la salle à manger sont particulièrement célèbres. La table repose sur quatre pieds qui, à chacun des coins, dominent le dessus de la table. Ces pieds supportent des lampes en verre peint, montées sur des tiges et laissant ainsi un espace pour des compositions florales. Une intention bien précise était à l'origine de cette conception: les compositions florales, les chandeliers et les bougies qui étaient habituellement placés au centre de la table formaient un obstacle visuel entre le maître, la maîtresse de maison et leurs invités. Ici par contre, les décorations et les éclairages sont placés aux coins de la table et libèrent l'espace central.

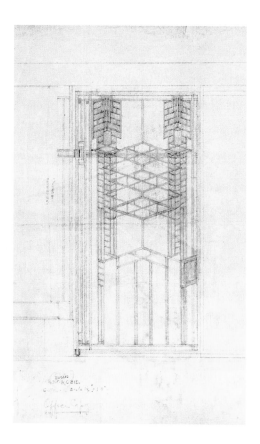

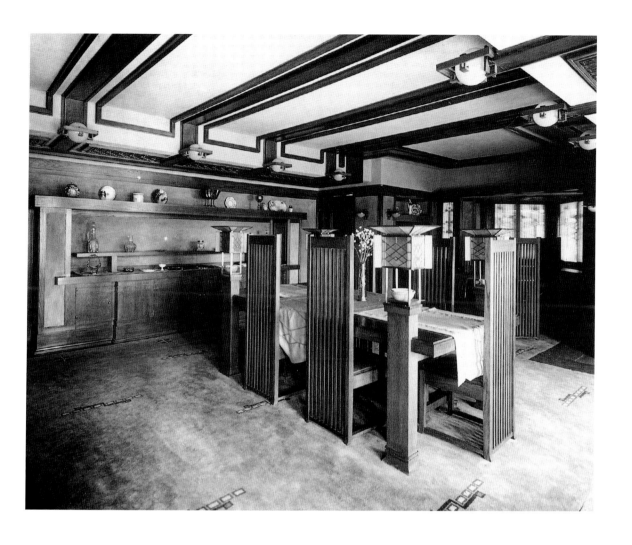

Mrs. Thomas Gale House, Oak Park, Illinois, 1909
Perspective drawing

Exhibition »Frank Lloyd Wright's Work« at The Art Institute of Chicago, 1907

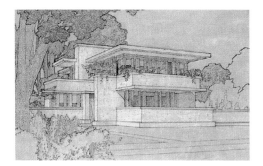

For a house as small as the Gale house, the elevation is strikingly modern with the projecting balconies and flat roof overhangs. Wright referred to the house as »the progenitor of Fallingwater,« and it is obvious how he made the association of the two. The living room and dining room of the house are not raised above ground, as was being done rather consistently with other prairie houses, and it has a full basement. The living room opens directly onto a low walled terrace, or porch. The lot is an unusually small one, which accounts for the compactness of the plan.

Bei dem recht kleinen Haus Gale wirkt der Aufriß mit den vorspringenden Balkonen und dem flachen, überstehenden Dach auffällig modern. Wright sprach von dem Haus als dem »Vorläufer von Fallingwater«, und es ist klar, wo er diese Verbindungen sah. Wohn- und Eßzimmer sind nicht wie bei fast allen anderen Präriehäusern im Obergeschoß gelegen, zudem ist das Haus voll unterkellert. Vom Wohnzimmer aus betritt man eine von einer niedrigen Mauer eingefaßte Terrasse. Das Grundstück ist ungewöhnlich klein, was die Kompaktheit des ganzen Entwurfs erklärt.

Pour une maison de dimensions aussi modestes, l'élévation est d'une modernité saisissante avec les balcons en saillie et les avant-toits plats. Wright désigne ce bâtiment comme le »précurseur de la maison sur la cascade«. Le lien entre les deux maisons est évident. La salle de séjour et la salle à manger ne sont pas surélevées, comme c'est presque toujours le cas dans les autres maisons de la Prairie, et la maison est complètement construite sur des caves. La salle de séjour donne sur une terrasse entourée de murets. Les dimensions du terrain sont plus restreintes que d'habitude et expliquent le caractère compact du plan.

Between 1894 and 1907, Wright was exhibited at nine annual exhibitions of the Chicago Architectural Club, held in The Art Institute of Chicago. The exhibition of 1907 ran from March 29 to April 26, and was the largest, up to that time, of Wright's work. It included drawings, photographs, models, stained glass, decorative objects such as vases and flower holders, and furniture. The layout of the exhibition, as well as the selection of objects and drawings, was done in a manner extremely sensitive to the work, as well as showing an innovative way of framing and hanging the drawings themselves.

Zwischen 1894 und 1907 wurden neun Ausstellungen über Wright vom Chicago Architectural Club im Institute of Chicago organisiert. Die Ausstellung des Jahres 1907 lief vom 29. März bis 26. April und war die bis dahin größte Dokumentation seiner Arbeiten. Sie umfaßte Zeichnungen, Fotografien, Modelle, Bleiglasfenster, Dekorationsobjekte wie Vasen und Möbel. Die Gestaltung der Ausstellung wie auch die Auswahl der Exponate waren äußerst feinfühlig, außerdem ging man neue Wege bei der Rahmung und Hängung der Zeichnungen.

Entre 1894 et 1907, Wright a présenté ses ouvrages à neuf expositions qui furent organisées par le Club des Architectes de Chicago et eurent lieu au Chicago Art Institute. L'exposition de 1907 se déroula du 29 mars au 26 avril. Jamais autant de travaux de Wright n'avaient été exposés: dessins, photographies, modèles, verres peints, objets décoratifs tels que des vases et des jardinières ainsi que des meubles. L'agencement de l'exposition ainsi que la sélection des objets et des dessins mettaient les travaux parfaitement en valeur tout en montrant de façon innovatrice comment encadrer et accrocher au mur ces dessins.

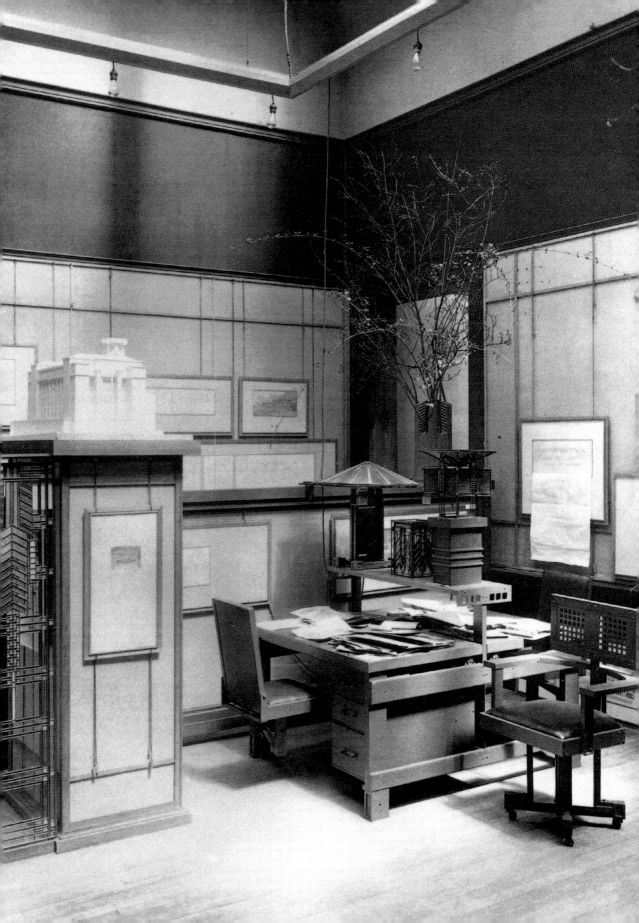

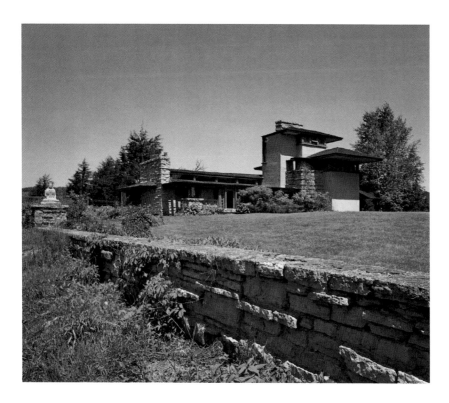

Taliesin, Spring Green, Wisconsin, 1911
View and dining area

The word »Taliesin« is Welsh for shining brow, and Wright chose it as the name for his home in southwestern Wisconsin for two reasons: his Welsh ancestry and the placement of the house on the brow of the hill. The low one story structure was wrapped around the brow of the hill with spectacular views over the lake below and surrounding hills. The other side of the long L-shaped house and studio opened onto secluded garden courts. Twice destroyed by fire, the building that stands today, Taliesin III, is a much larger, more expansive structure, which still preserves the harmonious relationship to the hillside, the garden courts and hill crown.

»Taliesin« bedeutet im Walisischen soviel wie leuchtende Bergkuppe. Wright entschied sich für diesen Namen seines Hauses im Südwesten Wisconsins aus zwei Gründen: wegen seiner walisischen Abstammung und der Situierung des Hauses auf einer Bergkuppe. Das niedrige, einstöckige Gebäude schmiegte sich an den Hügel und bot einen eindrucksvollen Ausblick auf die umliegenden Anhöhen und den im Tal liegenden See. Die abgewandte Seite des langgezogenen, L-förmigen Hauses öffnete sich auf einen abgeschlossenen Garten. Zweimal von Feuer zerstört, ist das heute stehende Gebäude, »Taliesin III«, wesentlich größer und raumgreifender, bewahrt aber immer noch die harmonische Beziehung zum Hang, zur Bergkuppe und den Gärten.

»Taliesin« est un mot gallois qui signifie le sommet radieux. Deux raisons expliquent le choix de ce nom pour la maison du sud-ouest du Wisconsin: les origines galloises de Wright et l'emplacement de la maison sur le sommet de la colline. La construction basse à un étage enserrait le sommet de la colline et offrait une vue spectaculaire sur le lac dans la vallée et sur les collines environnantes. L'autre côté de la maison et de l'atelier, qui formaient un L allongé, donnait sur une cour et un jardin. Deux fois détruit par le feu, le bâtiment qui existe aujourd'hui, Taliesin III, est une construction bien plus vaste qui a encore conservé la relation harmonieuse avec le flanc de la colline, les jardins et la crête de la colline.

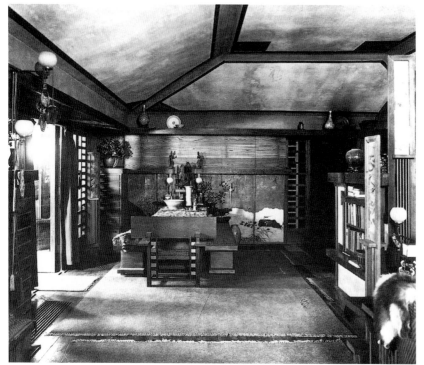

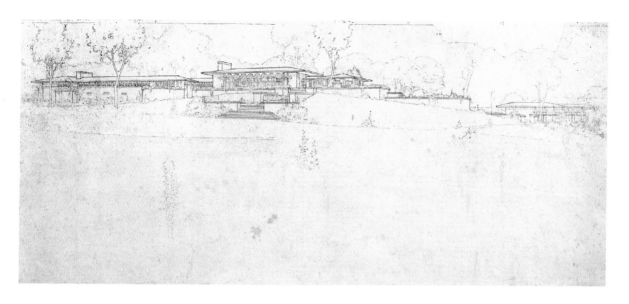

In 1900 Wright designed and built a home for Francis Little in Peoria, Illinois. In 1908, the Littles requested designs for a summer home on the shores of Lake Minnetonka, near Minneapolis, which never went beyond preliminary planning. In 1911/12, the Littles asked Wright to design a more substantial residence, but his travels to Europe and Japan intervened, and it was not until 1913 that a scheme was finally ready. The house stretched across a low hill facing the lake. A rather monumental flight of concrete steps bordered by low brick walls ascended to the main level, which contained living room, library and bedrooms. A lower level contained a dining room with a terrace bordering the lake, a kitchen and an additional bedroom for guests. The house was demolished in 1972, but the main rooms and art glass were saved. The living room is located now in New York's Metropolitan Museum of Art, the library in Pennsylvania's Allentown Museum.

1900 entwarf und baute Wright ein Haus für Francis Little in Peoria, Illinois. 1908 erbaten dann die Littles Zeichnungen für ein Sommerhaus am Ufer des Minnetonka-Sees, nahe Minneapolis. Dieses Projekt gelangte jedoch nie über Vorstudien hinaus. 1911/12 beauftragte die Familie Wright mit dem Entwurf eines größeren Wohnhauses, aber seine Reisen nach Europa und Japan verschoben die Ausführung, die schließlich 1913 erfolgte.
Das Haus erstreckte sich längs eines flachen Hügels am See. Eine ziemlich monumentale, von niedrigen Ziegelmauern gefaßte Betontreppe stieg bis zum Hauptgeschoß auf, das Bibliothek, Wohn- und Schlafzimmer beherbergte. Im Erdgeschoß befanden sich ein Gästezimmer, die Küche und das Eßzimmer mit einer an den See grenzenden Terrasse. Das Haus wurde 1972 abgerissen, aber die Haupträume und Glasarbeiten konnten bewahrt werden. Das Wohnzimmer befindet sich heute im New Yorker Metropolitan Museum of Art, die Bibliothek im Allentown Museum in Pennsylvania.

En 1900, Wright dessina les plans et construisit une maison pour Francis Little à Peoria, Illinois. En 1908, les Little lui demandèrent d'établir les plans pour une maison d'été sur les bords du lac Minnetonka, près de Minneapolis. Plans qui toutefois ne dépassèrent pas le stade du tracé préliminaire. En 1911/12, les Little prièrent Wright de dessiner les plans d'une maison plus vaste. Pris par ses voyages en Europe et au Japon, ce n'est qu'en 1913 qu'il put enfin les terminer.
La maison s'étendait sur un petit vallon qui fait face au lac. Un escalier assez monumental, avec des marches en béton et encadré de murets en brique, conduisait au niveau principal qui comprend la salle de séjour, la bibliothèque et les chambres. Au niveau inférieur se trouvaient une salle à manger avec une terrasse au bord du lac, une cuisine et une chambre pour amis. La maison fut démolie en 1972, mais les pièces principales et les travaux en verre furent épargnés. La salle de séjour se trouve maintenant au Metropolitan Museum of Art de New York et la bibliothèque au Allentown Museum en Pennsylvanie.

»Northome«, Francis W. Little House,
Wayzata, Minnesota, 1912–1914
Installation of the living room at the
Metropolitan Museum of Art, New York

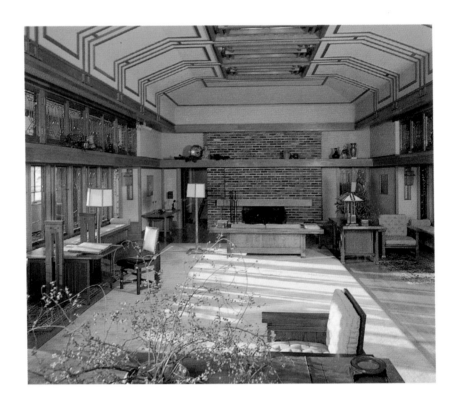

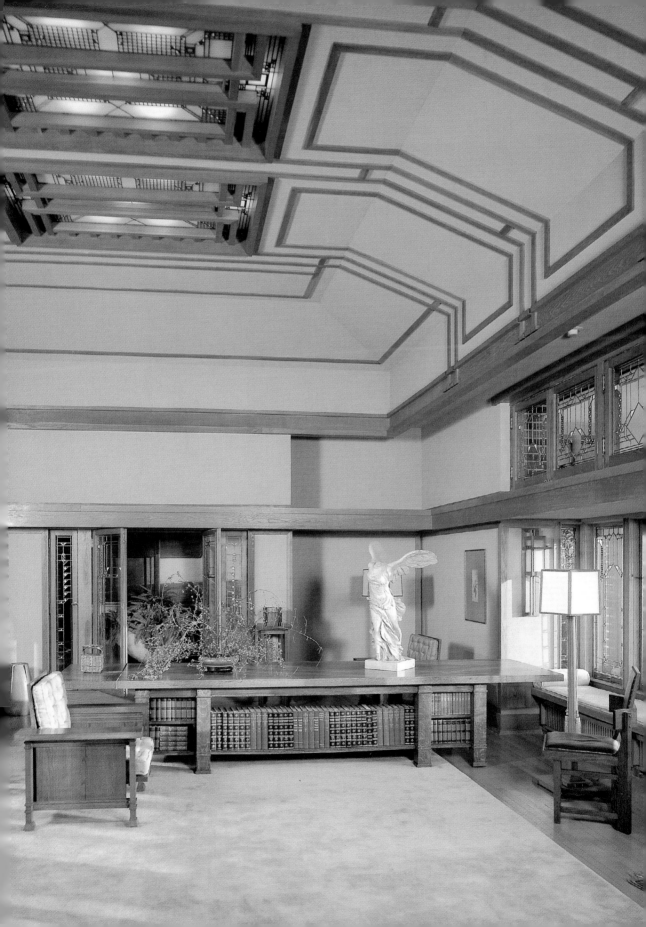

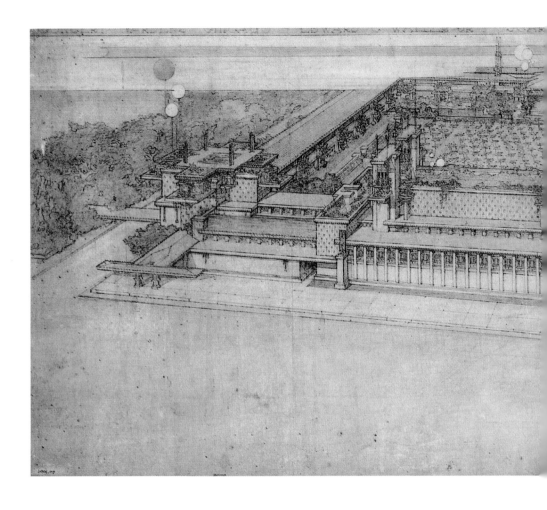

One particular element of the European life-style that greatly appealed to Frank Lloyd Wright was the German and Austrian beer garden. Ed Waller, son of an early client in Chicago, and a close friend to Wright, shared the same interest and suggested Wright design just such a place down on the Midway, in South Chicago. To make it available all the year round it was decided to incorporate an indoor winter garden as well, with the dining area surrounding a dance floor. By 1914 the Gardens were mainly completed, and opened to the public. In this building the architect became the master not only of architecture, but the related arts as well. Furniture, murals, sculpture, tableware, lamps, lights and textiles were incorporated into a harmonious relationship with the building. Wright wrote of this complex, »Here in the Midway Gardens painting and sculpture were to be bidden back again to their original places and to the original offices in architecture, where they belonged.«

Ein Element des europäischen Lebensstils, das Frank Lloyd Wright ganz besonders faszinierte, waren die Biergärten Österreichs und Deutschlands. Ed Waller, der Sohn eines Klienten aus frühen Chicagoer Tagen und ein enger Freund Wrights, empfand ebenso und schlug vor, Wright solle solch eine Anlage für den Midway im Süden Chicagos entwerfen. Man entschied sich, einen Wintergarten mit einem Restaurant und einer Tanzfläche mit einzuplanen, damit der Betrieb ganzjährig laufen konnte. 1914 war der Komplex im wesentlichen fertig und wurde dem Publikum zugänglich gemacht. Wright erwies sich hier nicht nur als Meister der Architektur, sondern auch der verwandten Künste: Mobiliar und Ge-

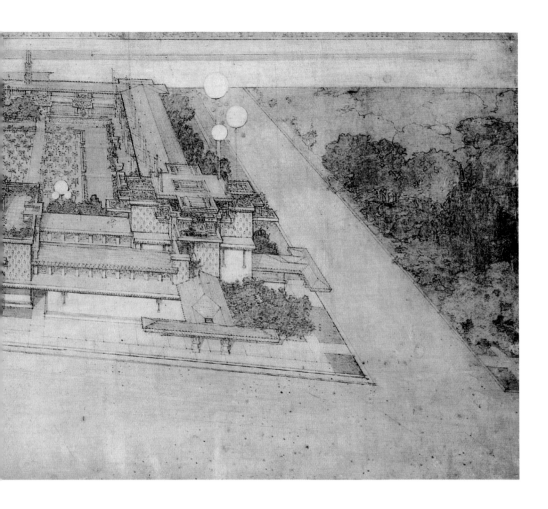

schirr, Wandgemälde, Skulpturen, Lampen und Stoffe gingen eine harmonische Beziehung mit dem Gebäude ein. Wright schrieb, daß »hier bei den Midway Gardens Malerei und Bildhauerei zu ihrem ursprünglichen Ort und ihren ursprünglichen Aufgaben in der Architektur zurückgeführt wurden.«

Wright apprécia grandement un élément particulier du style de vie européen: les cafés en plein air allemands et autrichiens. Ed Waller, fils de l'un de ses clients de Chicago et ami intime de Wright, partageait le même intérêt. C'est lui qui suggéra à Wright de dessiner un tel endroit à Midway, dans la partie sud de Chicago. Afin que l'on puisse en jouir toute l'année, il décida d'y intégrer un jardin d'hiver intérieur, avec une salle de restaurant entourant une piste de danse. En 1914, les »Gardens« étaient en grande partie terminés et furent ouverts au public. Avec ce bâtiment, Wright révéla non seulement sa maîtrise de l'architecture, mais aussi des autres arts. Mobilier, peintures murales, sculptures, articles de table,

lampes, éclairages et tissus étaient en harmonie avec le bâtiment. Wright écrivait sur ce complexe: »Dans les Midway Gardens, la peinture et la sculpture avaient repris leurs places et leurs fonctions d'origine.«

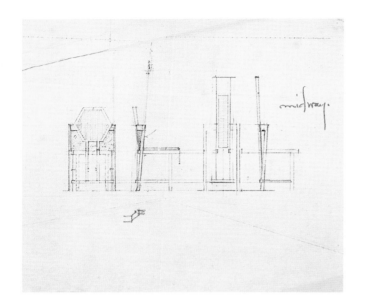

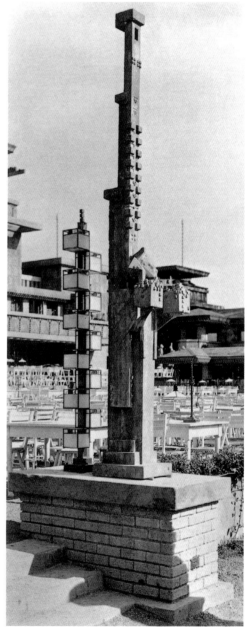

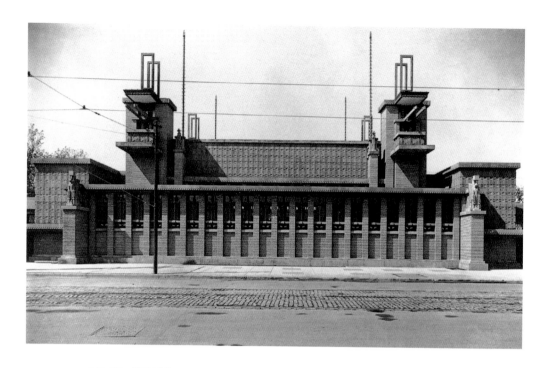

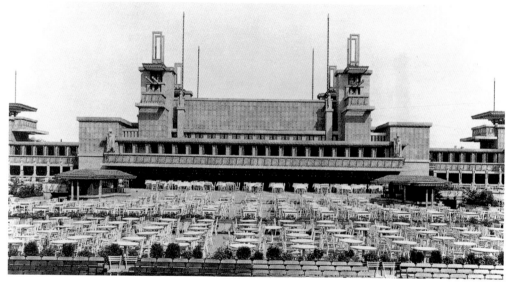

Midway Gardens, Chicago, Illinois,
1913–1914
Chair design, vintage photographs

Imperial Hotel, Tokyo, 1915–1922
Section, vintage photographs

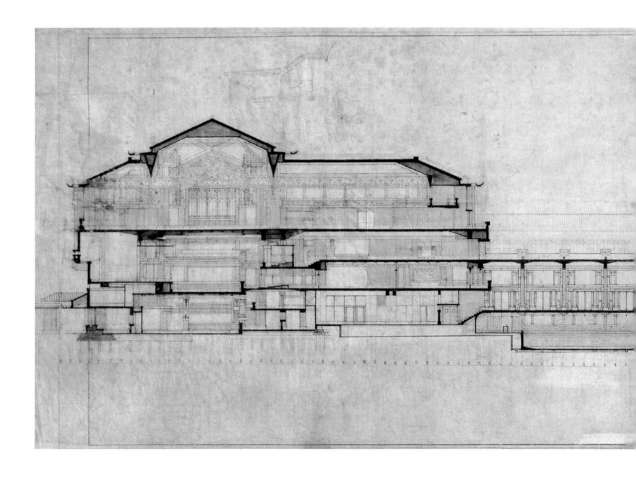

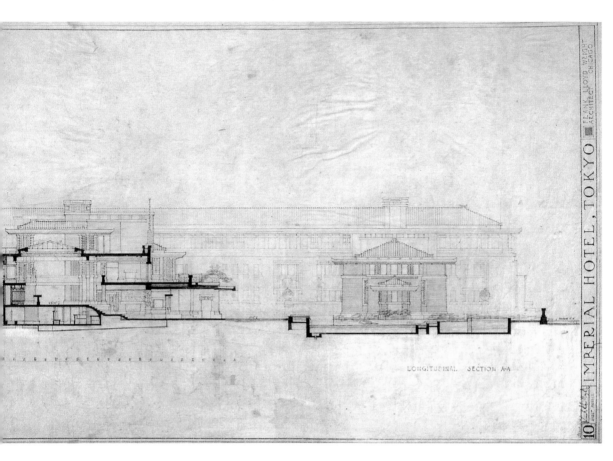

IMPERIAL HOTEL, TOKYO   FRANK LLOYD WRIGHT ARCHITECT CHICAGO

LONGITUDINAL SECTION A-A

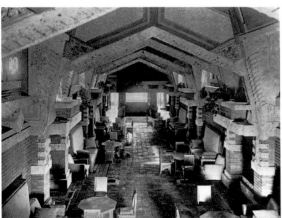

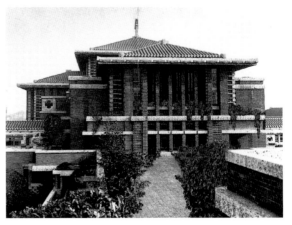

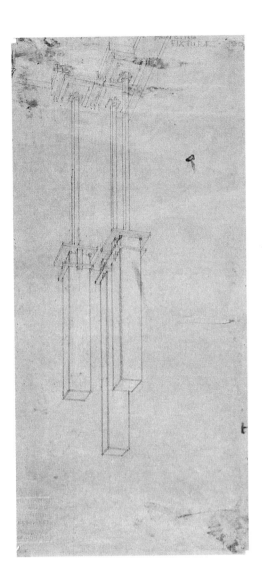

Imperial Hotel, Tokyo, 1915–1922
Drawings for lamp and fireplaces in the parlor

A supreme example of the use of reinforced concrete is the Imperial Hotel in Tokyo. In this building two considerations were paramount: a structure that would withstand earthquakes and be fireproof against the infernos that inevitably follow.

For this to be a fireproof structure the traditional wood and paper architecture of Japan had to give way to reinforced concrete, stone and brick. To render the building capable of surviving earthquakes, Wright developed a system of foundations and structural support hitherto unseen in architecture. The principle at work was the cantilever, the balanced load, not unlike the tray held overhead on the outstretched hand of a waiter. In place of heavy tile roofs of traditional Japanese architecture, the roof of the Imperial Hotel was made of thin copper plates. The whole structure rode on a network of thin concrete pins, nine feet deep and two feet apart throughout, that connected the building above to a mud substrata below. Flexibility, by means of reinforced concrete, was the principle which saved the building in the Kanto Quake of 1923.

Das Imperial Hotel in Tokio stellt ein herausragendes Beispiel für den Einsatz von Stahlbeton dar. Zwei Überlegungen waren hier bestimmend: Die Konstruktion sollte erdbebensicher und ebenso gegen die nach einem Erdbeben unausweichlichen Feuerbrünste gefeit sein. Daher mußten statt der traditionellen japanischen Bauweise mit Holz und Papier Stahlbeton, Stein und Ziegel eingesetzt werden. Um das Gebäude erdbebensicher zu machen, entwickelte Wright ein bislang in der Architektur unbekanntes System aus Fundamenten und Tragstrukturen. Dieses arbeitete nach dem Prinzip des freitragenden Kragarms beziehungsweise der balancierten Last, etwa so wie ein vom Kellner mit ausgestreckter Hand hochgehaltenes Tablett. Statt des traditionell japanischen, schweren Ziegeldachs wurden dünne Kupferplatten für die Eindachung verwendet. Die gesamte Konstruktion ruhte auf einem Netzwerk von Betonpflöcken, die im Abstand von 60 Zentimetern fast drei Meter in den lehmigen Untergrund gerammt waren. Diese mit Stahlbeton erreichte Flexibilität ließ das Gebäude das Kanto-Erdbeben des Jahres 1923 überstehen.

L'Hôtel Impérial de Tokyo est un exemple suprême de l'utilisation du béton armé. Dans ce bâtiment, deux considérations étaient de la plus haute importance: d'une part, la construction devait résister aux tremblements de terre et d'autre part, elle devait être protégée contre les incendies qui suivaient ces derniers. Pour assurer une protection contre les incendies, il fallait abandonner les matériaux traditionnels – bois et papier – de l'architecture japonaise et se tourner vers le béton armé, la pierre et la brique. Afin que le bâtiment soit capable de survivre aux séismes, Wright développa un système de fondations, allié à une charpente de soutien, qui était encore totalement inconnu en architecture. Le principe était le porte-à-faux, la charge en équilibre, évoquant le plateau que le garçon de restaurant tient à bout de bras au-dessus de sa tête. A la place des toits aux lourdes tuiles de l'architecture japonaise traditionnelle, le toit de l'Hôtel Impérial était recouvert de minces plaques de cuivre. Toute la construction reposait sur un ensemble de minces montants en béton, d'une profondeur de neuf pieds et ayant un intervalle de deux pieds, qui reliaient le bâtiment à une couche d'argile. La souplesse – obtenue grâce au béton armé – fut le principe qui sauva le bâtiment lors du séisme Kanto de 1923.

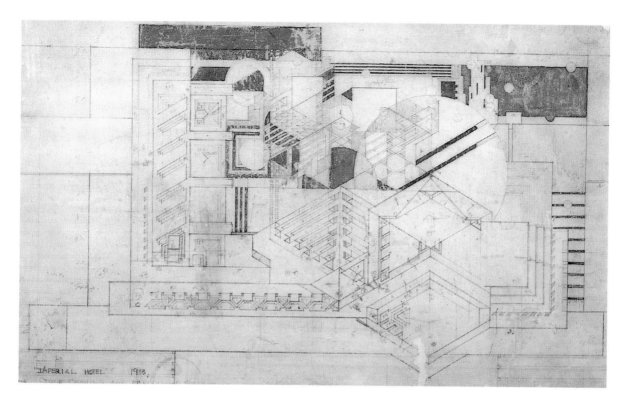

IMPERIAL HOTEL 1913

CARVING AND POLYCHROME DECORATION
IMPERIAL HOTEL 1913

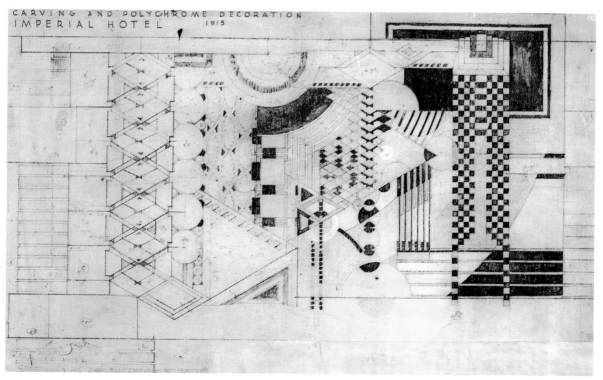

Jiyu Gakuen School, Tokyo, 1921
Elevation, interior

For this school building in the heart of Tokyo, Wright fashioned every detail with young children in mind. The scale of the rooms themselves, as with the furniture, likewise considers a child's point of view. Wright and Arato Endo, his associate in Japan, wrote: »This little school building was designed for the Jiyu Gakuen – in the same spirit implied by the name of the school – a free spirit. It was intended to be a simple happy place for happy children – unpretentious – genuine.«
When Madame Hani, the founder of the school, died in 1957, Wright sent this *in memoriam* to the school: »Dear Madame Honor Hani was an inspiration to us all! With Endo San I was building in Tokyo the little School of the Free Spirit for the Hanis while we were building the Imperial Hotel for the Mikado. Madame Hani's large group of pupils – pretty sloe-eyed ebony-haired young girls – made a picture I shall never forget as Endo San and I attended the dedication exercises when our school building was finished for the Hanis. Madame Hani presided. I felt then as now that she was an education wise beyond her time. The cultural ideals of her nation she understood and loved but – as important she knew how to inculcate the love of beauty in the young entrusted to her care.«

Bei diesem Schulgebäude im Herzen Tokios gestaltete Wright jedes Detail mit dem Blick auf die Bedürfnisse von Kindern. Die Größe der Räume und der Möbel berücksichtigt die Perspektive eines Kindes. Wright und sein japanischer Mitarbeiter Arato Endo notierten während ihrer Arbeit: »Dieses kleine Schulgebäude wurde für jenen freiheitlichen Geist von Jiyu Gakuen entworfen, wie ihn auch der Name des Hauses schon ausdrückt. Es sollte ein einfacher und glücklicher Platz für glückliche Kinder werden: möglichst unprätentiös und natürlich.« Als Madame Hani, die Gründerin der Schule, 1957 starb, schickte Wright zum Gedenken die folgenden Worte: »Die verehrte Madame Hani war uns allen eine Inspiration! Ich habe gemeinsam mit Endo die kleine ›Schule des freien Geistes gebaut‹, während wir zur gleichen Zeit in Tokio an dem Imperial Hotel für Mikado arbeiteten. Als Endo und ich an der feierlichen Übergabe des fertigen Gebäudes teilnahmen, gaben Madame Hanis viele Schülerinnen – hübsche mandeläugige Mädchen mit ebenholzschwarzen Haaren – ein Bild ab, das ich nie vergessen werde. Ich bin sicher, heute wie damals, daß Madame Hani in allen Fragen der Erziehung über eine Weisheit verfügte, die den Anschauungen ihrer Zeit weit voraus war. Sie verstand und liebte die kulturellen Ideale ihres Volkes, und sie wußte, wie wichtig es ist, in den ihr anvertrauten Kindern die Liebe zur Schönheit zu wecken.«

Pour ce bâtiment situé en plein cœur de Tokyo, Wright réalisa tous les détails en gardant à l'esprit qu'il s'adressait à de jeunes enfants. Les dimensions des salles, tout comme celles du mobilier, ont été calculées en fonction de la taille des enfants. Wright et Arato Endo, son associé au Japon, écrivirent: »Ce petit bâtiment scolaire a été conçu pour le Jiyu Gakuen – dans le même esprit que celui sous-entendu par le nom de l'école – un esprit libre. Il s'agissait de réaliser un lieu simple et gai pour des enfants heureux – sans prétention – sans affectation.« Lorsque Madame Hani, la fondatrice de l'école, décéda en 1957, Wright adressa à l'école ces lignes à sa mémoire: »Notre chère Madame Honor Hani fut notre inspiration à nous tous! Avec Endo San, je construisis à Tokyo la petite Ecole du Libre Esprit pour les Hani pendant que nous réalisions l'Hôtel Impérial pour le Mikado. Lorsque nous eûmes terminé la construction de l'école, le groupe d'élèves de Madame Hani – de jolies petites filles aux yeux de prunelle et à la chevelure d'ébène – exécuta un tableau que je n'oublierai jamais. Il avait été réalisé pour la cérémonie d'inauguration, à laquelle Enio et moi-même avions été conviés. Madame Hani présidait. Je ressentis alors comme maintenant qu'elle était un sage en matière d'éducation et bien en avance sur son époque. Elle comprenait et aimait les idées culturelles de sa nation, mais – ce qui est tout aussi important – elle savait comment inculquer l'amour de la beauté aux jeunes esprits confiés à ses soins«.

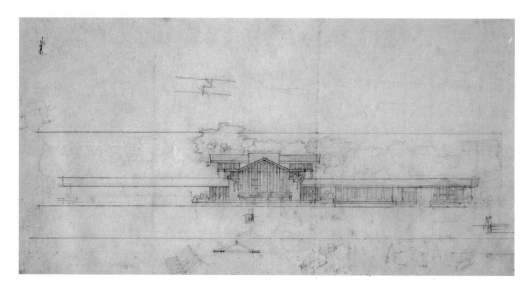

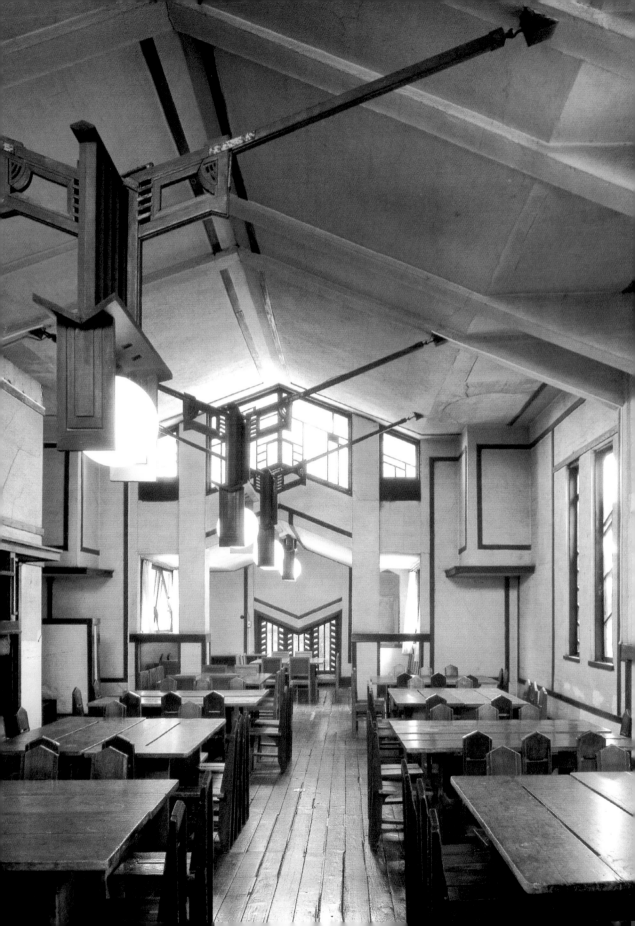

**»Hollyhock House« for Aline Barns-
dall, Los Angeles, California,
1917–1920**
West façade, garden court and dining
room

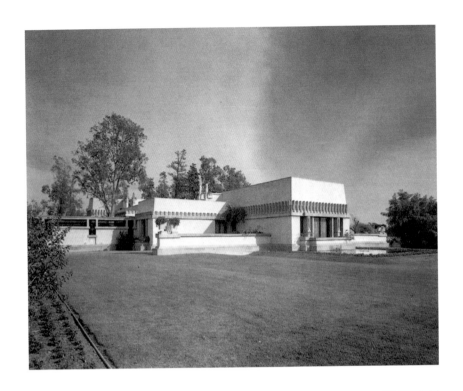

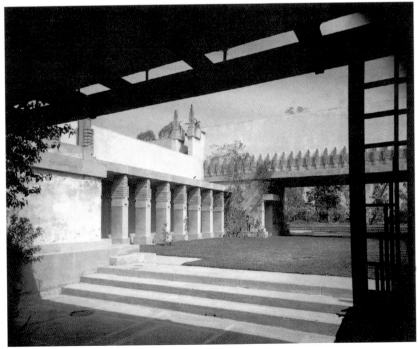

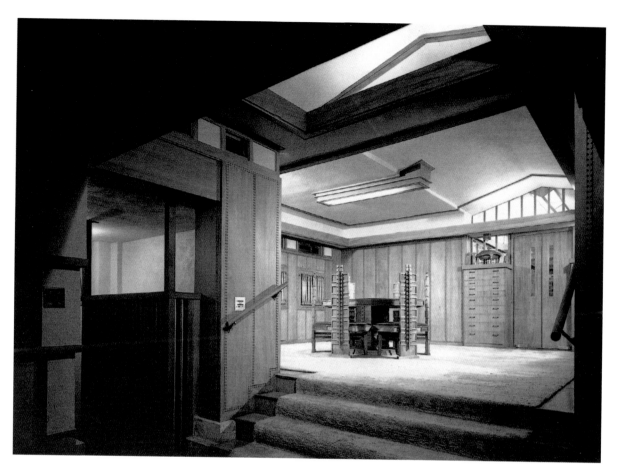

By 1922, Wright had returned from Japan, the hotel completed, and had established himself in Los Angeles to continue with work for Aline Barnsdall. Her love was drama and she had purchased a substantial piece of property in the heart of Los Angeles called Olive Hill. At the hill's base, she planned a large theatre, motion picture theatre, residences for actors and directors, and a series of shops and stores. On the hill above was to be her own home, Hollyhock House. None of her theatre plans were carried out, but her own house and two others, called Residence A and Residence B, were built. The house was designed with the south-west climate in mind: walls facing the hot California sun have a minimum of exposed glass, while generous areas of glass doors open into a central, cool green patio.

1922 war das Imperial Hotel fertig, Wright kehrte aus Japan zurück und ließ sich in Los Angeles nieder, um die Arbeit für Aline Barnsdall fortzusetzen. Sie hatte mitten in der Stadt ein ziemlich weitläufiges Grundstück namens Olive Hill erworben. Ihre Liebe galt der Bühne, und so plante sie am Fuß des Hügels ein großes Theater, ein Kino, Wohnungen für Schauspieler und Regisseure sowie einige Geschäfte und Läden. Oben auf der Kuppe sollte ihre eigene Villa, das »Hollyhock House«, stehen. Zwar wurde keiner ihrer Theaterpläne ausgeführt, doch neben ihrem eigenen Wohnhaus entstanden zwei weitere, die Residence A und Residence B genannt wurden. Der Entwurf zu ihrem eigenen Wohnhaus ging von den Bedingungen des kalifornischen Klimas aus: Wände, die der Sonne ausgesetzt sind, zeigen nur kleine Öffnungen, während großzügig bemessene Glastüren auf einen begrünten, kühlen Innenhof im Zentrum führen.

En 1922, Wright retourna aux Etats-Unis après avoir achevé la construction de son hôtel au Japon. Il s'installa à Los Angeles afin de poursuivre le travail qu'il réalisait pour Aline Barnsdall. La passion de Mme Barnsdall était le théâtre. Elle avait acheté une très grande propriété dans le centre de Los Angeles, appelée Olive Hill. Au pied de la colline, elle avait prévu un grand théâtre, un cinéma, des habitations pour acteurs et directeurs et une série de boutiques et de magasins. Au sommet de la colline devait être édifiée sa propre maison »Hollyhock House« (»La rose trémière«). Aucun des plans pour le théâtre ne fut réalisé. Sa maison, toutefois, ainsi que deux autres, nommées Résidence A et Résidence B, furent construites. La maison s'adaptait au climat du sud-ouest: les murs qui doivent affronter le chaud soleil de Californie ont un minimum de vitrage, tandis que de grandes portes en verre s'ouvrent sur un patio central, plein de fraîcheur et de verdure.

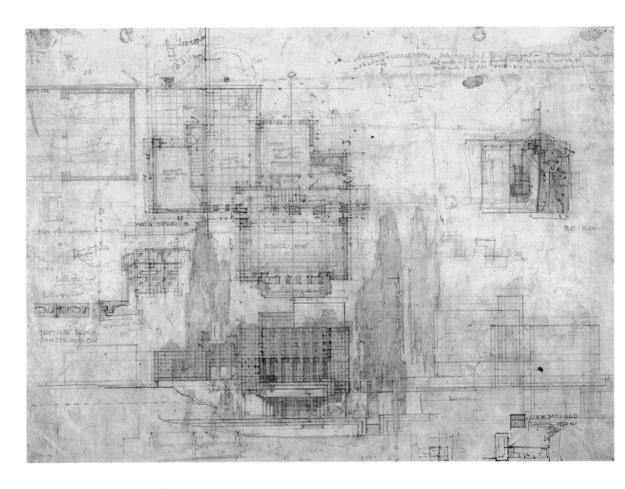

»La Miniatura«, House for George Millard, Pasadena, California, 1922–1923
Drawing with plan and elevation, entrance side

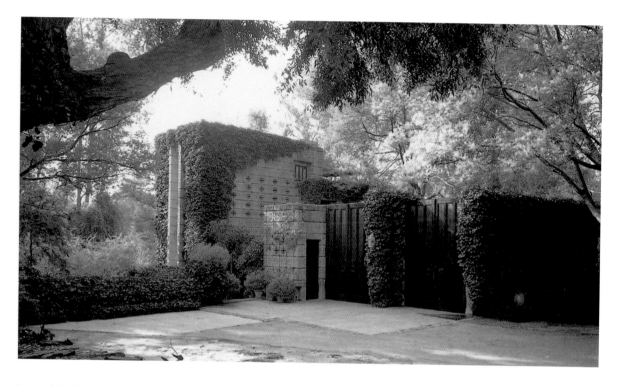

In general, Wright's work is predominantly horizontal: certainly the great majority of the prairie houses were such, and some of the larger non-residential work, such as Midway Gardens and the Imperial Hotel bear this distinctive characteristic. With the prairie it was his intention to accentuate the long, low horizontal line, and in the Midway Gardens and Imperial Hotel that same emphasis prevailed. But here, in a narrow ravine in Pasadena, is a work that has strongly vertical elements and vertical significance. This was the first house to be built of the new system he had innovated and named »textile block construction«. »We would take that despised outcast of the building industry – the concrete block . . . find hitherto unsuspected soul in it – make it live as a thing of beauty – textured like the trees. All we would have to do would be to educate the concrete block, refine it and knit it together with steel in the joints . . . The walls would thus become thin but solid reinforced slabs and yield to any desire for form imaginable.«

Normalerweise betonen Wrights Entwürfe überwiegend die Horizontale; dies trifft sicherlich auf die meisten Präriehäuser und auf einige der größeren kommerziellen Bauten wie Midway Gardens und das Imperial Hotel zu. Bei all diesen Entwürfen war die Intention, die langgestreckte, niedrige, waagerechte Linie zu betonen. Hier aber, in einer engen Schlucht in Pasadena, findet sich eine Arbeit, die stark vertikale Elemente und Ausrichtung zeigt. Es war das erste Haus, das nach seinem neu erfundenen System – Gewebe-Block-Konstruktion genannt – gebaut wurde: »Nehmen wir uns des verachteten Ausgestoßenen der Bauindustrie an – des Betonblocksteins . . ., entdecken wir eine unerwartete Seele in ihm, erwekken wir lebendige Schönheit in ihm, mit einer Textur wie die Bäume. Alles, was wir tun müssen, ist, den Blockstein zu kultivieren, ihn zu verfeinern und mit Stahl an den Verbindungspunkten zu versehen . . . So werden die Hauswände zu dünnen, aber soliden Stahlbetonplatten, die jede gewünschte Form annehmen können.«

En règle générale, les travaux de Wright sont horizontaux; assurément, la grande majorité des »Prairie houses« ont cette forme et certains ouvrages plus importants comme les Midway Gardens et l'Hôtel Impérial présentent cette caractéristique. Son intention était d'en accentuer la longue et basse ligne horizontale. Mais ici, dans un ravin étroit de Pasadena, le travail présente des éléments très verticaux et a une signification verticale. C'était la première maison à être construite selon un nouveau système qu'il avait inventé et nommé »construction avec blocs en texture«. »En prenant ce matériau proscrit et dédaigné de l'industrie du bâtiment – le bloc de ciment . . . nous découvrîmes en lui une âme insoupçonnée – qui l'anime et lui prête une beauté – dont la texture est semblable à celle des arbres. Tout ce que nous avions à faire était de le travailler, de l'affiner et de le lier avec de l'acier dans les joints . . . Les murs devenaient alors des plaques fines, mais solidement renforcées, et se prêtaient à toutes les formes imaginables.«

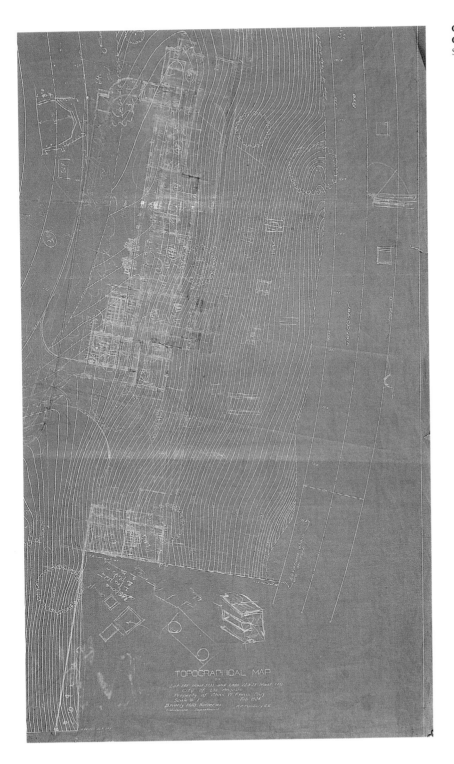

TOPOGRAPHICAL MAP
OF
Lot 115, Tract 3733 and Lots 22 & 23, Tract 1411
City of Los Angeles
Property of Chas. W. Ennis Esq.
Scale 1"
Beverly Hills Nurseries   Feb 1924

A large portion of the Ennis house is given over to the massive concrete block retaining walls that support the building on the steeply-pitched hillside. The other concrete block houses by Frank Lloyd Wright, built in the same region and at about the same time, have a scale that is more typical of his treatment of residential architecture. He calls it »human scale«, meaning to bring the traditional unnecessary heights down to a scale more in keeping with the occupants. But the Ennis house is a definite break in this rule: the rooms are high, with lofty ceilings, which accounts for the massing of concrete block rising above the window lines. In plan the house is basically a two bedroom house with guest room adjacent to the dining room. Bedrooms for the original owners are spaced apart from each other, connected by a long enclosed gallery and an open terrace. The dining room, kitchen and guest room are set on a raised level above the living room. This is one of the last residences by Frank Lloyd Wright to employ stained glass, and one of the first resi-

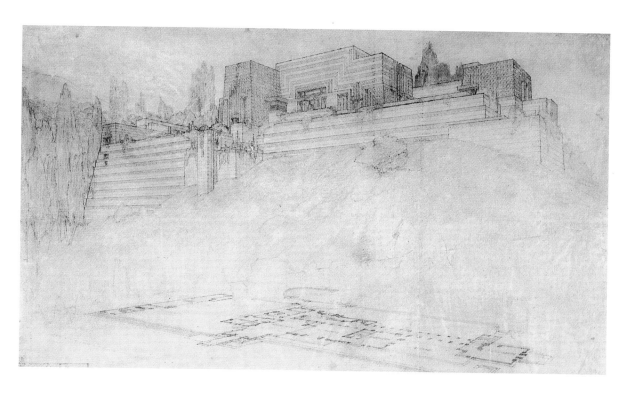

dences, along with the nearby Freeman house, to employ mitred glass windows. The monumental nature of the design throughout is somewhat softened and made more human by the scale of the concrete block, and the combination of plain and patterned blocks.

Ein ganz wesentlicher Teil des Ennis-Hauses sind die mächtigen Mauern aus Betonblocksteinen, die das Gebäude am steilen Berghang abstützen. Andere Betonblock-Häuser, die Frank Lloyd Wright in der gleichen Gegend und zur gleichen Zeit baute, sind vom Maßstab her typischer für seine Wohnhaus-Architektur. Er sprach von »menschlichem Maßstab«, womit gemeint war, daß er die üblichen unnötigen Höhen auf ein eher auf die Bewohner abgestimmtes Maß reduzierte. Das Haus Ennis aber bricht entschieden mit diesem Prinzip: Die Decken liegen sehr hoch, und das erklärt auch die vielen Betonblöcke oberhalb der Fensterlinien. Das Haus hat zwei Schlafzimmer sowie ein Gästezimmer neben dem Eßzimmer.

Die Schlafzimmer der ersten Besitzer waren durch einen langen Gang und eine offene Terrasse voneinander getrennt. Eßzimmer, Küche und Gästezimmer befinden sich auf erhöhtem Niveau über dem Wohnzimmer. Dies war eines der letzten Wohnhäuser von Frank Lloyd Wright, bei dem er mit Bleiglas arbeitete, und neben dem nahe gelegenen Haus Freeman eines der ersten, bei dem er mit mitriertem Glas arbeitete. Die monumentale Wucht des Entwurfes wird durch das Format des verwendeten Betonblocksteins und den Wechsel zwischen strukturierten und glatten Blöcken etwas gemildert.

Une grande partie de la maison Ennis doit son effet aux murs de soutènement en blocs massifs de béton, qui soutiennent l'édifice sur le versant abrupt de la colline. Les autres maisons en blocs de béton, construites par Wright dans la même région et à la même époque, ont été édifiées à une échelle qui est plus typique de sa conception de l'architecture d'habitation. C'est ce qu'il appelait »l'échelle humaine«, indiquant ainsi le

rabaissement des hauteurs inutiles à une échelle plus conforme à ses occupants. La maison Ennis représente toutefois une exception catégorique à cette règle: les pièces sont hautes, avec des plafonds élevés justifiant la masse de béton qui, vue de l'extérieur, s'élève au-dessus des fenêtres. Sur le plan, la maison est principalement composée de deux chambres et d'une chambre d'amis adjacente à la salle à manger. Les chambres, conçues pour les premiers propriétaires, sont éloignées l'une de l'autre et reliées par une longue galerie couverte et une terrasse en plein-air. La salle à manger, la cuisine et la chambre d'amis sont à un niveau surélevé par rapport à la salle de séjour. Cette maison fut l'une des dernières où Wright employa des vitraux et l'une des premières, avec la maison Freeman, où il utilisa des fenêtres à onglet. L'aspect monumental de toute la construction est quelque peu adouci et rendu plus humain par les dimensions des blocs en béton et par l'association des blocs lisses aux blocs graufrés.

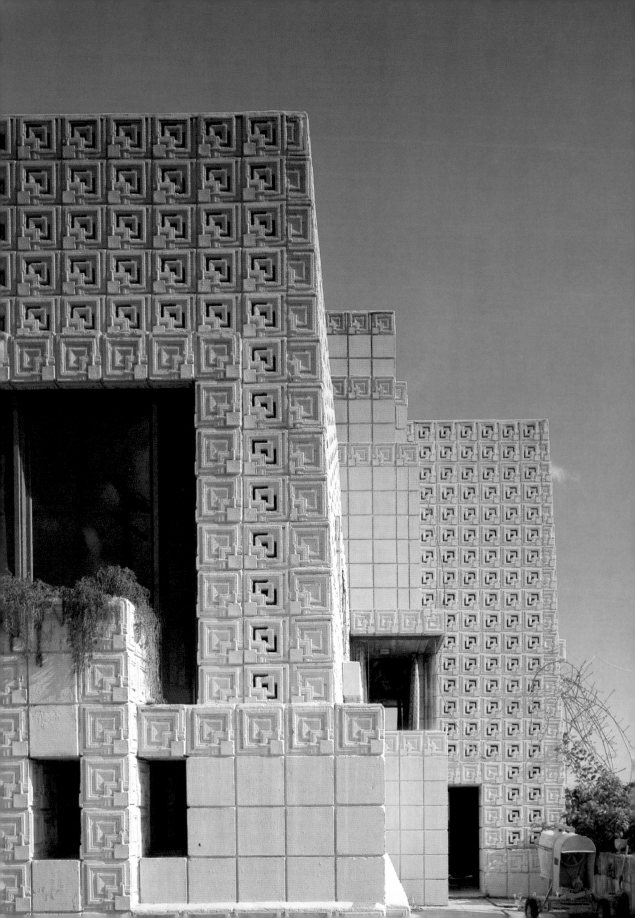

**Charles Ennis House, Los Angeles,
California, 1923–1924**
West façade, fireplace in the living
room

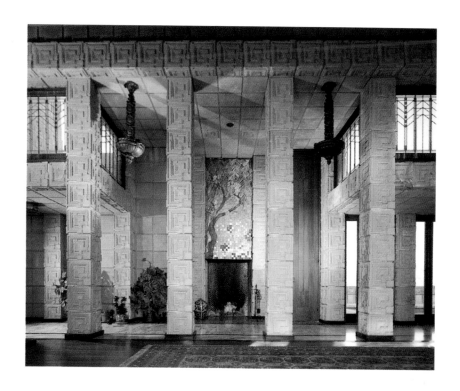

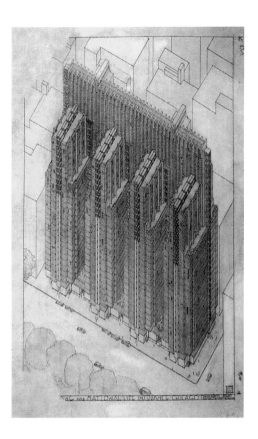

National Life Insurance Company Office Building, Chicago, Illinois, 1924 (project)

Skyscraper Regulation Scheme, 1926 (project)

Albert Johnson, President of the National Life Insurance Company of Chicago, came to the office of Frank Lloyd Wright early in the year 1924. He was immensely »impressed by the performance of the Imperial Hotel during the Kanto earthquake in 1923« and wanted an office building that employed the same principle of construction: the reinforced concrete cantilevered floor slab. Wright's design for the 39-storey office tower was his answer to Johnson's request, with one other very special request: not too much glass on the exterior wall surface. In this case, the floors are cantilevered from centrally placed interior supports, and from the slab edges the screen walls are composed of glass and sheet metal (copper).

Der Präsident der Chicagoer Niederlassung der National Life Insurance Company, Albert Johnson, suchte im Frühjahr 1924 das Büro von Frank Lloyd Wright auf. Er zeigte sich immens »beeindruckt von der Stabilität, die das Imperial Hotel während des Kanto-Erdbebens 1923 gezeigt hatte«, und wünschte sich ein nach denselben Konstruktionsprinzipien – mit auskragenden Bodenplatten aus Stahlbeton – entworfenes Bürohaus. Wrights Entwurf eines neununddreißigstöckigen Hochhauses berücksichtigte Johnsons weitere besondere Bitte, nicht zuviel Glas an den Fassaden zu verwenden. In diesem Fall kragten die Decken von zentral gesetzten Stützen aus, am Ende der Platten schlossen Wände aus Glas und Kupferblech den Raum ab.

Albert Johnson, président de la Compagnie nationale d'assurance-vie de Chicago, se présenta au bureau de Frank Lloyd Wright au début de l'année 1924. Il avait été vivement »impressionné par la solidité de l'Hôtel Impérial pendant le séisme de Kanto en 1923« et désirait un immeuble de bureaux construit selon le même principe: sur une dalle en porte-à-faux de béton armé. Le plan de Wright pour la tour à 39 étages fut sa réponse à Johnson qui avait émis une autre exigence: pas trop de verre sur la surface extérieure des murs. Les étages sont à porte-à-faux à partir de supports intérieurs placés au centre; les parois, en verre et en métal (cuivre), sont posées en retrait sur les socles.

Frank Lloyd Wright firmly believed that the city was essentially evil, a condition abhorrent to man, which placed him in an environment that was unnatural. But he offered a solution when he designed a project called »Skyscraper Regulation«. Taking six or eight blocks, on the usual grid pattern common to most American cities, he planned the skyscrapers and tall buildings to be spaced and regulated in height so that sunshine, light and air fell upon the streets and sidewalks. The top levels of the lower buildings were planted with trees and shrubs, sidewalks were located on the second floor level, crossing over the streets below as bridges so as to separate the pedestrians from the hustle and bustle of traffic.

Für Frank Lloyd Wright war die Stadt im Grunde etwas Teuflisches, ein dem Menschen widerstrebendes und unnatürliches Lebensumfeld. Mit seinem »Skyscraper Regulation«-Schema bot er jedoch eine Lösung an. Er faßte sechs oder acht Blocks der typischen Schachbrett-Anlage amerikanischer Städte zusammen und ordnete Wolkenkratzer und andere hohe Gebäude so an, daß genügend Sonne, Licht und Luft auf Straßen und Gehwegen gelangen konnte. Die Dächer der niedrigeren Gebäude wurden parkartig bepflanzt, die Gehsteige in den ersten Stock verlegt. Fußgängerbrücken führten über die Straßen und trennten so die Passanten vom Verkehrstreiben.

Frank Lloyd était persuadé que la ville était, par essence, néfaste à l'homme, qu'elle représentait une situation odieuse à celui-ci en le plaçant dans un environnement non naturel. Avec son projet qu'il avait nommé »Réglementation des gratte-ciel«, Wright offrait une solution. Ayant pris six ou huit blocs sur le modèle habituel en damier de la plupart des villes américaines, il prévoyait d'espacer et de réglementer la hauteur des gratte-ciel et des hauts bâtiments, de telle sorte que les rayons du soleil, la lumière et l'air frais se déversaient dans les rues et sur les trottoirs. Le niveau supérieur du bâtiment les plus bas était aménagé en espaces verts. Les trottoirs étaient situés au deuxième étage et traversaient les rues comme des ponts, ce qui permettait de tenir les piétons à l'écart de l'intense circulation routière.

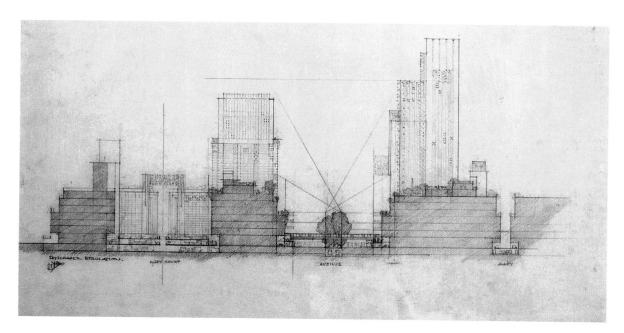

SKYSCRAPER REGULATION.   ALLEY COURT   AVENUE   ALLEY

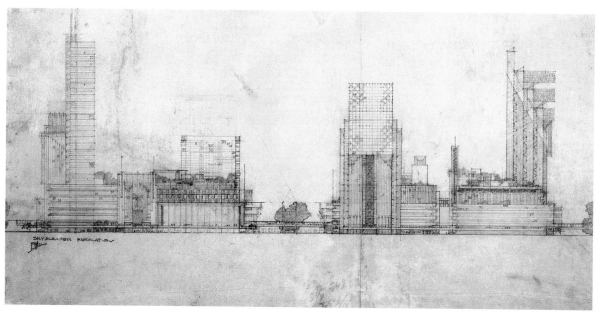

SKYSCRAPER REGULATION.

107

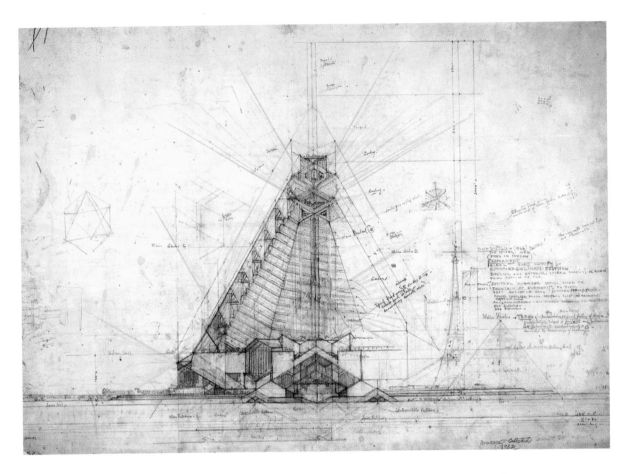

William Norman Guthrie, the flamboyant and unconventional pastor of St. Mark's on the Bouwerie, an episcopalian church in lower Manhattan, asked friend Frank Lloyd Wright to design an immense edifice of nine major cathedrals and several minor chapels capable of accommodating one million people. The response to his request was this hexagon-based design which places the cathedrals and chapels at the outer edge with a great pyramid rising above a vast open central court. Along with many other unbuilt projects of the 1920's, this design demonstrates Wright's approach to structural engineering in his innovative use of steel in suspension, glass and sheet metal in an architecture he believed befitting the twentieth century.

William Norman Guthrie, der flamboyante, unkonventionelle Pastor von St. Mark's on the Bouwerie, einer episkopalischen Kirche im Süden von Manhattan, bat seinen Freund Frank Lloyd Wright, ein riesiges Bauwerk mit neun großen Kathedralen und mehreren kleineren Kapellen zu planen, das eine Million Menschen fassen könnte. Wrights Antwort war dieser auf einem Sechseck basierende Entwurf, der die Kathedralen und Kapellen an den äußeren Enden plazierte, während sich über dem freien zentralen Hof eine gewaltige Pyramide erhob. Wie viele andere nicht realisierte Projekte aus den 20er Jahren zeigt dieser Entwurf Wrights Zugang zu Konstruktionstechniken; durch die innovative Verwendung von Stahlverspannungen, Glas und Metallplatten in einer Architektur, die er dem 20. Jahrhundert für angemessen hielt.

William Norman Guthrie, pasteur fougueux et non-conformiste de l'église épiscopale St. Mark's on the Bouwerie dans la partie sud de Manhattan, demanda à son ami Frank Lloyd Wright, d'établir les plans pour un immense édifice réunissant neuf grandes cathédrales et plusieurs petites chapelles et pouvant accueillir un million de fidèles. La réponse de Wright fut ce plan hexagonal: les cathédrales et les chapelles sont situées aux angles extérieurs et une grande pyramide surplombe une vaste cour centrale ouverte. A l'instar de nombreux autres projets non réalisés des années vingt, cette étude montre bien comment Wright abordait les techniques de construction, en employant de façon innovatrice l'acier en suspension, le verre et les plaques de métal dans une architecture, dont il pensait que le XXème siècle tirerait profit.

**Gordon Strong Automobile Objective
and Planetarium, Sugarloaf Mountain,
Maryland, 1924 (project)**

The purpose of this building was two-fold: first to provide visitors with a spectacular view of the surrounding countryside, accessible by car, and then entered into by descending a special pedestrian ramp; and second to relate the celestial to the terrestial by providing a planetarium accessible at ground level. On the one hand, man is placed in the terrain, able to study and appreciate the earth and its rocks, trees, flowers and foliage, while on the other hand, in the planetarium, man contemplates the mysteries and miracles of the cosmos. This was Wright's first major use of the spiral ramp; eighteen years later it would come into its own, this time as the interior of the building in the Guggenheim Museum.

Der Entwurf begegnete zwei Bauaufgaben: Erstens sollten Besucher vom Wagen aus die eindrucksvolle Aussicht genießen können, um dann über eine Fußgängerrampe ins Gebäude zu gelangen, und zweitens sollten Himmel und Erde durch ein Planetarium, dessen Zugang im Erdgeschoß lag, in Beziehung gebracht werden. Einerseits befindet sich der Besucher also mitten im Gelände und kann die Erde mit ihren Felsen, Bäumen und Blumen studieren und würdigen, andererseits kann er sich im Planetarium mit den Wundern und Mysterien des Kosmos befassen. Bei diesem Entwurf setzte Wright erstmals in größerem Maßstab eine spiralförmige Rampe ein; achtzehn Jahre später wird sie im Inneren des Guggenheim-Museums zu ihrer vollen Geltung kommen.

Ce bâtiment devait remplir deux objectifs: le premier était d'offrir aux visiteurs une vue spectaculaire des environs, à laquelle on avait accès en voiture. On pénétrait ensuite dans le bâtiment et descendait par le moyen d'une rampe spéciale réservée aux piétons. Le second était de relier les beautés célestes aux beautés terrestres en proposant un planétarium au rez-de-chaussée. D'un côté, on peut apprécier et étudier la terre et les rochers, les arbres, les fleurs et les feuillages et de l'autre on peut contempler les mystères et les miracles du cosmos. Ce fut la première occasion pour Wright d'utiliser une rampe en spirale; dix-huit ans plus tard, il la reprit à l'intérieur du musée Guggenheim.

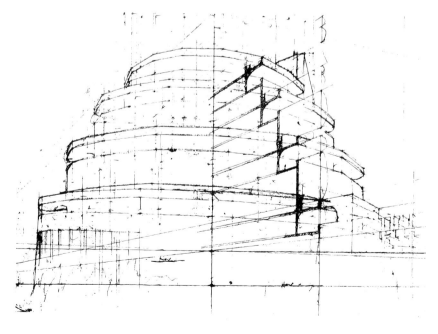

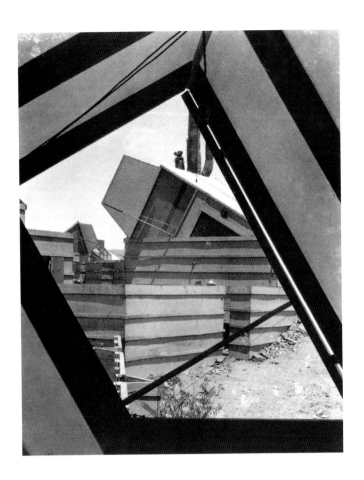

When Wright was called to Chandler, Arizona, to design the resort hotel San Marcos-in-the-Desert, the client, Dr. Alexander Chandler, presented him with two options: rent space in town for his family and draftsmen, or build something out on the desert not far from the site of the projected new hotel. Wright naturally chose to build, and Chandler let him have his pick of any site in the region. The desert encampment, called Ocotillo after the desert cactus in the region, was his first experiment with canvas as an architectural material.

Als Wright nach Chandler, Arizona, gerufen wurde, um dort für Dr. Alexander Chandler das Ferienhotel »San Marcos-in-the-Desert« zu bauen, wurden ihm zwei Möglichkeiten angeboten. Er konnte sich mit seiner Familie und dem Zeichnerteam entweder in der Stadt einmieten oder etwas für sie in der Wüste nahe dem Bauplatz entwerfen. Natürlich zog Wright das letztere vor, und Chandler ließ ihm freie Wahl für den Standort. Dieses Wüstencamp – nach den Kakteen der Region Ocotillo genannt – war Wrights erstes Experiment mit Leinwand als architektonischem Material.

Lorsque Wright se rendit à Chandler, en Arizona, pour établir le plan de l'hôtel San Marcos-in-the Desert, il put choisir, pour son lieu de résidence, entre deux possibilités que lui proposait son client, le Dr. Alexander Chandler: soit il louait une habitation pour sa famille et les dessinateurs, soit il construisait un abri dans le désert, à proximité de l'endroit où s'élèverait le nouvel hôtel. Wright choisit bien sûr la seconde solution et Chandler le laissa manier la pioche où il le désirait. Le campement dans le désert, baptisé Ocotillo d'après le cactus poussant dans la région, fut sa première expérience avec les textiles comme matériau d'architecture.

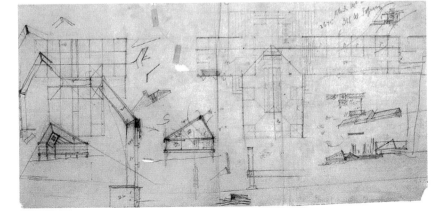

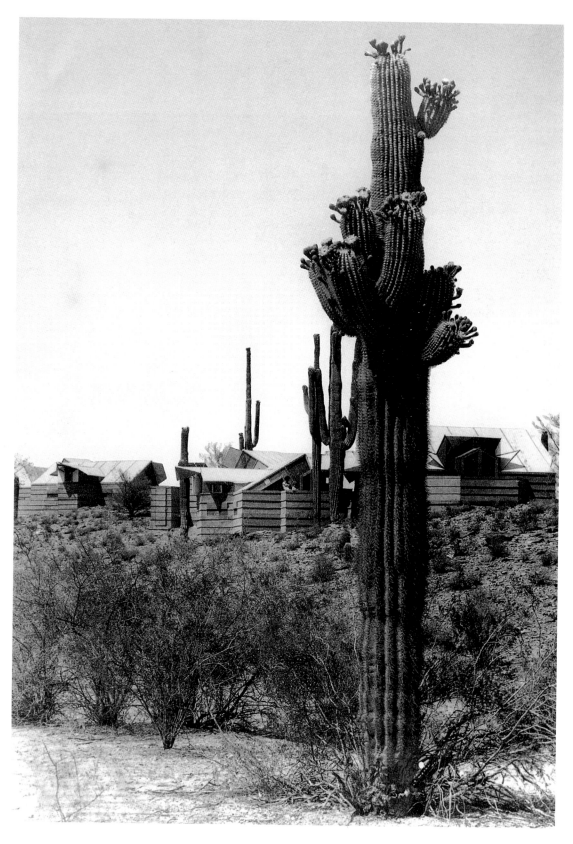

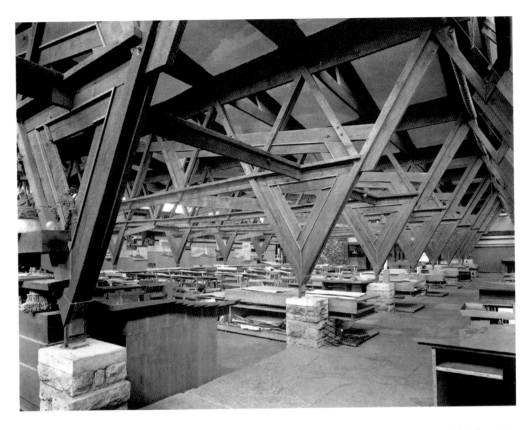

The Hillside Home School Building of
1902 was adapted to become the
Taliesin Fellowship Complex in 1932,
when the Taliesin Fellowship was
founded as a school for apprentice
training in architecture. To the north of
the original building was added the
large drafting room, completed in
1939, with eight apprentice rooms
along either side. Because of the intri-
cate truss work of oak beams, Wright
referred to this room as »the abstract
forest«. When this room was complete,
all architectural work was moved over
to Hillside from Taliesin, a quarter mile
away, and the original Taliesin studio
was then converted into Frank Lloyd
Wright's personal office.

Das Gebäude der Hillside Home
School aus dem Jahr 1902 sollte 1932
zum Taliesin Fellowship Complex um-
gestaltet werden, nachdem diese Stif-
tung als Schule für praktische Architek-
turausbildung gegründet worden war.
Nördlich des ursprünglichen Gebäudes
schloß sich der 1939 fertiggestellte
große Zeichensaal mit acht Studenten-
zimmern auf jeder Seite an. Wegen seines kunstvollen Fachwerks aus Eichen-
balken gab Wright diesem Raum den
Namen »Der abstrakte Wald«. Als dieser Raum fertiggestellt war, wurde alle
architektonische Arbeit von Taliesin
nach dem eine Viertelmeile entfernten
Hillside verlegt, und das ursprüngliche
Taliesin-Studio wurde zu Wrights per-
sönlichem Büro.

En 1932, le bâtiment de l'école privée
de Hillside, datant de 1902, fut l'objet
de transformations et devint le complexe de la Communauté Taliesin, afin
d'abriter l'école d'architectes nouvelle-
ment fondée. Au nord du bâtiment original, on ajouta une grande salle de
dessin, achevée en 1939, avec huit
pièces d'apprentissage de chaque côté.
A cause de l'armature enchevêtrée des
poutres de chêne, Wright désignait
cette salle sous le nom de »forêt abs-
traite«. Lorsque cette salle fut terminée,
tous les travaux architectoniques furent
transportés de Taliesin à Hillside, qui se
trouvait à peu près à cinq cent mètres, et
l'atelier d'origine de Taliesin fut alors
transformé en bureau personnel de
Wright.

Taliesin East, Spring Green, Wisconsin, 1911
The architect's studio

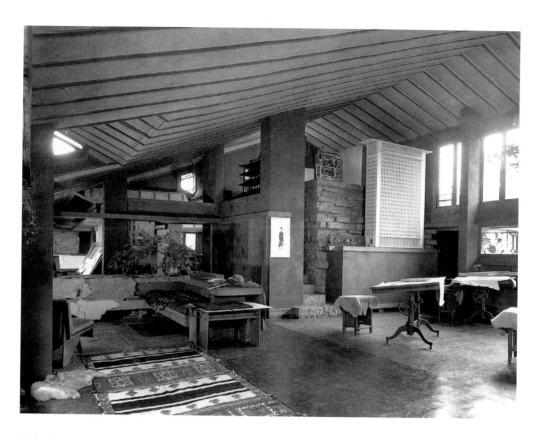

The fire that raged through Taliesin in the spring of 1925 destroyed only the architect's living quarters. A great number of oriental art treasures were lost at that time, but the rest of the building complex was undamaged. The studio at Taliesin, adjacent to the house (architect's living quarters) was likewise spared in both the fires, 1914 and 1925. The area behind the model of the Press Building contained the vault, in which were kept Wright's drawings and archives along with his collection of Japanese prints and folding screens.

Das Feuer, das im Frühjahr 1925 in Taliesin wütete, zerstörte lediglich die Wohnräume des Architekten. Eine große Anzahl orientalischer Kunstgegenstände verbrannte, doch der Rest des Gebäudes blieb unversehrt. Das an das Privathaus des Architekten angrenzende Studio in Taliesin blieb von den Bränden der Jahre 1914 und 1925 verschont. Hinter dem Modell des Pressegebäudes befand sich ein Tresorschrank, in dem Wrights Zeichnungen und Archive samt seiner Sammlung japanischer Drucke und Paravents aufbewahrt wurden.

L'incendie qui se déchaîna à Taliesin au printemps 1925 ne détruisit que les lieux d'habitation de l'architecte. De nombreux trésors d'art oriental furent certes perdus, mais les autres bâtiments du complexe furent épargnés. L'atelier de Taliesin, qui est adjacent à la maison (aux lieux d'habitation de l'architecte), fut lui aussi épargné lors des incendies de 1914 et de 1925. L'espace derrière la maquette du Press Building comprenait une chambre-forte, où étaient conservées les esquisses et les archives de Wright ainsi que sa collection d'estampes et de paravents.

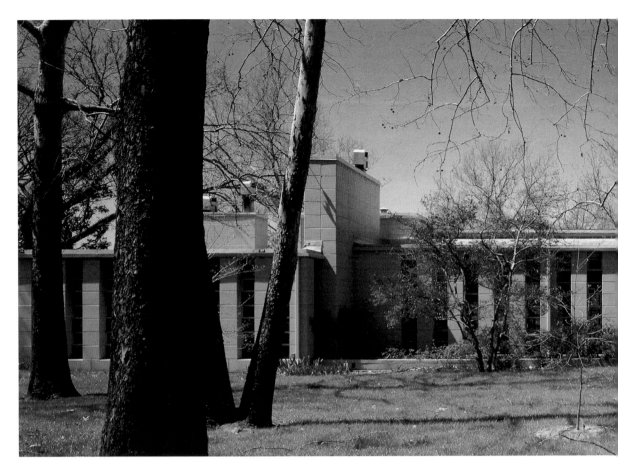

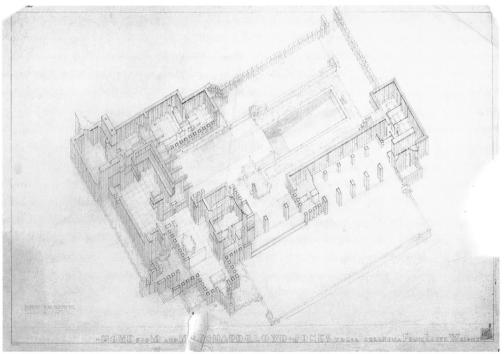

·HOME·FOR·MR·AND·MRS·RICHARD·LLOYD·JONES·TULSA·OKLAHOMA·FRANK·LLOYD·WRIGHT·

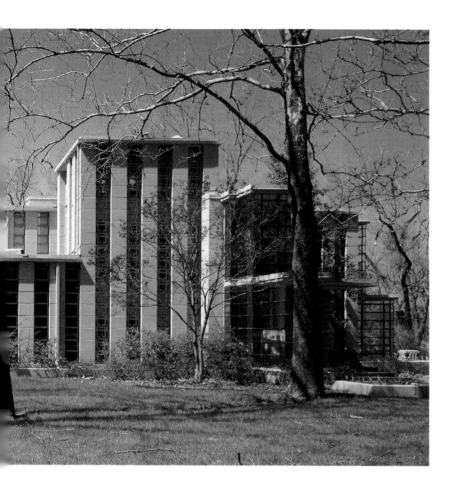

In 1931 a large exhibition of the work of Frank Lloyd Wright was seen in Brussels, Amsterdam and Berlin. A model of the Richard Lloyd Jones house was part of the show. In the earlier Californian houses the block was a total screen, with openings for windows and French doors. But the wall treatment in this house is entirely different. To explain this aspect of the walls to the European audience during that 1931 exhibition, Wright composed the accompanying caption as follows: »The dwelling house without walls. The palisades with steel sash and glass between substituted.« »Palisades« was Wright's term to describe the alternating vertical members of concrete block and glass.

1931 wurde eine große Frank-Lloyd-Wright-Werkschau in Brüssel, Amsterdam und Berlin gezeigt. Auch ein Modell des Hauses für Richard Lloyd Jones war Teil dieser Ausstellung. Während in den früheren kalifornischen Häusern der Block Flächen mit Öffnungen für Fenster und Glastüren bildete, wurde hier die Außenwand ganz anders behandelt. Um diesen Aspekt der Mauergestaltung den europäischen Ausstellungsbesuchern nahezubringen, formulierte Wright folgende Erläuterung zum Modell: »Das Wohnhaus ohne Mauern. Statt dessen Palisaden mit stahlgefaßtem Glas.« Mit »Palisaden« bezeichnete Wright die alternierenden senkrechten Elemente aus Betonblocksteinen und Glas.

En 1931, une grande exposition sur les travaux de Frank Lloyd Wright eut lieu à Bruxelles, à Amsterdam et à Berlin. Une maquette de la maison Richard Lloyd Jones comptait parmi les ouvrages exposés. Dans les maisons de Californie, le bloc était un écran total, avec des ouvertures pour les fenêtres et les portes à la française. Dans cette maison, le mur a un aspect complètement différent. Afin d'expliquer l'aspect de ces murs au public européen, pendant l'exposition de 1931, Wright rédigea la légende suivante: »Maison d'habitation sans murs. Ceux-ci sont remplacés par des palissades avec des cadres en acier et du verre.« »Palissades« était le mot employé par Wright pour décrire l'alternance des éléments verticaux en bloc de béton et en verre.

Malcolm Willey House, Minneapolis, Minnesota, 1933–1934
Drawing, garden side, kitchen

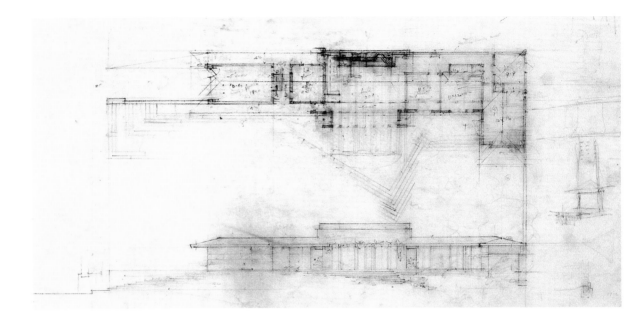

Two different designs were made for the Malcolm Willeys, the first one – a two-storey residence with many features that would later evolve into the »Usonian House«, proved too costly. The second one is a one-storey plan called »The Garden Wall« because the building is placed along a brick wall at the far extremity of the property. This was done so as to take best advantage of the site. The floor is paved with brick, employing two different color tones set in alternating bands, as was done in the walls. The original furniture was a new direction in Wright's designs, and leads quite naturally into the plywood furniture he would later develop for the »Usonian« houses.

Für die Willeys wurden zwei verschiedene Entwürfe angefertigt. Der erste, ein zweistöckiges Wohnhaus mit vielen Merkmalen, die später zum »Usonia«-Haustyp entwickelt wurden, erwies sich als zu kostspielig. Der zweite, einstöckige hieß »Die Gartenmauer«, da das Gebäude entlang einer Ziegelmauer am äußersten Ende der Besitzung plaziert ist. So wurde das Grundstück optimal genutzt. Der Fußboden ist in abwechselnden Reihen mit zweifarbigen Ziegeln gepflastert, auch die Hausmauern sind so gestaltet. Das Originalmobiliar stellte einen neuen Weg in Wrights Schaffen dar, der ganz natürlich zu den Sperrholzmöbeln der »Usonia-Häuser« führte.

Deux plans différents ont été réalisés pour les Willey. Le premier représentait une maison à deux étages avec de nombreuses caractéristiques – caractéristiques qu'il développera plus tard dans ses »Usonian houses« – et s'avéra trop coûteux. Le second est un plan à un étage, qu'il avait nommé »le mur du jardin« en raison de l'emplacement du bâtiment, le long d'un mur en brique, à l'extrémité de la propriété. Ceci afin de profiter le plus possible du paysage. Le plancher est recouvert de briques de deux couleurs différentes. Les rangées sont posées en alternance. Les murs sont recouverts de la même façon. Le mobilier d'origine reflète la nouvelle direction dans le désign et conduit presque naturellement aux meubles en contre-plaqué qui seront développés plus tard pour les »Usonian houses«.

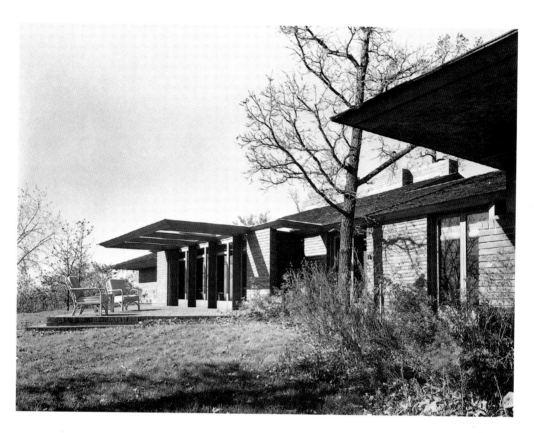

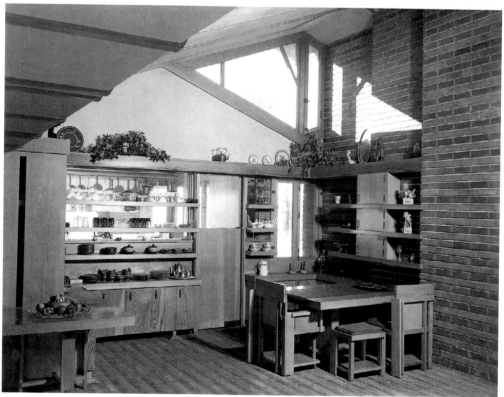

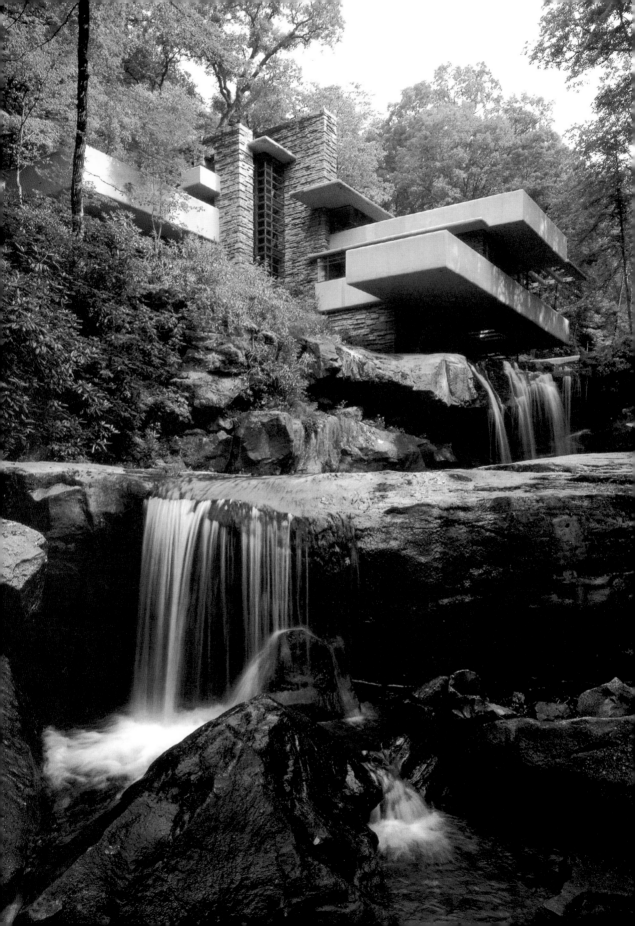

»Fallingwater«, House for Edgar J.
Kaufmann, Bear Run, Pennsylvania,
1935–1939
Views from the valley and the driveway

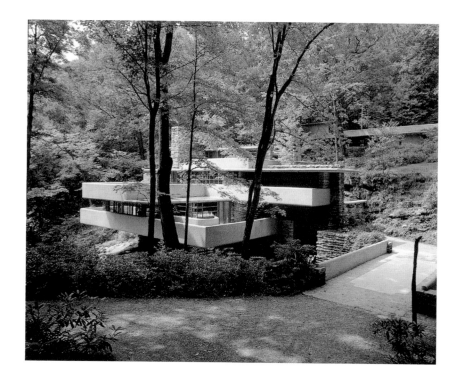

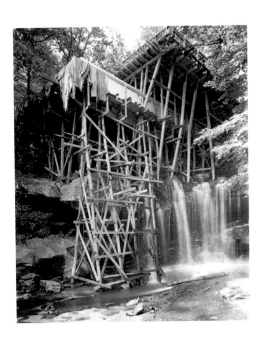

»Fallingwater«, House for Edgar J. Kaufmann, Bear Run, Pennsylvania, 1935 – 1939
The house under construction, floor plans

In a talk to the Taliesin Fellowship Frank Lloyd Wright said of this house, »Fallingwater is a great blessing – one of the great blessings to be experienced here on earth. I think nothing yet ever equalled the coordination, sympathetic expression of the great principle of repose where forest and stream and rock and all the elements of structure are combined so quietly that really you listen not to any noise whatsoever although the music of the stream is there. But you listen to Fallingwater the way you listen to the quiet of the country . . .« What the building achieves with perhaps more drama than any other single private residence is the placement of man in relation to nature. This important aspect of man and the landscape was deeply rooted in Wright. Fallingwater is famous the world over, principally as it is seen in photographs, from below the cascades looking up towards the cantilevered balconies and terraces. What Wright did in this house is to put the occupants in a close relationship to the glen, the trees, the foliage and wild flowers. Wherever one is within the building, the glory of the natural surrounding is accentuated, brought in, and made a component part of daily life. The main floor affords views in three directions, with terraces leading out in two: one terrace opens upstream, the other projects over the rocks and cascades. Each bedroom on the level above has its own terrace, and the study and gallery-bedroom on the third level have access, likewise, to yet another outdoor terrace. All the vertical elements of the house are constructed of native stone, with »stick-outs« or slightly projected stones to give a more sculptural quality to the stone masses. All horizontal elements are poured concrete. The floors throughout are paved in stone, the same as the walls, and the woodwork is a sap grain walnut, executed at an extremely fine level of craftsmanship. A semi-circular covered walk joins the main house to the guest house further up the hill.

In einer Ansprache an die Taliesin-Gemeinschaft sagte Frank Lloyd Wright über dieses Haus: »Fallingwater ist eine große Wohltat, wohl eine der größten, die man hier auf Erden erfahren kann. Vermutlich ist nichts wirklich mit dem Einklang und dem Ausdruck großer Ruhe und Gelassenheit zu vergleichen, wie sie dort aus der Kombination von Wald, Fluß und Fels und den Elementen der Struktur entstehen. Obwohl die Musik des Flusses immer da ist, achtet man auf kein Geräusch. Man hört Fallingwater so, wie man die Ruhe des Landes hört . . .« Bei diesem Haus wurde – vermutlich bewegender als bei jedem anderen Privatwohnhaus – der Bewohner in eine Beziehung zur Natur gebracht, ein Aspekt, der zutiefst in Wrights Persönlichkeit verwurzelt war. Fallingwater ist weltberühmt, hauptsächlich durch Fotografien, die gewöhnlich von unterhalb des Wasserfalls aufgenommen sind und die auskragenden Balkone und Terrassen zeigen. Wright gelang es mit diesem Haus, die Bewohner in ein inniges Verhältnis zur Schlucht, zu den Bäumen, dem Laubwerk und den wilden Pflanzen zu bringen. In jedem Teil des Gebäudes wird die Herrlichkeit der umgebenden Natur betont, einbezogen und zu einem festen Bestandteil des täglichen Lebens gemacht. Das Geschoß bietet Ausblicke in drei Richtungen. Zwei Terrassen gehen von ihm aus, eine davon zeigt flußaufwärts, die andere springt über die Felsen und den Wasserfall vor. Im Stockwerk darüber hat jedes Schlafzimmer eine eigene Terrasse, und auch vom Arbeitszimmer und vom Galerie-Schlafzimmer im dritten Stock aus kann je eine eigene Außenterrasse betreten werden. Sämtliche vertikalen Elemente des Hauses sind in einheimischem Stein ausgeführt, mit leicht vorstehenden Steinen, um den Mauerflächen eine skulpturhafte Wirkung zu verleihen. Alle horizontalen Teile bestehen aus gegossenem Beton. Die Fußböden sind ebenso wie die Wände mit Stein belegt, die Holzarbeiten in außerordentlich fein verarbeitetem gemasertem Walnußholz ausgeführt. Das Haupthaus ist durch einen halbkreisförmigen Fußweg mit dem weiter oben liegenden Gästehaus verbunden.

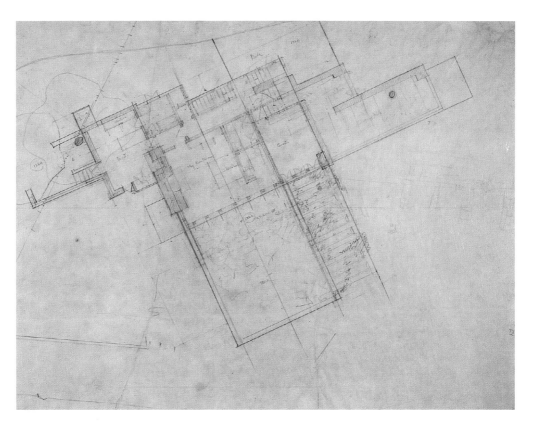

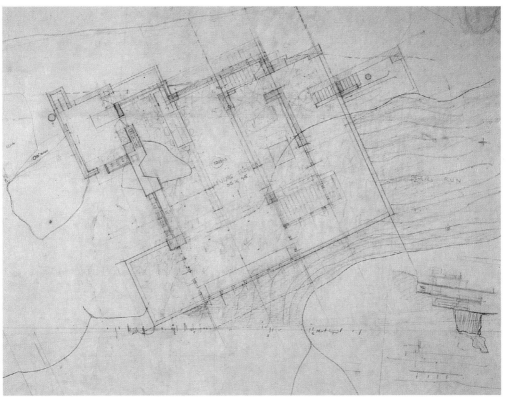

121

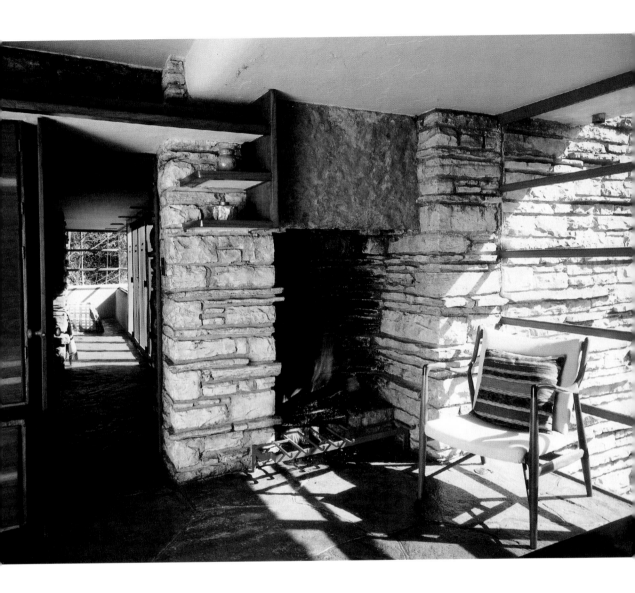

Lors d'une discussion avec les membres de la Communauté Taliesin, Frank Wright dit en parlant de cette maison: »Fallingwater est une grande bénédiction parmi celles que l'on peut recevoir ici sur terre. Je pense que rien n'a encore jamais égalé la coordination, l'expression vibrante du principe de sérénité où forêt, rivière, rocher et tous les éléments de la construction forment une association si tranquille qu'en fait vous ne percevez aucun bruit quel qu'il soit bien que la musique du torrent existe. Vous écoutez Fallingwater de la façon dont vous écoutez le calme de la campagne . . .« Ce que le bâtiment arrive à accomplir avec peut-être plus d'emphase que n'importe quelle autre habitation privée, c'est de placer l'homme en relation avec la nature. Cet important aspect de l'homme et du paysage était profondément ancré en Wright. Fallingwater est célèbre dans le monde entier, en particulier par les photographies prises à la base de la cascade et représentant les balcons et les terrasses en encorbellement. Dans cette maison, Wright a placé ses occupants en relation étroite avec la gorge de la montagne, les arbres, le feuillage et les fleurs sauvages. A l'intérieur du bâtiment, la gloire de l'environnement naturel est partout accentuée, introduite et transformée en partie intégrante de la vie quotidienne. L'étage principal s'ouvre sur trois vues différentes; les terrasses sont situées dans deux directions: la première donne sur le côté en amont, la seconde surplombe les rochers et la cascade. Les chambres des niveaux supérieurs ont chacune leur terrasse. Le cabinet de travail et la chambre en galerie du troisième étage donnent aussi sur une terrasse extérieure. Tous les éléments verticaux de la maison sont construits en pierre du pays, avec des »saillies« ou pierres légèrement en relief afin de prêter à la surface des murs un aspect plus sculptural. Tous les éléments horizontaux sont en béton coulé. Les sols sont partout recouverts de pierre; il en est de même pour les murs. Les travaux de menuiserie sont en noyer madré et ont été réalisés avec beaucoup de dextérité. Un chemin protégé, en forme de demi-cercle, relie la maison principale à la maison pour invités située plus haut dans la colline.

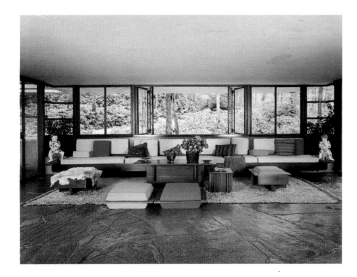

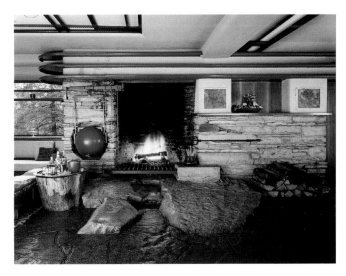

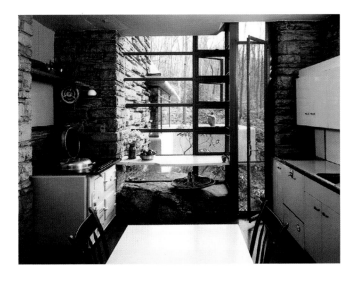

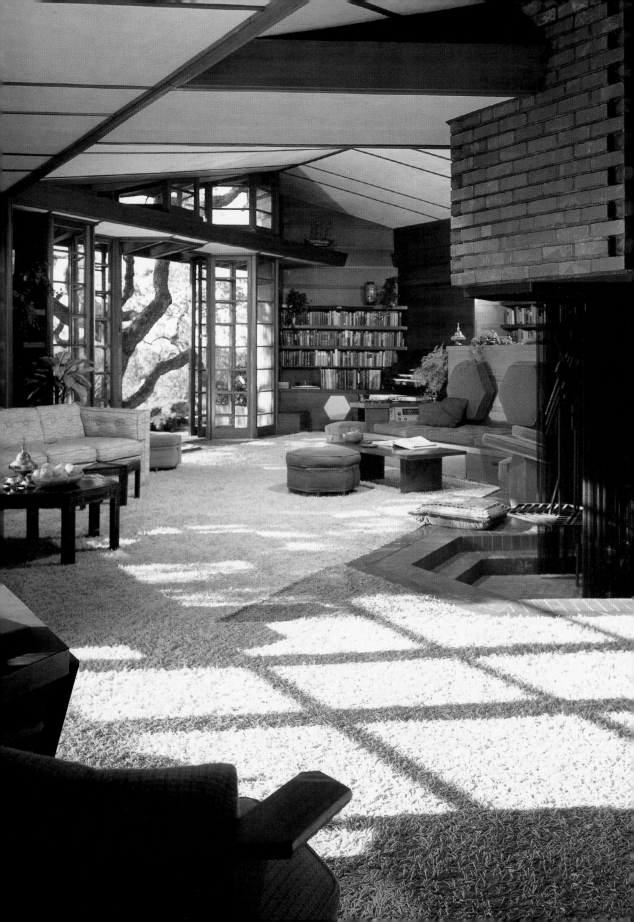

»Honeycomb House« for Paul R. and
Jean Hanna, Stanford, California,
1936–1937
Living room, views from street and
garden

In his continuing quest to find a more
flexible plan form, one that would result
likewise in more flexible interior space,
Wright found the hexagon, and the hexagonal unit, more desirable than either
the square or rectangle. In its first application at the Hanna house the hexagonal unit provides the basis for the
plan. The house itself is not a hexagon,
but has a free-flowing plan with wider
angles (120 degrees) than the usual 90
degrees. Being a prototype, the project
required a great number of architectural
drawings to develop the scheme and
then to produce a set of working drawings that could be easily understood by
contractor and workmen.

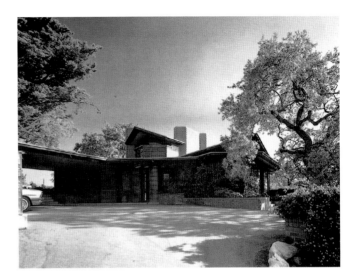

Auf seiner ständigen Suche nach einer
flexibleren Grundrißform, die in ebenfalls flexibleren Innenraumlösungen re-
sultieren sollte, fand Wright das Sechseck erstrebenswerter als quadratische
oder rechteckige Einheiten. Eine erste
Anwendung fand die Sechseckform
beim Plan des Hauses Hanna. Es ist allerdings kein Sechseck als ganzes, sondern hat einen eher fließenden Grundriß mit größeren Winkeln – nämlich
120 Grad – statt der üblichen rechten
Winkel. Da dies ein echter Prototyp
war, erforderte das Projekt zahlreiche
Entwurfs- und Ausführungszeichnun-
gen, um vom ausführenden Unternehmer und von den Arbeitern verstanden
werden zu können.

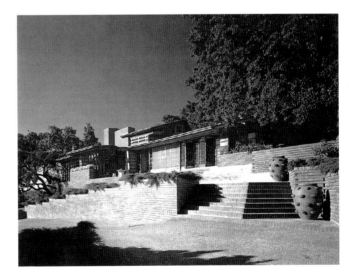

Dans sa continuelle recherche pour un
plan plus flexible, un plan qui aurait
pour résultat un espace intérieur également plus souple, Wright adopta
l'hexagone, et la trame hexagonale,
qui'il préféra au carré ou au rectangle.
Dans sa première application avec la
maison Hanna, la trame hexagonale
fournit la base du plan. La maison elle-
même n'est pas un hexagone, mais a un
plan dont les angles (120 degrés) sont
plus larges que les angles habituels de
90 degrés. En tant que prototype, le
projet exigeait un grand nombre de dessins pour développer le plan et pour
fournir des plans de construction faciles
à comprendre pour l'entrepreneur et les
ouvriers.

»Honeycomb House« for Paul R. and
Jean Hanna, Stanford, California,
1936–1937
Ground plan

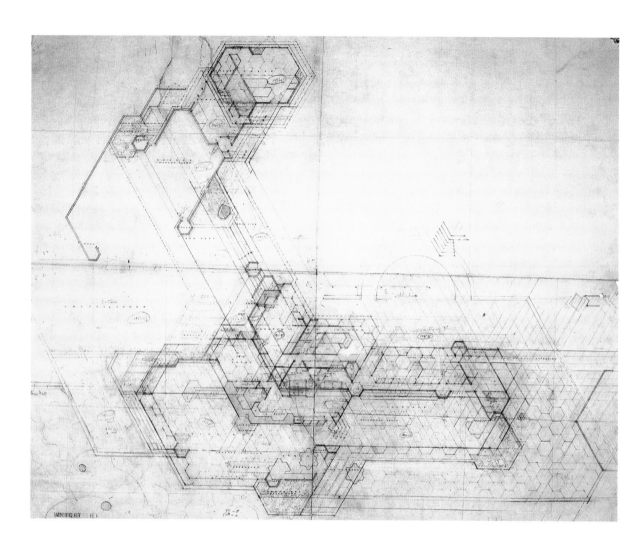

Robert D. Lusk House, Huron, South Dakota, 1936 (project)

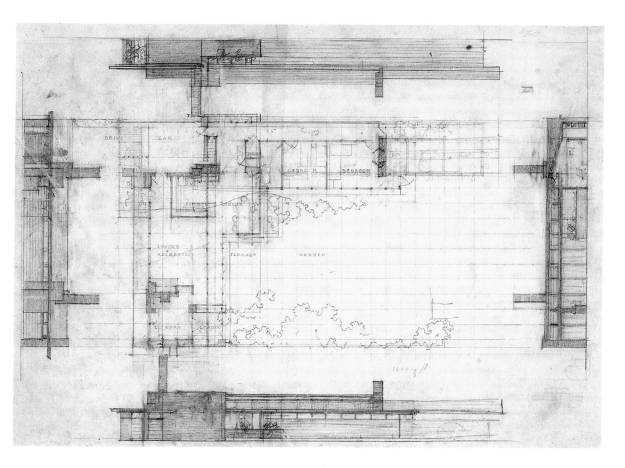

The Robert Lusk house was the first in a series that Wright called »Usonian houses«. It was his answer to the ever-growing need and demand for moderate cost housing. In 1936, moderate cost housing in the United States was almost exclusively confined to the Colonial box-type seen all over the nation. Although the Lusk house was not built, its plan and general construction system were developed further and next built for Herbert Jacobs.

Der Entwurf des Hauses für Robert Lusk war der erste in einer Reihe, die Wright »Usonia-Häuser« nannte und die seine Antwort auf den stets zunehmenden Bedarf an preisgünstigen Bauweisen darstellte. 1936 war bezahlbarer Hausbau noch fast vollständig auf den kolonialen Kastenbaustil beschränkt, wie man ihn in ganz Nordamerika finden konnte. Obwohl das Haus Lusk nie gebaut wurde, wurden der Grundriß und die allgemeine Konstruktionsweise weiterentwickelt und gingen in den Entwurf für Herbert Jacob ein.

La maison Robert Lusk fut la première d'une série de maisons portant le nom de »Usonian houses« (maisons usaniennes). Wright répondait ainsi aux demandes toujours plus nombreuses réclamant des maisons à prix modérés. En 1936 aux Etats-Unis, seules les maisons coloniales »en forme de caisse«, que l'on voyait dans tout le pays, étaient proposées à un prix modéré. Bien que la maison Lusk ne fut pas construite, ses plans et son système général de construction furent développés et concrétisés peu après dans la maison pour Herbert Jacobs.

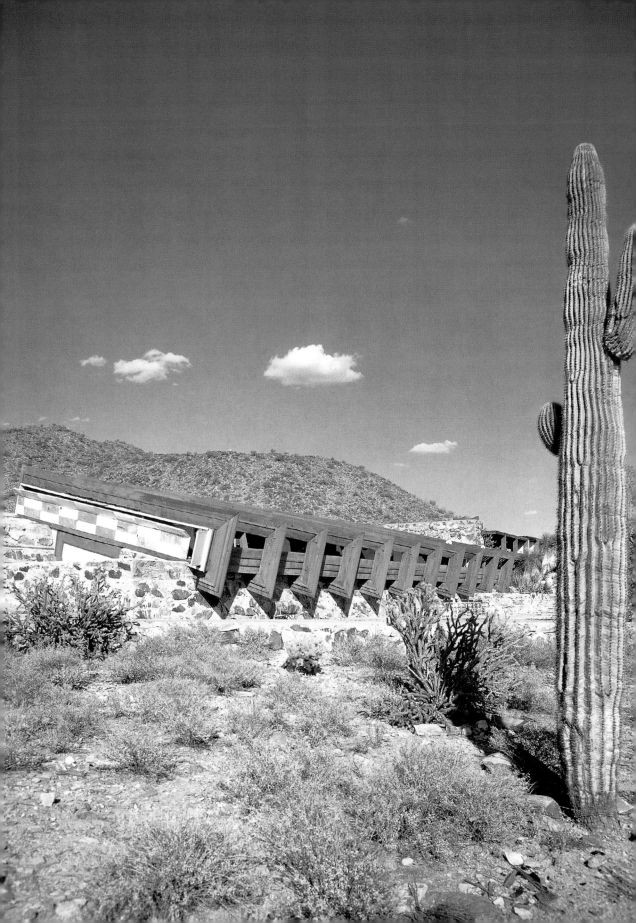

**Taliesin West, Scottsdale, Arizona,
1937–1938**
South side, drawing room

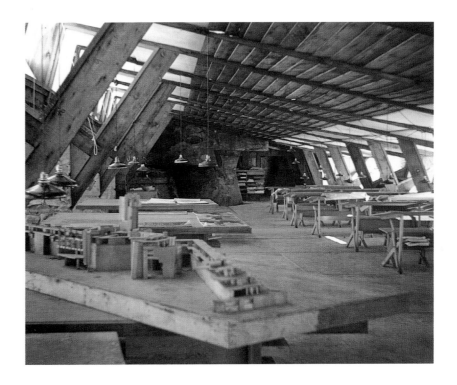

Ever since his first long-term stay in
Arizona in 1927, Wright was anxious to
return to this region of the Sonoran desert in order to escape the intensely cold
winters of Wisconsin. Finally, in 1937,
he and his wife made a trip to Phoenix
in search of land. Out on the desert
north of Phoenix, up against the
McDowell Mountain range, they discovered property which he described as
»a look over the rim of the world«. The
designs for the new buildings came
quickly out of Wright's fertile imagination. As he sat making designs for the
various buildings that would form the
complex, stone and sand were
gathered, the ground made ready, and
wooden forms erected for making the
masonry walls. The overhead structure,
inspired by its use in Ocotillo ten years
earlier, was a truss-work of redwood
beams, with white canvas stretched
over wooden frames and inserted between the sloping beams. Eventually he
sought to make it more permanent,
bringing in glass and steel and trans-
forming its original »camp-like« aspect
to one of more durability.

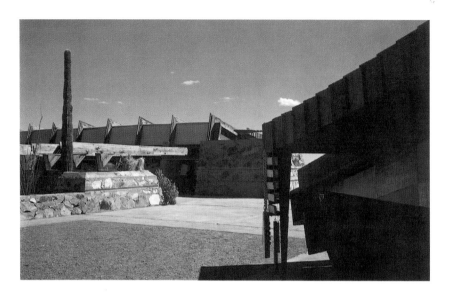

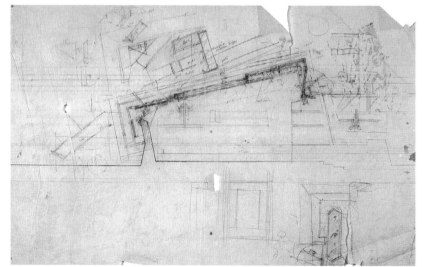

Schon seit seinem ersten längeren Aufenthalt in Arizona 1927 beschäftigte Wright die Idee, den strengen Wintern Wisconsins in der Sonora-Wüste zu entgehen. 1937 schließlich fuhr er mit seiner Frau nach Phoenix, um sich nach Bauland umzusehen. Im Norden von Phoenix entdeckten sie ein Stück Wüstenland vor der McDowell-Hügelkette, das Wright als »einen Blick über den Rand der Erde« beschrieb. Schnell waren erste Ideen für die neuen Gebäude entwickelt. Noch während er an den Zeichnungen arbeitete, wurden bereits der Baugrund vorbereitet, Sand und Steine herangeschafft und die Holzschalungen für die Natursteinwände aufgerichtet. Der obere Teil der Struktur war vom Camp Ocotillo inspiriert; es handelte sich um Binder aus Rotholz mit dazwischengesetzten Holzrahmen, die mit weißer Zeltleinwand bespannt waren. Schließlich aber wollte Wright Taliesin West dauerhafter machen und verlieh dem ursprünglich »campartigen« Eindruck mit Hilfe von Stahl und Glas mehr Beständigkeit.

Depuis l'époque de son premier long séjour en Arizona, en 1927, Wright avait toujours désiré retourner dans cette région du désert Sonoran afin de fuir les rigoureux hivers du Wisconsin. En 1937 finalement, Wright et sa femme firent un voyage à Phoenix pour chercher un terrain. Dans le désert au nord de Phoenix, et aux pieds des monts McDowell, ils découvrirent une propriété que Wright qualifiait de »regard sur les confins du monde«. Grâce à son imagination créatrice, les plans pour les nouveaux bâtiments furent rapidement réalisés. Pendant qu'il faisait les plans pour les différents bâtiments du complexe, on rassemblait les pierres et le sable, on préparait le sol et on érigeait la charpente pour la maçonnerie des murs. La structure du toit, s'inspirant du plafond d'Ocotillo d'il y a dix ans, était une construction de poutres en bois de séquoia. Une toile blanche était tendue sur les cadres en bois et le tout était intercalé entre les poutres inclinées. Par la suite, il chercha à la rendre plus durable et plus résistante, en y ajoutant du verre et de l'acier et en modifiant son aspect original de »campement«.

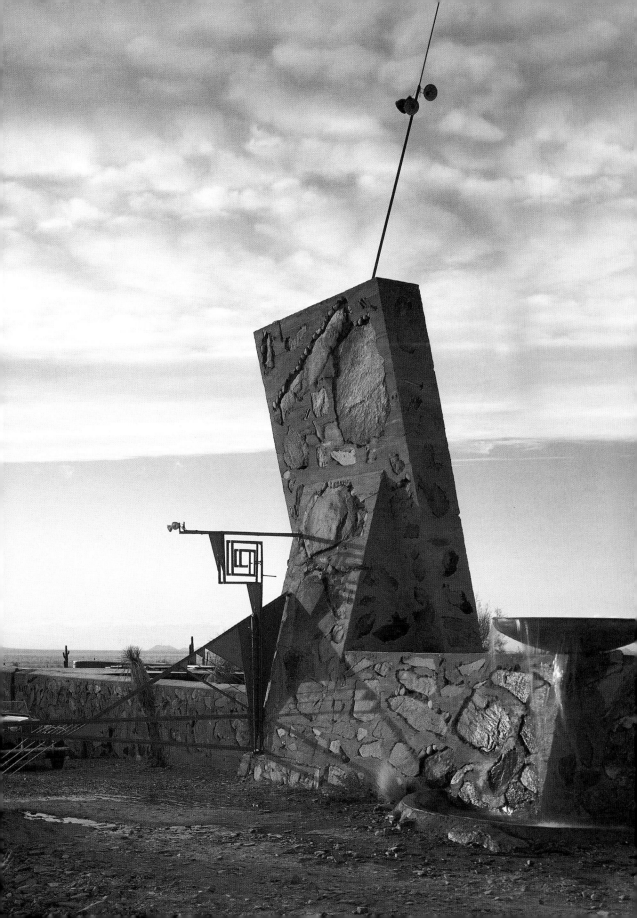

**Ralph Jester House, Palos Verdes,
California, 1938 (project), executed
for Arthur E. and Bruce Brooks Pfeiffer
in Taliesin West, Scottsdale, Arizona,
1971–1972**
Drawing, entrance view

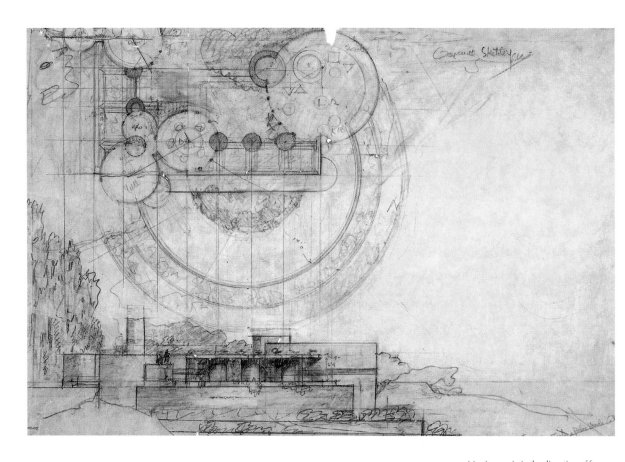

Moving again in the direction of freer plan forms, from square or rectangle to hexagon, Wright's next venture in this direction was the circle. In the Ralph Jester house every major room is a complete circle, the circles spaced apart on a square grid, connected by a covered patio so as to avoid the constriction of the interstices. The circular plan for each room obliterates corners and space flows in a more even line. The windows on the exterior are narrow continuous bands of glass 18" high, at a level where the view is seen when sitting down. But the glass doors that open onto the shaded patio give ample light to balance and compensate for the narrow bands of light on the exterior.

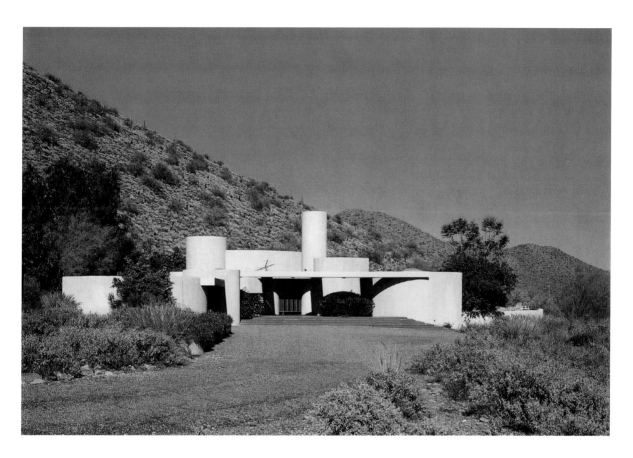

Bei seinen Experimenten mit freieren Grundrißformen kam Wright vom Quadrat oder Rechteck über das Sechseck zum Kreis. Im Haus Jester ist jeder größere Raum aus einem vollen Kreis gebildet, wobei die einzelnen Kreisformen so auf einem quadratischen Raster angeordnet und auf einen Innenhof ausgerichtet sind, daß keine engen Resträume entstehen. Durch den runden Grundriß jedes Zimmers gibt es keine Ecken, und der Raum bewegt sich auf einer ausgewogenen Linie. Die Außenfenster sind als schmale, 40 Zentimeter hohe Glasbänder so niedrig eingeschnitten, daß sie den besten Ausblick ermöglichen, wenn man sitzt. Doch die auf den schattigen Innenhof führenden Glastüren gleichen die schmalen Fenster der Außenseiten aus und sorgen für ausreichende Beleuchtung.

Ayant abandonné le carré et le rectangle pour l'hexagone, Wright voulait progresser vers des plans encore plus libres. Sa prochaine démarche fut l'emploi du cercle. Dans la maison Ralph Jester, toutes les salles principales ont la forme du cercle; les cercles sont placés à intervalle sur une trame carrée et sont reliés par un patio couvert afin d'éviter que les espaces intermédiaires soient trop étroits. Dans ce plan circulaire, les angles ont été effacés et l'espace intérieur acquiert une ligne plus régulière. Les fenêtres sont disposées en rangées étroites et les vitres ont une hauteur de 45,7 cm. Elles sont placées de telle sorte que l'on a encore une vue sur l'extérieur, même en étant assis. Les portes-fenêtres, qui s'ouvrent sur le patio ombragé, amènent une grande clarté afin de contre-balancer les étroites bandes de lumière qui proviennent des fenêtres.

John C. Pew House, Madison, Wisconsin, 1938–1940
Drawing, preliminary sketch and view
from the lakeside

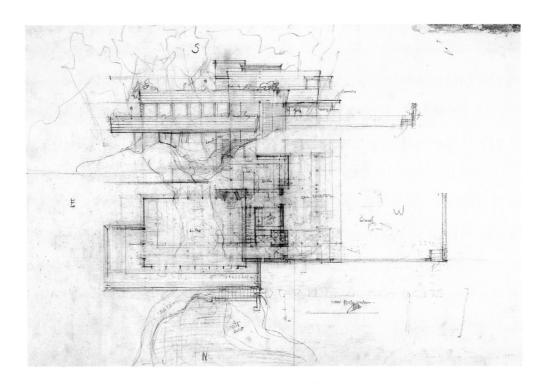

The property John Pew chose for his Wisconsin house was narrow, with neighbors close by on either side. But the steep slope of the lot from the road above to the water's edge below and the profusion of trees and bushes made it possible for Wright to design a home that appears quite isolated and private. This was achieved by setting the house at an angle to the lake below, what the architect called »on the reflex.« The building is really one large balcony composed of smaller ones, and the effect is not one of a house on a confined site, but of a house placed out and among the branches of the trees, looking down through the foliage onto the lake below.

Das Grundstück, das John Pew für sein Haus in Wisconsin ausgesucht hatte, war schmal, der Abstand zu den Nachbarhäusern gering. Aber der steile Hang zwischen Straße und Ufer und sein dichter Bewuchs ermöglichten es Wright, ein Haus zu entwerfen, das durchaus zurückgezogen und privat wirkt. Dies wurde vor allem durch den Winkel erzielt, den das Haus zum See bildet – eine Anordnung, die Wright »on the reflex« nannte. Das Haus ist im Grunde ein einziger großer Balkon, der sich aus kleineren zusammensetzt, und wirkt dadurch nicht eingeengt und kompakt, sondern wie ein Haus, das zwischen die Zweige der Bäume hineingebaut ist und durch das Laubwerk auf den See hinunterblickt.

John Pew avait choisi pour sa maison du Wisconsin un terrain étroit et encadré, de chaque côté, par des maisons voisines. Toutefois, la pente accentuée de la parcelle, située entre la route en haut et le bord de l'eau en bas, ainsi que la profusion d'arbres et de buissons, permirent à Wright de concevoir une maison qui semble complètement isolée et préserve l'intimité. Ceci fut possible en plaçant la maison dans un angle formé par le lac, dans »l'angle rentrant« pour reprendre les termes de l'architecte. Le bâtiment est à vrai dire un grand balcon composé de petits balcons et l'effet qu'il produit n'est pas celui d'une maison sur un terrain enserré, mais d'une maison placée parmi les branches des arbres, dont le regard plonge à travers le feuillage sur le lac à ses pieds.

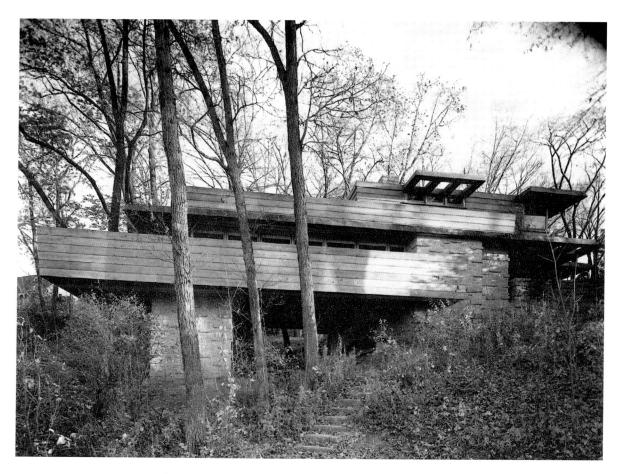

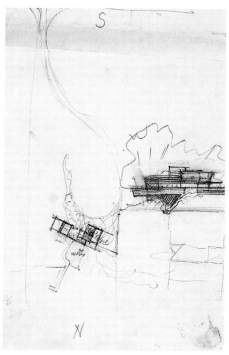

135

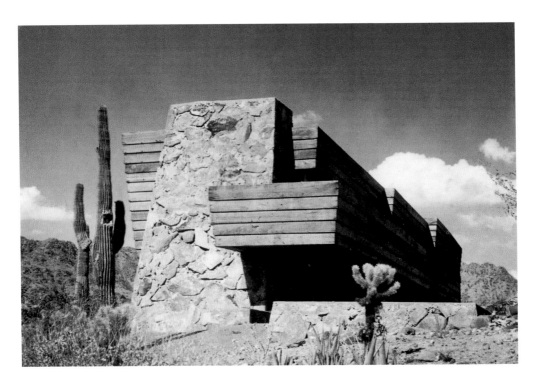

The perspective drawing for this work demonstrates the close, harmonious association of house and desert. It would seem, from this view, that the desert and dwelling were made at one and the same moment. Since the living room faced north, there was no need for an overhang, and the two-storey glass gives a view onto a mountain range beyond. Rose Pauson and her sister Gertrude only lived in the house one season; when they returned to their native San Francisco, they rented the house, and it was destroyed by a fire. It was one of the most exquisite of Wright's residential works, its loss was indeed tragic.

Die perspektivische Zeichnung für dieses Projekt führt bereits die enge, harmonische Beziehung zwischen Haus und Wüste vor Augen. In dieser Studie scheint es so, als seien Wüste und Haus gleichzeitig geschaffen worden. Da das Wohnzimmer nach Norden lag, war ein Dachüberstand hier unnötig, und die über zwei Stockwerke reichende Glasfläche gewährte Ausblick auf die jenseitige Hügelkette. Rose Pauson und ihre Schwester Gertrude konnten nur eine Saison in dem Haus verbringen. Als sie in ihre Heimatstadt San Francisco zurückkehrten, wurde es vermietet und dann durch ein Feuer zerstört. Dieser Verlust eines der vorzüglichsten von Wrights Wohnhäusern ist wirklich zu bedauern.

La vue en perspective dessinée pour ce projet montre bien l'étroite et harmonieuse association entre la maison et le désert. Avec cette vue, on a l'impression que la maison et le désert sont apparus simultanément. La salle de séjour étant exposée au nord, il n'était pas nécessaire de construire un avant-toit; les fenêtres du deuxième étage donnent sur une chaîne de montagnes au loin. Rose Pauson et sa soeur Gertrude n'y habitèrent que pendant une saison. Lorsqu'elles retournèrent à San Francisco, leur ville natale, elles louèrent la maison qui fut ensuite détruite par un incendie. Comptant parmi les ouvrages d'habitation les plus raffinés, sa perte était vraiment tragique.

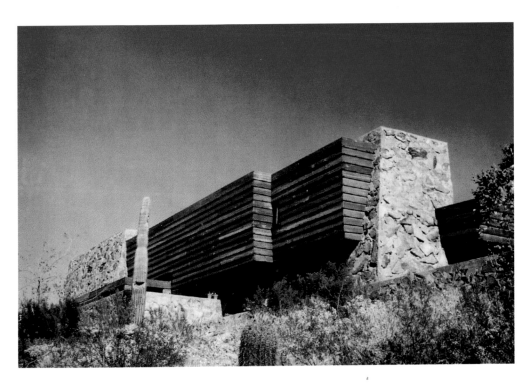

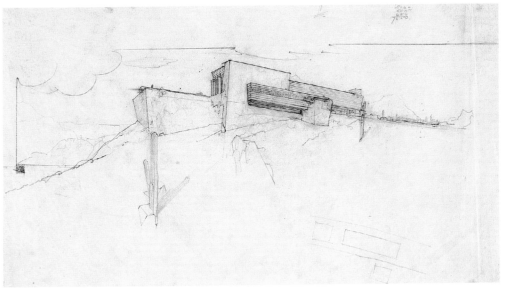

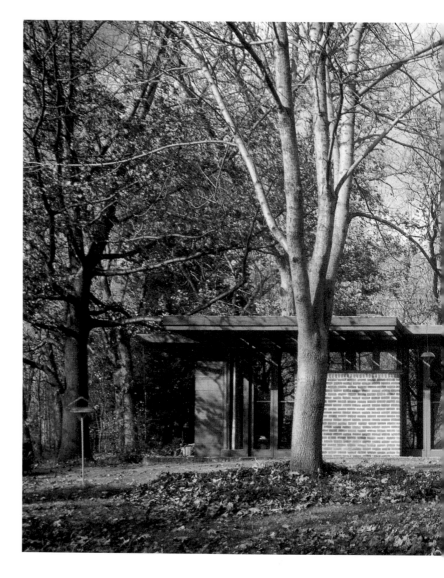

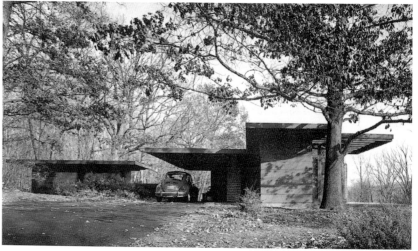

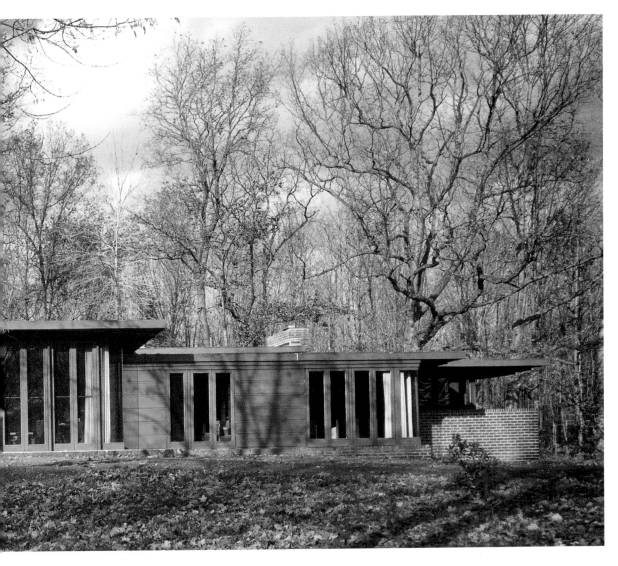

The Baird house backs up against a forest with a sloping meadow to the south. Access is from the side and rear of the house to leave open the magnificent views of hills and mountains. This was a typical Wright solution. The north side of the house is basically a brick wall with few openings in the way of doors and windows. On the opposite side, however, the rooms open generously out through glass doors and windows that welcome this sunny, southern exposure. The concrete floor rests on heating pipes that circulate hot water throughout the slab, warming it sufficiently to give an even, comfortable heat. The plan, though simple, eliminates the sense of confinement often found in homes as small as this one.

Das Haus Baird steht mit der Rückseite zu einem Wald, der nach Süden hin in eine sanft abfallende Wiese übergeht. Die Zugänge zum Haus liegen an der Seite und hinten, um den herrlichen Blick auf Hügel und Berge frei zu lassen. Diese Lösung war typisch für Wright. Die Nordseite des Hauses ist eine Ziegelwand mit wenigen Fenstern und Türen. Die gegenüberliegende Südseite hingegen öffnet sich mit großzügigen Glasflächen zur Sonne. Der Betonboden liegt auf Heizröhren, durch die heißes Wasser zirkuliert. Sie erwärmen den Boden ausreichend und geben eine gleichmäßige, angenehme Raumtemperatur. Auch wenn der Plan einfach ist, so wirkt er dem Eindruck von Enge entgegen, der kleine Häuser wie dieses oft bestimmt.

La maison Baird se tient contre une forêt avec une prairie en pente orientée vers le sud. L'accès à la maison se fait sur le côté et par derrière afin que rien n'entrave la magnifique vue sur les collines et les montagnes. Le côté nord de la maison est essentiellement constitué d'un mur de briques percé de quelques portes et fenêtres. De l'autre côté les pièces s'ouvrent largement sur des baies vitrées et jouissent de l'exposition ensoleillée au sud. Le plancher en béton repose sur des conduites de chauffage qui transportent l'eau chaude, réussissant à chauffer suffisamment la dalle du rez-de-chaussée pour que l'on obtienne une température égale et agréable. Bien qu'il s'agisse d'un plan simple, il ôte ainsi cette sensation d'emprisonnement que l'on ressent souvent dans des maisons de si petites dimensions.

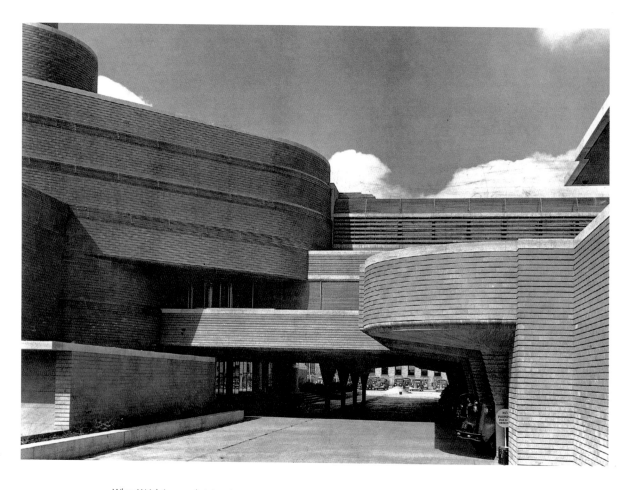

When Wright's new administration building for the S.C. Johnson & Son Company opened its doors after three years of construction, it immediately created a sensation around the world. *Life* magazine featured it in its May 8, 1939 issue with remarks such as »Spectacular as the showiest Hollywood set, it represents simply the result of creative genius applied to the problem of designing the most efficient and comfortable, as well as beautiful, place in which Johnson Wax executives and clerks could do their work.« The building was set in an industrial zone and Wright decided again to create an enclosed, sealed space and light it from above, as he had done in the Larkin Building. In the main workroom a forest of thin, white concrete columns rises to spread out at the top and forms the ceil-

ing, the spaces in between the circles set with skylights made of glass tubes. At the corners, where the walls usually meet the ceiling, the walls stop short of the ceiling and glass tubes continue up, over, and connect to the skylights. The entrance is within the structure, penetrating the building on one side with a covered carport on the other. All the furniture, manufactured by Steelcase, was designed for the building. The warm, reddish brown hue of the bricks is used in the concrete floor slab as well; the white stone trim and white concrete columns make a subtle contrast.

Als nach dreijähriger Bauzeit Wrights neues Verwaltungsgebäude für die S.C. Johnson & Son Company seiner Bestimmung übergeben wurde, war dies eine weltweite Sensation. Das *Life*-Magazin

berichtete darüber in seiner Ausgabe vom 8. Mai 1939 und brachte Kommentare wie: »Spektakulär wie die aufwendigste Hollywood-Inszenierung, stellt es schlicht die Antwort eines kreativen Genies auf die Problemstellung dar, das effizienteste, komfortabelste und schönstmögliche Gebäude für die Angestellten von Johnson Wax zu entwerfen.« Das Gebäude entstand in einem Industriegebiet, daher entschloß sich Wright, wie beim Larkin-Gebäude einen nach außen geschlossenen, abgeschotteten Raum zu schaffen, der sein Licht ausschließlich von oben erhält. Im großen Arbeitsraum erhebt sich ein »Wald« aus dünnen, weißen Betonpfeilern, die sich oben aufspreizen, um die Decke zu formen. In die Flächen zwischen diesen Kreisen sind Oberlichter aus Glasröhren eingelassen. In den

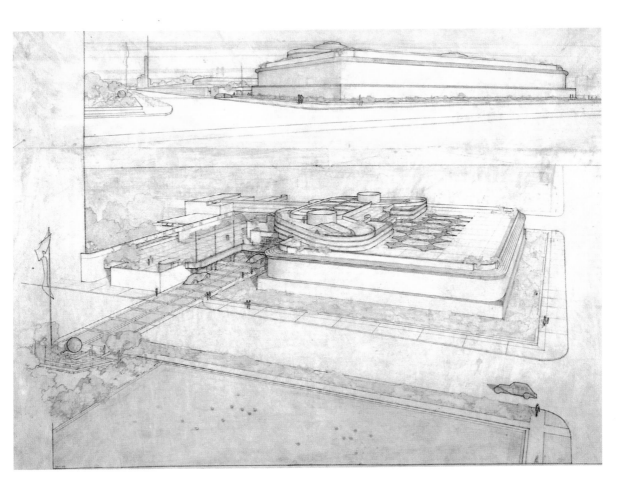

Ecken, wo gemeinhin Wand und Zimmerdecke sich treffen, hört die Wand vorzeitig auf, die Fortsetzung und Verbindung zu den Oberlichtern wird ebenfalls von Glasröhren hergestellt. Der Eingang befindet sich innerhalb des Komplexes auf der einen Seite einer Durchfahrt, mit überdachten Garagen auf der anderen Seite. Sämtliches Mobiliar wurde speziell für das Gebäude entworfen und von der Firma Steelcase gebaut. Das warme Rotbraun der Ziegelwände wird auch für die Betonböden übernommen. Die weißen Steinbänderungen und Betonsäulen ergeben dazu einen subtilen Kontrast.

Quand le nouveau bâtiment administratif de la société S.C. Johnson et Fils ouvrit ses portes, après trois ans de construction, il fit immédiatement sensation dans le monde entier. Dans son numéro du 8 mars 1939, le magazine *Life* le caractérisait de la façon suivante: »Spectaculaire comme le plus prestigieux décor d'Hollywood, il représente simplement la solution du génie créatif au problème posé par la conception d'un lieu, qui doit être le plus fonctionnel et le plus confortable tout en étant beau, et où directeurs et employés de la sociéte Johnson Wax peuvent travailler.« L'immeuble était situé dans une zone industrielle et Wright décida à nouveau de créer un espace fermé et hermétique avec un éclairage zénithal, comme il l'avait fait avec le bâtiment Larkin. Dans la grande salle de travail, une multitude de colonnes en béton s'élevaient en s'arrondissant au sommet et formaient le plafond. Dans les espaces entre les cercles étaient placés des faisceaux de tubes de verre. Aux angles, là où les murs rejoignent habituellement le plafond, des tubes de verre avaient été encastrés, montaient jusqu'au plafond et étaient reliés aux espaces zénithaux. Tout le mobilier, fabriqué par Steelcase, a été conçu spécialement pour le bâtiment. Le rouge-brun chaud des briques recouvre également la dalle de béton du rez-de-chaussée; les ornements en pierre blanche et les colonnes en béton forment un contraste subtil.

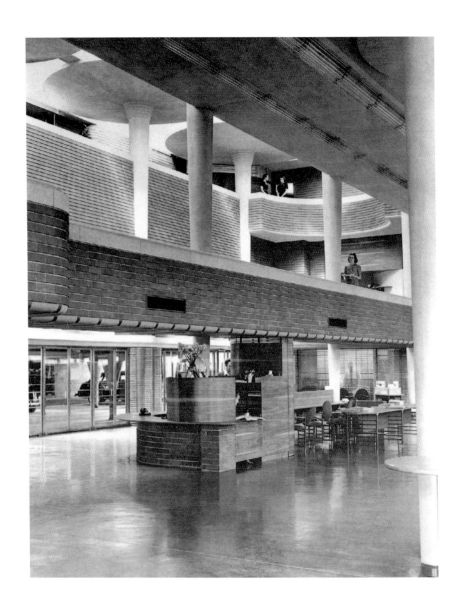

**S.C. Johnson and Son Company
Administration Building, Racine,
Wisconsin, 1936–1939**
Lobby and elevator

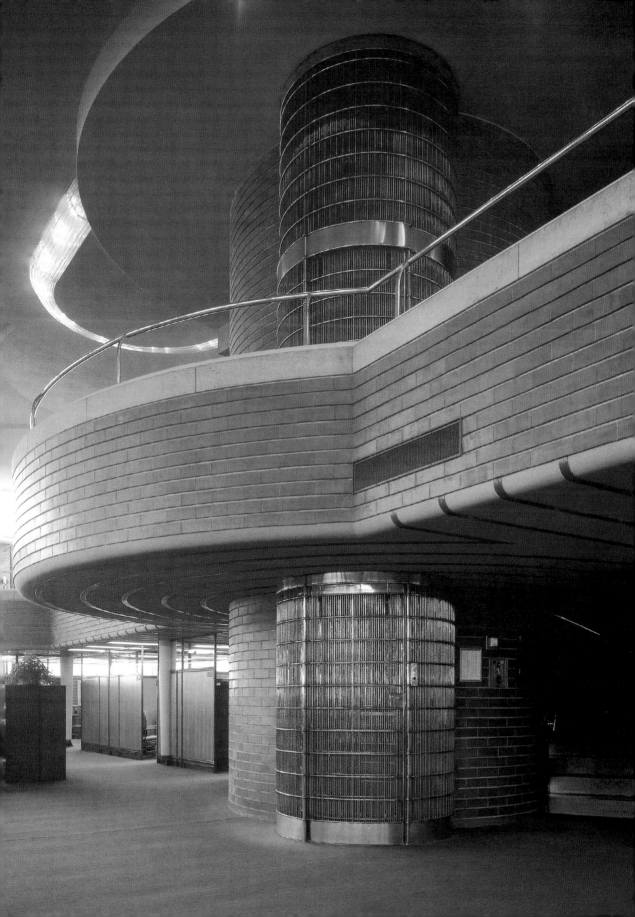

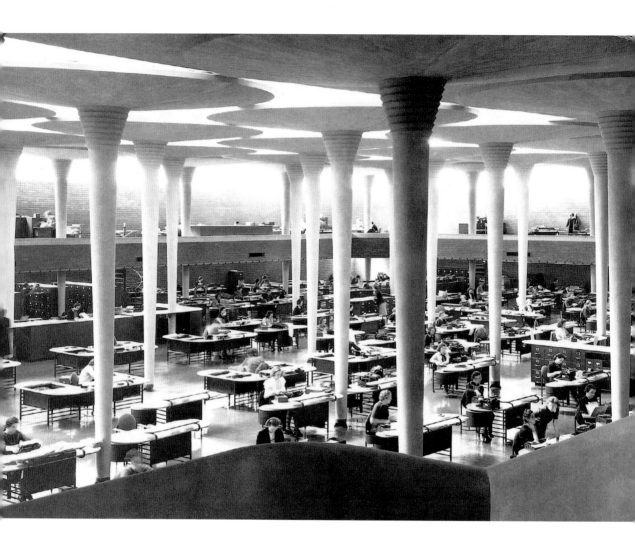

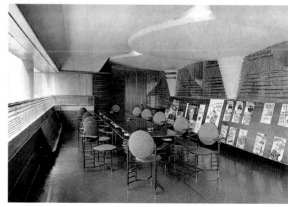

S.C. Johnson and Son Company
Research Tower, Racine, Wisconsin,
1944–1950

When the S.C. Johnson & Son Company was contemplating the addition of a research laboratory to its plant in Racine, many of its officials considered the project one that any competent engineer could handle. But Herbert F. Johnson, who had commissioned Wright in 1936 for the office building, realized that any structure tangent to the famous administration building would have to respect the character of the former. »I had seen several meandering flat piles called laboratories«, Wright wrote, »ducts running here, there and everywhere and a walkaround for everybody.« The design he proposed consisted of fourteen levels, seven as square plans, with a circular mezzanine above each square level. The entire outside surface was sheathed in glass tubes, like the adjacent office structure, with plate glass clipped onto the inside surface for further insulation. »This seemed to me to be a natural solution and this sun-centered laboratory we now call the Heliolab came alive doing its own breathing and affording all kinds of delightful sun-lit, directly united, work space.«
Cantilevered from the giant stack, the floor slabs spread out like tree branches, providing sufficient segregation of departments vertically. Elevator and stairway channels up the central stack link all these departments to each other. Like the cellular pattern of the tree trunk, all utilities and the many laboratory intake and exhaust pipes run up and down in their own central utility groves. The single reinforced concrete foundation for this central core was termed »tap root«, and was based on an idea proposed by Frank Lloyd Wright for the St. Mark's Tower, New York, in 1929. The same »tap root« foundation was used again in the H.C. Price Tower in Bartlesville, Oklahoma, in 1952. Thus freed from peripheral supporting elements, the Tower rises gracefully from a garden and fountain pools that surround its base while a spacious court on three sides provides ample parking.

Als die S.C. Johnson & Son Company plante, ihr Werk in Racine durch ein Forschungslabor zu ergänzen, glaubten viele der Firmenvertreter, dieses Projekt könne von jedem begabten Ingenieur ausgeführt werden. Herbert F. Johnson jedoch, der Wright 1936 den Auftrag für das Bürohaus gegeben hatte, er-

kannte, daß jeder Bau, der das berühmte Verwaltungsgebäude berührte, dessen speziellen Charakter würde berücksichtigen müssen. »Ich hatte schon viele verwinkelte Gebäudekomplexe gesehen, die Laboratorien genannt wurden«, schrieb Wright, »überall nur Leitungen und ein einziger Rundweg für jedermann.« Sein Entwurf bestand aus vierzehn Stockwerken, wobei über sieben quadratischen Stockwerken jeweils ein runder Zwischenstock lag. Die gesamte Außenfläche des Gebäudes bestand aus Glasröhren, wie sie auch beim angrenzenden Bürohaus verwendet worden waren, und wurde von innen mit Glasplatten zusätzlich isoliert. »Dies schien mir eine natürliche Lösung zu sein, und dieses so auf die Sonne bezogene Labor, das wir inzwischen ›Helio-Lab‹ nennen, begann ein eigenes Leben zu bekommen, schien zu atmen und bot jene gewünschten herrlich hellen, kompakten Arbeitsflächen.«
Von der mächtigen Hauptstütze des Gebäudes aus kragen die Stockwerke wie die Zweige eines Baumes aus, wodurch die einzelnen Bereiche vertikal deutlich voneinander abgegrenzt werden. Wie beim Nährstoffsystem des Baumstammes laufen alle Versorgungsleitungen und die zahlreichen zu- und ableitenden Rohre des Laboratoriums zentral in ihren eigenen Schächten auf und ab. »Das Stahlbetonfundament für diesen Gebäudekern geht auf eine Idee Frank Lloyd Wrights für den St. Mark's Tower in New York von 1929 zurück und wurde »Pfahlwurzel« genannt. Das gleiche »Pfahlwurzel«-Fundament fand 1952 beim H.C. Price Tower in Bartlesville, Oklahoma, Anwendung. Der Turm ist also von allen außenliegenden Stützelementen befreit und erhebt sich anmutig aus einem Areal mit Gärten und Springbrunnen, während ein geräumiger Platz an drei Seiten reichlich Parkfläche bietet.

Lorsque la société S.C. Johnson et Fils envisagea d'ajouter un laboratoire de recherche à ses établissements de Racine, un grand nombre de ses employés pensaient que ce projet pouvait être réalisé par n'importe quel ingénieur capable. Herbert F. Johnson, qui avait chargé Wright en 1936 de la construction des bureaux, s'aperçut toutefois que le bâtiment qui s'élèverait à côté du bâtiment administratif devrait s'harmo-

niser avec le caractère de celui-ci. »J'ai vu bon nombre de ces édifices plats et à méandres appelés laboratoires« écrivait Wright »les conduits courent ici et là et partout, et sont une course d'obstacles pour tout le monde«. Ce qu'il proposait était un ensemble de quatorze niveaux: sept avec un plan carré et surmontés chacun d'une mezzanine circulaire. Toute la surface extérieure était gainée de tubes de verre, comme le bâtiment administratif adjacent, avec une plaque de verre insérée dans l'espace intérieur pour accroître l'isolation. »Ceci me sembla être une solution naturelle et ce laboratoire solaire, que nous appelons maintenant ›Helio-lab‹, vint à la vie grâce à son propre souffle et en offrant toutes les possibilités d'un ravissant lieu de travail ensoleillé, aux liaisons directes.
Construits en porte-à-faux, les étages s'étendent comme les branches de l'arbre, offrant suffisamment de séparations verticales pour les différents services. L'ascenseur et les escaliers sont situés dans la partie centrale et relient tous ces services les uns aux autres. Pareil au modèle cellulaire du tronc de l'arbre, les systèmes d'alimentation et les nombreux tuyaux d'arrivée et d'échappement du laboratoire montent et descendent jusqu'au dispositif central d'alimentation.« Les fondations en béton armé pour ce noyau central portaient le nom de »tap root« (pile enfoncée dans le terrain) et reposaient sur une idée proposée par Frank Lloyd Wright, en 1929, pour la tour St. Marc de New York. Le même type de fondations fut encore utilisé, en 1952, dans la tour H.C. Price, à Bartlesville, Oklahoma. Libérée ainsi d'éléments de soutènement périphériques, la tour s'élève gracieusement, avec un jardin et des pièces d'eau qui entourent sa base, tandis qu'un vaste espace abrité offre sur les trois côtés un grand parking.

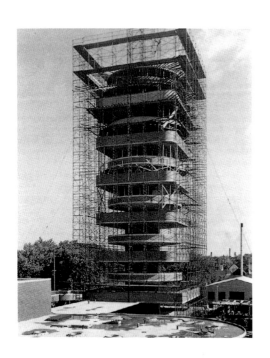

S.C. Johnson and Son Company
Research Tower, Racine, Wisconsin,
1944–1950
Tower under construction, street view

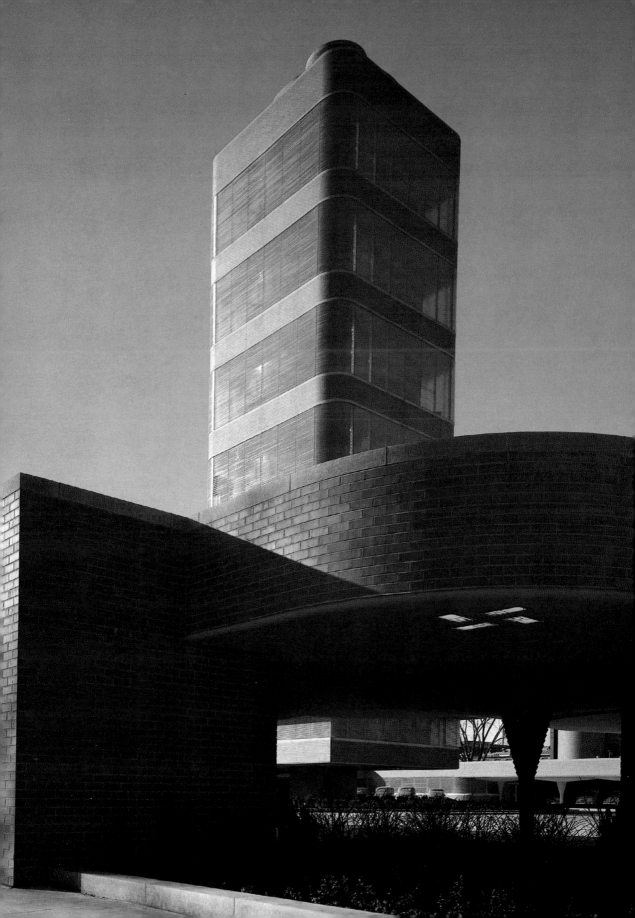

S.C. Johnson and Son Company
Research Tower, Racine, Wisconsin,
1944–1950
Round and square laboratories

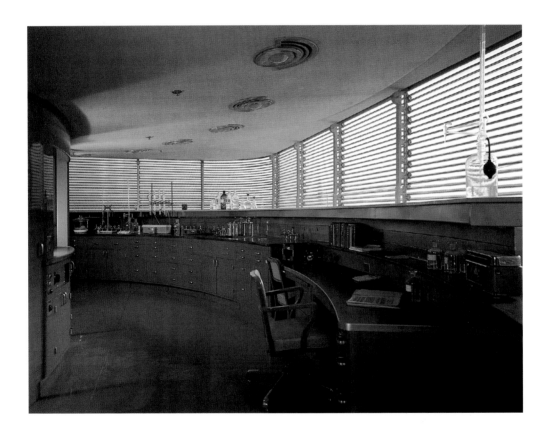

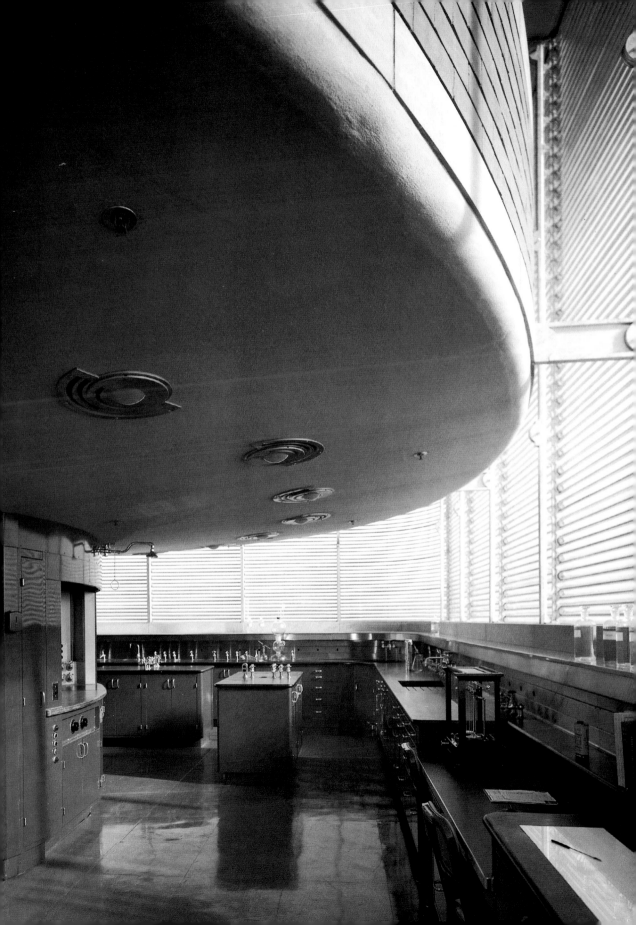

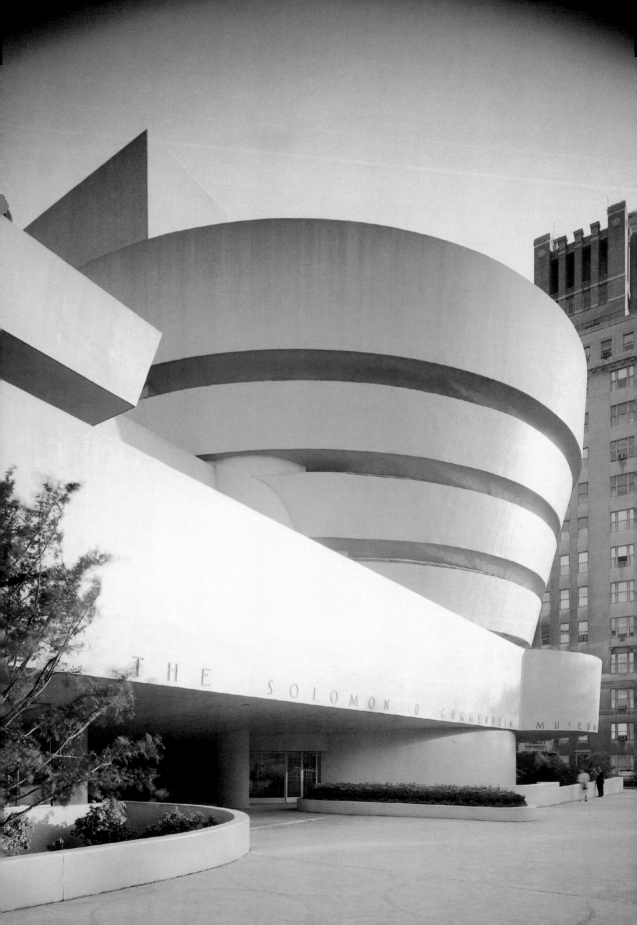

Solomon R. Guggenheim Museum, New York, N.Y., 1943–1946, 1955–1959
Entrance view

When asked why he chose the ramp, instead of level floors in the conventional stack, Wright explained that he felt the museum-goer would find it far more convenient to enter the building, take the elevator to the top ramp, gradually descend around an open court, always have the option, as the ramp touched the elevator stack at each level, to either go back, or skip down to further levels, and finally, at the end of the exhibition, he would find himself on the ground floor, near the exit. Wright further reasoned that in so many conventional museums, the public traverses long galleries of exhibitions only to have to retrace its steps to get back to the beginning in order to leave. Guggenheim was overwhelmed with this concept of an ascending spiral, and supported the project until his death in 1949. The building underwent many delays from 1943 to 1956, due to changes in site conditions, building codes, the museum's own change of its program, and to the rising costs of materials and construction. But finally, on August 16, 1956, ground was broken and construction begun. When Wright died in April of 1959, the building was mainly complete, waiting for final details. Six months later, on October 21, the museum was opened to the world. While the building was in construction, a letter was sent to the director and trustees of the museum, signed by a long list of artists complaining that the sloped walls and ramped floor would be unsuitable for the exhibition of paintings. »Why do you think the walls of the Solomon R. Guggenheim Museum are gently sloping outward? They gently slope because the donor and his architect believed that pictures placed against the walls slightly tilted backward would be seen in better perspective and be better lighted than if set bolt upright. This is the chief characteristic of our building and was the hypothesis upon which the museum was fashioned. This idea is new but sound, one that can set a precedent of great value.«

Befragt, warum er hier die Spiralrampe den üblichen aufgeschichteten Stockwerken vorgezogen habe, erklärte Wright, der Museumsbesucher müsse es doch als sehr viel angenehmer empfinden, das Gebäude zu betreten, mit dem Aufzug ins oberste Stockwerk zu fahren, allmählich um einen offenen Hof herum abwärts zu gehen – immer mit der Möglichkeit, von jedem Niveau der Rampe aus mit dem Lift auf- oder abwärts zu fahren –, um sich schließlich, am Ende der Ausstellung, im untersten Stockwerk und nahe dem Ausgang wiederzufinden. Wright führte weiter aus, daß in so vielen konventionellen Museen das Publikum lange Enfiladen durchwandern müsse, nur um später denselben Weg zum Ausgang wieder zurückgehen zu müssen. Guggenheim war vom Konzept der ansteigenden Spirale begeistert und unterstützte das Vorhaben bis zu seinem Tod im Jahr 1949. Das Projekt wurde von 1943 bis 1956 mehrfach durch Bauplatzänderungen, Bauauflagen, Änderungen der Museumsleitung am Programm und ansteigende Kosten für Material und Ausführung verzögert. Aber schließlich konnten am 16. August 1956 die Erdarbeiten begonnen werden. Als Wright im April 1959 starb, war der Bau im wesentlichen fertiggestellt und bedurfte nur noch einiger letzter Detailüberarbeitungen. Sechs Monate später, am 21. Oktober, wurde das Museum eröffnet.
Noch während der Bauarbeiten erreichte den Direktor und die Treuhänder des Museums ein von einer langen Liste von Künstlern unterzeichneter Brief, in dem es hieß, daß die geneigten Wände und die abfallende Rampe ungeeignet für die Präsentation von Gemälden seien. »Warum, glauben Sie, sind die Wände des Guggenheim-Museums leicht nach außen geneigt? Weil der Stifter des Museums und sein Architekt glaubten, daß Gemälde, die an einer leicht gekippten Wand angebracht wären, besser beleuchtet und gesehen werden könnten, als wenn sie lotrecht hängen würden. Dies ist das Hauptcharakteristikum unseres Gebäudes und war die Arbeitshypothese für seine Entwicklung. Die Idee ist neu, aber überzeugend und kann ein wertvoller Präzedenzfall für die Zukunft sein.«

Quand on lui demanda pourquoi il avait choisi la rampe au lieu des planchers plats traditionnels, Wright répondit qu'il croyait que le visiteur du musée trouverait bien plus pratique d'entrer dans le bâtiment, de prendre l'ascenseur jusqu'à la rampe supérieure, de redescendre petit à petit la rampe qui domine une cour ouverte, d'avoir toujours la possibilité de prendre l'ascenseur, vu que la rampe conduit à celui-ci à chaque niveau, pour remonter ou pour descendre aux niveaux inférieurs, et de se trouver finalement, au terme de la visite, au rez-de-chaussée près de la sortie. Wright ajoutait que dans de nombreux musées traditionnels, le public doit traverser de longues galeries et refaire le chemin parcouru simplement pour retrouver le point de départ et quitter le musée. Guggenheim était rempli d'enthousiasme pour ce concept de spirale ascendante et il soutint le projet jusqu'à sa mort en 1949. Entre 1943 et 1956, la construction du bâtiment fut plusieurs fois repoussée, en raison des changements dans les conditions de l'emplacement, des règlements relatifs à la construction, des changements de programme du musée et des augmentations dans le coût des matériaux et de la construction. Enfin, le 16 août 1956, on ouvrit le sol et la construction de l'édifice commença. Quand Wright mourut en avril 1956, le bâtiment était en grande partie terminé, et il ne manquait que les derniers détails. Six mois plus tard, le 21 octobre, le musée fut ouvert au grand public.
Pendant la construction du bâtiment, une lettre fut envoyée au directeur et aux administrateurs du musée. Elle était signée par de nombreux artistes qui se plaignaient que les murs et les rampes inclinés ne conviendraient pas à une exposition de tableaux. »Pourquoi croyez-vous que les murs du musée Solomon R. Guggenheim sont légèrement inclinés vers l'extérieur? Parce que le fondateur et son architecte pensent que les tableaux accrochés à des murs s'inclinant légèrement vers l'arrière peuvent être vus sous une meilleure perspective et sont mieux éclairés que s'ils étaient placés droits comme des piquets. Ceci est la caractéristique principale de notre bâtiment et c'est en se basant sur cette hypothèse que le musée fut construit. Cette idée est nouvelle, mais elle est juste. C'est une idée qui peut servir de précédent de grande valeur.«

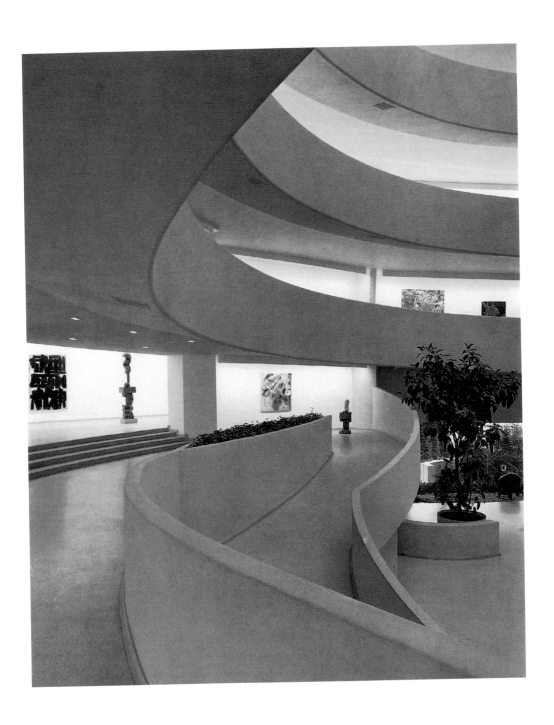

**Solomon R. Guggenheim Museum,
New York, N.Y., 1943–1946,
1955–1959**
Interior view, conceptual drawings

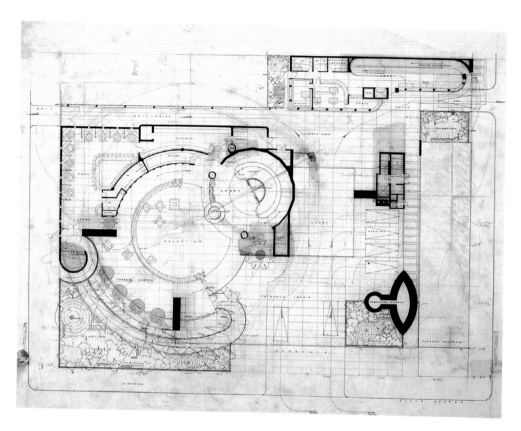

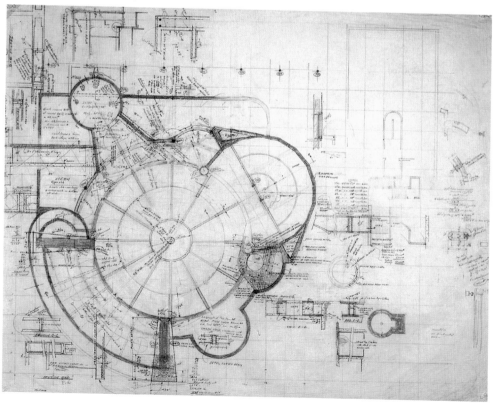

153

For a house in the northern climate,
Wright devised a scheme that he named »Solar Hemicycle«. The building is designed on a hemicycle plan, with earth
piled up against the northern wall, in a
berm, for insulation, with the southern
wall composed of two-storey glass windows and doors to bring in the sun's
warmth in winter. The southern overhang is designed so that in summer
shade is cast upon the glass, while in
winter, the glass faces directly into the
desired warmth of the sunshine, thus
taking advantage of the elliptical solar
path. The balcony, which contains the
bedrooms, is hung from the ceiling raf-
ters above by means of steel rods com-
ing down through the partitions and
locking into the floor beams. In this
way, the space on the ground floor is
altogether freed from any supports for
the upper floor.

Für ein Haus, das dem nördlichen
Klima angepaßt wäre, entwickelte
Wright ein Schema, das er »Solar Hemicycle« nannte. Das Gebäude steht auf
einem halbkreisförmigen Grundriß, auf
der Nordseite ist das Erdreich zu einem
Wall angeschüttet, die Südseite hingegen besteht nur aus einer über beide
Stockwerke reichenden Glaswand, die
im Winter die Sonnenwärme in das
Haus bringt. Der südliche Dachüberstand ist so bemessen, daß die Glasflächen im Sommer beschattet, im Winter
aber von den willkommenen Sonnen-
strahlen erreicht werden können, und
nimmt so Rücksicht auf den wechseln-
den Sonnenstand. Die Galerie mit den
Schlafzimmern ist mit Stahlstäben von
den Dachsparren abgehängt. Dadurch
konnte das Erdgeschoß von allen Stütz-
konstruktionen freigehalten werden.

Pour une maison située dans un site au
climat froid, Wright avait imaginé un
plan qu'il nomma »Solar Hemicycle«.
Le bâtiment est conçu sur un plan en
hémicycle; le mur exposé au nord est
protégé par un remblai pour une meilleure isolation et le mur exposé au sud
s'élève sur deux étages et est constitué
de fenêtres et de portes en verre qui
captent la chaleur du soleil en hiver.
L'avant-toit de la face sud projette, en
été, son ombre sur les baies vitrées, tandis qu'en hiver celles-ci sont directement exposées à la chaleur du soleil,
profitant ainsi de la course elliptique du
soleil. Le balcon, qui contient les chambres à coucher, est accroché aux che-
vrons du plafond et soutenu par des
montants en acier qui sont intégrés aux
parois et encastrés dans les solives du
plancher. De cette façon, on obtient un
espace continu au rez-de-chaussée qui
est dépourvu de toute paroi soutenant le
niveau supérieur.

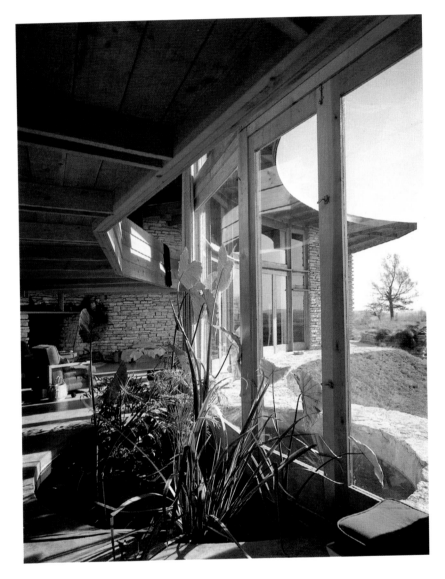

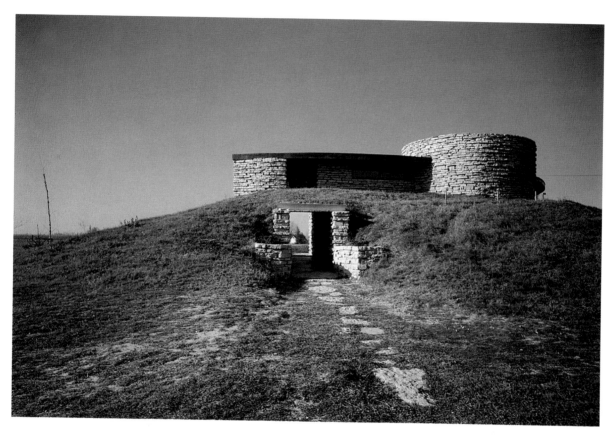

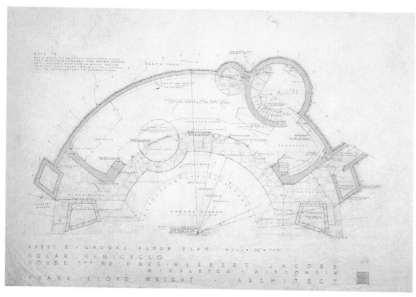

SHEET 2 · GROUND FLOOR PLAN
SOLAR · HEMICYCLO
HOUSE · FOR · MR · & MRS · HERBERT · JACOBS
MIDDLETON · WISCONSIN
FRANK · LLOYD · WRIGHT · ARCHITECT

Lowell Walter House, Cedar Rock,
Quasqueton, Iowa, 1945
View from diveway, site plan

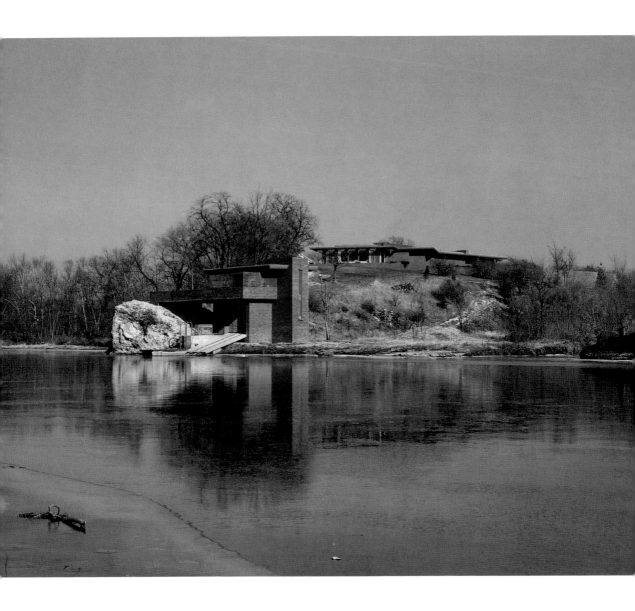

Lowell Walter Boat House, Cedar Rock, Quasqueton, Iowa, 1948
View from the lake

The home sits on a bluff overlooking the Wapsipinicon River and surrounding woodlands. In this location the need for privacy did not exist, and Wright was free to let the Garden Room serve as a viewing room from which the area's natural beauty could be viewed. A section of the Garden Room floor is left unpaved and planted as an interior garden near the fireplace, with a series of skylights overhead which fill the room with light. Workspace, utilities, baths and bedrooms extend out from this central area into a separate, more private, wing of their own.

Das Haus liegt auf einer Anhöhe, von der aus man den Wapsipinicon River und die umliegenden Wälder überblickt. In dieser Lage bestand kein Bedürfnis nach Abgeschlossenheit, und so war es Wright möglich, jenes Gartenzimmer als einen Raum zu nutzen, der sich der natürlichen Schönheit der Umgebung öffnete. Ein Teil des Fußbodens blieb hier unbelegt und als »Zimmergarten« am Kamin gestaltet, mit Oberlichtern, die dem Raum Helligkeit geben. Arbeitsraum, Küche, Bäder und Schlafzimmer sind in einem eigenen, privateren Flügel zu diesem zentralen Bereich geordnet.

La maison domine à pic la rivière Wapsipinicon et les bois environnants. Cet emplacement ne permettant aucune intimité, Wright eut le loisir de faire de la gloriette une salle panoramique, à partir de laquelle on pouvait admirer les merveilles naturelles de la région. Une partie du plancher de la gloriette est non pavé, mais offre l'aspect d'un jardin intérieur, près de la cheminée. Toute une série de percées zénithales laissent la lumière se répandre dans la pièce. Dans le prolongement de cet espace central, le cabinet de travail, les pièces réservées à la lessive et au repassage, les salles de bains et les chambres se trouvent dans une aile séparée et plus intime.

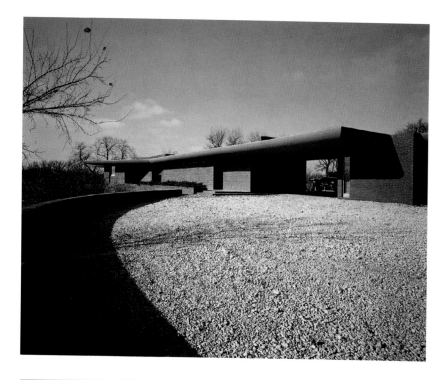

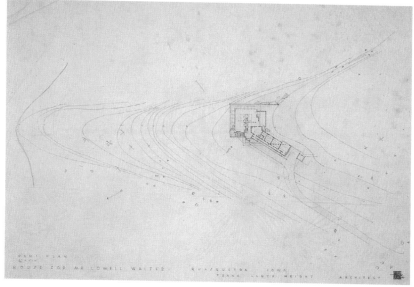

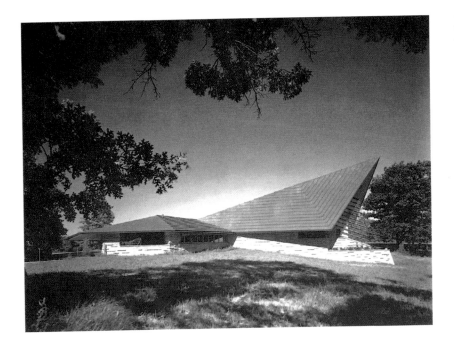

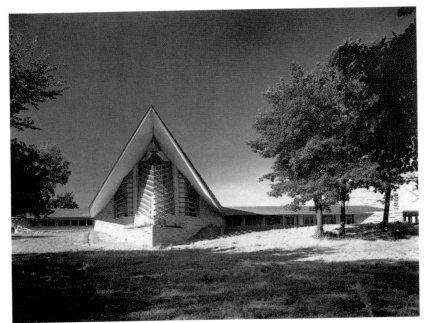

The usual small or moderate-sized church in the United States at that time, 1947, was a slender Colonial box, a tall steeple on top of it, and frequently a Classical porch of some sort. Wright felt these forms to be highly inappropriate to the United States, or to the twentieth century. »Unitarians«, he said, »believed in the unity of all things. Well, I tried to build a building here that expressed that over-all sense of unity. The plan you see is triangular. The roof is triangular and out of this – triangulation – (aspiration) you get this expression of reverence without recourse to the steeple.«

Die üblicherweise kleine oder mittelgroße Kirche der späten vierziger Jahren in den Vereinigten Staaten war eine schmächtige Schachtel mit einem hohen Kirchturm und irgendeiner Art von klassischem Portal. Wright fand, daß diese Formen weder zu den Vereinigten Staaten noch in das 20. Jahrhundert paßten. »Die Unitarier«, sagte er, »glauben an die Einheit aller Dinge. Nun, also versuchte ich ein Gebäude zu entwerfen, das diesen übergreifenden Gedanken einer alles verbindenden Einheit vermittelt. Wie Sie sehen, ist der Grundriß dreieckig. Auch das Dach ist dreieckig, und aus dieser Dreieckigkeit – diesem Streben – entsteht ganz ohne einen Kirchturm dieser tiefe Ausdruck von Ehrerbietung.«

A cette époque, en 1947, l'église petite ou moyenne aux Etats-Unis était une longue caisse de style colonial, avec un haut clocher posé dessus et, fréquemment, un porche classique quelconque. Wright sentait que ces formes ne convenaient ni aux Etats-Unis, ni au XXième siècle. »Les Unitariens« dit-il »croient en l'unité de toutes choses. J'essayais donc de construire ici un bâtiment qui exprime ce sens suprême de l'unité. Le plan que vous voyez est triangulaire. Le toit est triangulaire et de cette – triangulation – (aspiration) vous obtenez cette expression de vénération sans avoir recours au clocher.«

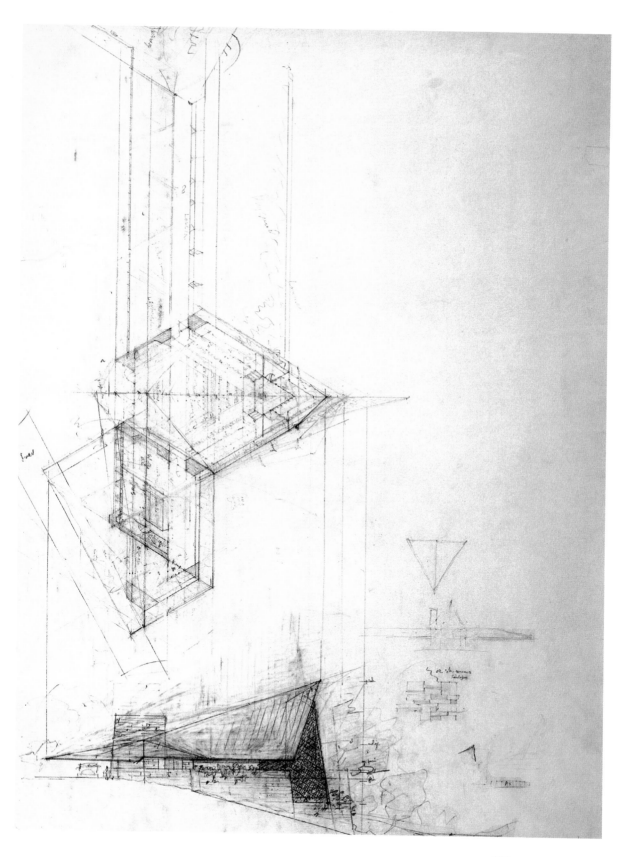

**V.C. Morris Gift Shop, San Francisco,
California, 1948–1950**
Entrance, interior

Since the Morris Shop on Maiden Lane,
San Francisco, was built in 1949, and
the Guggenheim Museum started construction in 1956, it is often and erro-
neously supposed that the design for the
shop came before, and somewhat inspired, the design for the museum. It
was in the museum, first designed in
1943, that Wright employed the interior
ramp as a feature of the building. But in
the Morris Shop the ramp is not so much
a feature, although its presence
dominates the sense of design inside, as
it is a means of getting from ground floor
up to second level. The entire shop is a
remodelling of a previous space, but in
place of the usual store front window,
Wright has placed a blank brick curtain
wall, with an arched opening of brick
and glass.

Da das Morris-Kaufhaus an der Maiden
Lane in San Francisco 1949 gebaut
wurde, die Bauarbeiten am Guggenheim-Museum aber erst 1956 aufgenommen wurden, wird oft irrtümlicher-
weise angenommen, daß der Entwurf
des Kaufhauses zeitlich vor dem des
Museums lag und diesen inspiriert
hatte. Aber Wright benutzte die Innen-
rampe als ein das Gebäude bestimmen-
des Merkmal bereits 1943 beim Mu-
seumsentwurf. Im Morris-Kaufhaus ist
die Rampe weniger charakterisierend,
bestimmt aber dennoch die Innenge-
staltung als Bewegungslinie vom Erdgeschoß zum ersten Stock. Der ganze
Kaufhausentwurf war nur der Umbau
eines bestehenden Gebäudes, aber anstatt des üblichen Schaufensters setzte
Wright einen Bogen aus Ziegeln und
Glas in die ansonsten glatte, geschlossene Mauerfläche.

Etant donné que le magasin Morris, situé sur la Maiden Lane à San Fransisco,
fut édifié en 1949 et que le musée Guggenheim fut commencé en 1956, on
croit souvent à tort que les plans du
magasin furent réalisés en premier et
qu'ils servirent plus ou moins d'inspiration pour la conception du musée. En
fait ce fut dans le musée, dont les premiers plans remontent à 1943, que
Wright utilisa pour la première fois la
rampe comme élément caractéristique
du bâtiment. Toutefois, dans le magasin
Morris, la rampe est moins une caractéristique, bien que sa présence domine
le plan intérieur, qu'un passage reliant
le rez-de-chaussée au premier étage. Le
magasin qui existait auparavant a été
complètement transformé. A la place
de la vitrine habituelle, Wright a construit un pan de mur en brique avec une
arcade en brique et en verre.

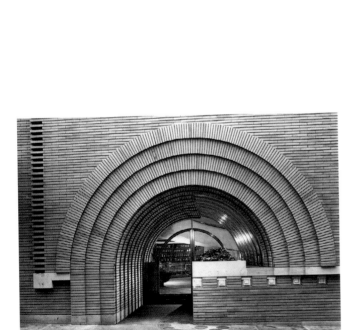

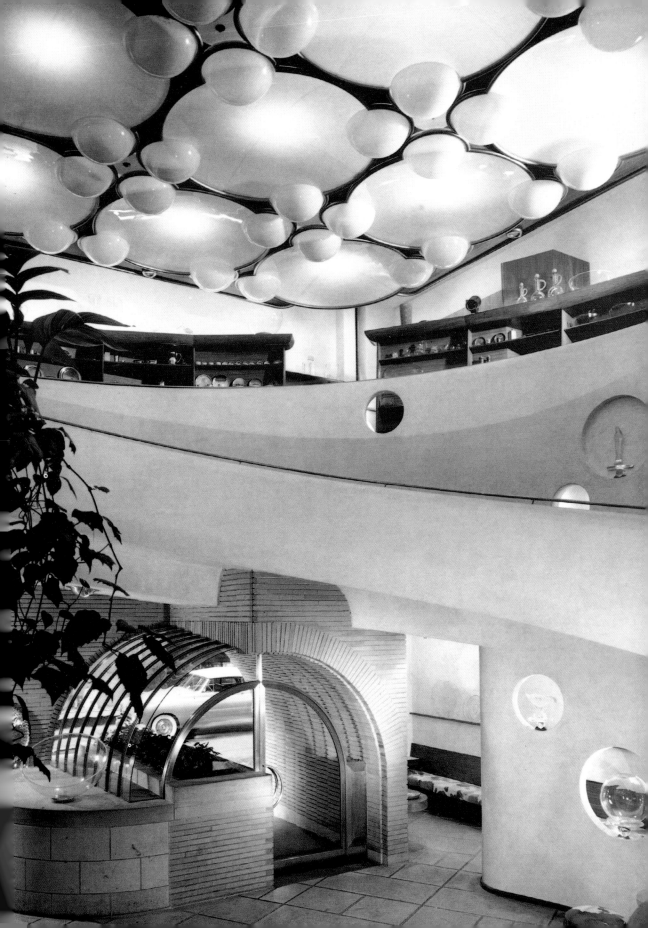

»How to Live in the Southwest«, House for David Wright, Phoenix, Arizona, 1950
Living room, drawing

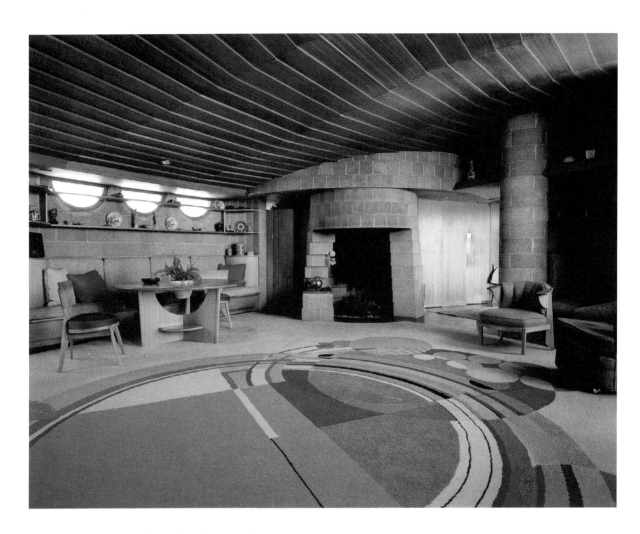

»How to live in the Southwest« was the title that Wright lettered on his conceptual sketch for this house. Placed in a citrus orchard located near Camelback Mountain, the advantage of elevating the main living quarters above the ground level is twofold: first, it provides a fine view over the branches of the surrounding citrus trees to the mountain range beyond; second, it creates a ground level of shaded gardens and cool breezes, desirable in this region, especially in summer. The plan follows a circular rim, approached by a gradual ramp which is also a garden. Living room with dining space occupies the larger segment of this circular ring, while the bedrooms extend along the

arc. The conceptual sketch for this house is among the most fascinating and delicately rendered drawings by Wright. Not only is the kernel of the idea aptly drawn, but also the more detailed plan, section and elevation, complete with interior dimensions noted.

»Wie lebt man im Südwesten« schrieb Wright auf die Entwurfsskizze dieses Hauses. Da es in einem Zitronenhain nahe dem Camelback Mountain liegt, war es in zweifacher Hinsicht vorteilhaft, den zentralen Wohnbereich in den ersten Stock zu legen: Zum einen eröffnet sich so ein schöner Blick über die Zweige der Zitronenbäume hinweg auf die Berge; zum anderen werden

damit auf Erdgeschoßniveau schattige Gärten und luftige Plätze geschaffen, die die Sommerhitze dieser Region erträglicher machen. Der Grundriß zeichnet einen Kreis nach. Der Zugang ist mit einer sanft ansteigenden, terrassenartigen Rampe gelöst. Die Entwurfsskizze zu diesem Projekt gehört zu Wrights faszinierendsten und subtilsten Zeichnungen. Sie stellt nicht nur die zentrale Idee überzeugend dar, sondern auch Schnitt, Aufriß und einen detaillierten Grundriß mit Maßangaben.

»Comment vivre dans le Sud-Ouest«, est le titre inscrit par Wright sur l'esquisse de cette maison. Vu son emplacement au milieu d'orangers et de ci-

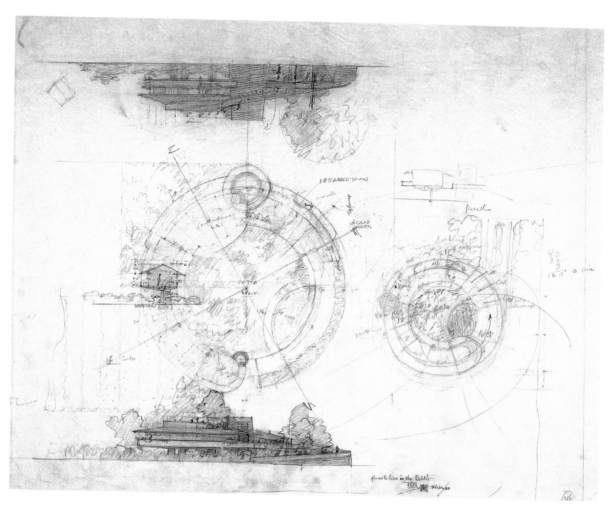

tronniers et à proximité des monts Ca-
melbak, le fait de surélever les pièces
habitables présentait deux avantages: le
premier était d'obtenir une vue superbe
au-dessus des arbres sur la chaîne des
monts en arrière-plan et le second de
créer un niveau du sol, qui était aménagé en jardins ombragés et où soufflait
une légère brise, ce qui est tout à fait
souhaitable dans cette région, surtout
en été. Le plan présente une forme circulaire, introduite par une rampe en
pente douce qui sert également de jardin. La salle de séjour, comprenant un
espace pour la salle à manger, occupe
la partie la plus large de cet anneau
circulaire, tandis que les chambres s'or-
donnent le long de l'arc. L'esquisse

conceptuelle de cette maison compte
parmi les plus fascinantes et les plus
minutieuses que Wright ait réalisées.
Non seulement l'idée centrale est repré-
sentée avec justesse, mais les détails du
plan, coupe et élevation, figurent également au complet et sont accompagnés
des dimensions intérieures.

163

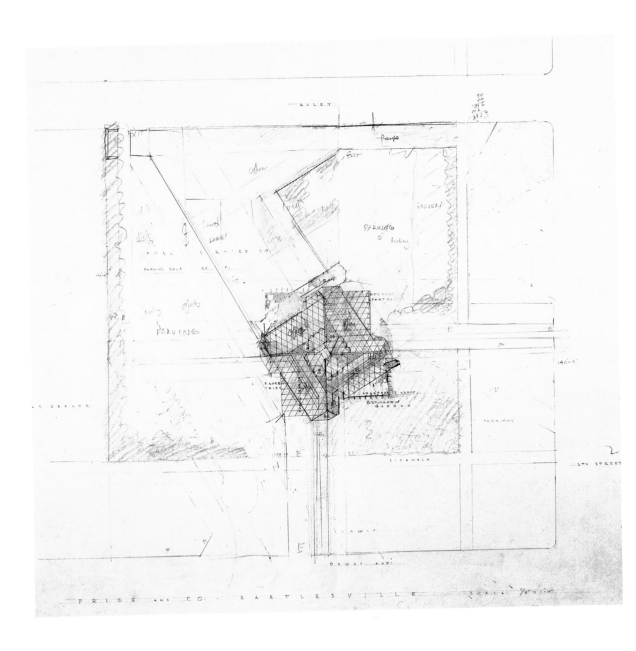

**Harold C. Price Company Tower,
Bartlesville, Oklahoma, 1952–1956**
Site plan, view

The quadruple plan as used in the H.C.
Price Tower was a further development
of the plan for the St. Mark's Tower of
1929. In the earlier tower Wright proposed a »tap-root« foundation supporting a central core out from which all the
floors of reinforced concrete are cantilevered. In St. Mark's, since the tower
was completely devoted to apartments,
the living room occupies a two story
quadrant, with two bedrooms on the
mezzanine overlooking it and opening
onto side balconies outdoors. The Price
tower was primarily intended for office
space, with only one quadrant per floor
given over to apartments.

Der viergliedrige Entwurf für den H.C.
Price Tower stellt eine Weiterentwick-
lung der Pläne für den St. Mark's Tower
von 1929 dar. Schon für diesen Turm
hatte Wright ein »Pfahlwurzel«-Funda-
ment vorgeschlagen, das den zentralen
Gebäudekern trug, von dem wiederum
die Stockwerksplatten aus Stahlbeton
auskragten. Da der St. Mark's Tower
komplett für Wohnungen vorgesehen
war, konnten die Grundrisse so aufgeteilt sein, daß ein Viertel jeweils von
einem zweistöckigen Wohnraum eingenommen wurde; die beiden Schlafzimmer waren auf dem Zwischenstock
untergebracht und öffneten sich zu Au-
ßenbalkonen. Der H.C. Price Tower jedoch war hauptsächlich für Büros bestimmt, und nur ein Viertel jedes Stockwerks wurde für Wohnungen genutzt.

Le plan quadruple, tel qu'il fut employé
dans la tour H.C. Price en 1952, se
référait au plan de la tour St. Marc,
construite en 1929. Dans ce projet an-
térieur, Wright proposait des fondations
en »tap root« qui soutenaient un noyau
central à partir duquel tous les étages en
béton armé sont en porte-à-faux. Dans
la tour St. Marc, qui était exclusivement
une tour d'habitation, la salle de séjour
était située sur un quadrant de deux
étages, avec deux chambres surplombant la mezzanine et s'ouvrant sur des
balcons extérieurs latéraux. La tour
Price, qui à l'origine était réservée aux
bureaux, ne possédait qu'un seul quadrant par étage pour les appartements.

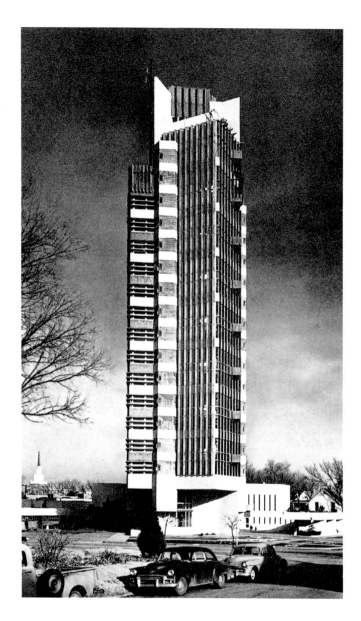

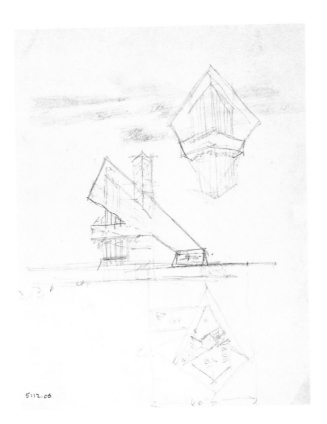

»Sun Bonnet« was the name that Wright gave this small house when it was first proposed for a client in California. That particular commission was for a seaside cottage on the sandy beaches near Carmel. But the house was not built until the following year when Mrs. Boomer asked for a similar cottage in the Arizona desert. The »sun bonnet« idea is evident in the steeply-pitched roof that rides up the back of the building and projects out over the front, shielding glass windows on the upper floor from direct sunlight during the summer. A balcony extending out from this upper level provides shade for the windows on the lower floor.

Wright nannte dieses Haus, das eigentlich für einen Bauherrn in Kalifornien bestimmt war, »Sonnenkappe«. Es war der Auftrag für ein Strandhaus in der Nähe von Carmel. Gebaut wurde das Haus jedoch erst im folgenden Jahr, als Mrs. Boomer ein ähnliches Ferienhaus in der Wüste Arizonas wünschte. Die Idee der »Sonnenkappe« wird deutlich, wenn man sich das steile Dach ansieht, das von der Rückseite des Gebäudes ansteigt und über die Vorderseite hinausragt, so daß die Fenster des oberen Stockwerks im Sommer vor direktem Sonnenlicht geschützt sind. Der Balkon des ersten Stocks gibt den Zimmern der unteren Etage Schatten.

»Bonnet ensoleillé«, c'est ainsi que cette petite maison fut baptisée lorsque Wright la proposa pour la première fois à un client californien. Cette commande particulière comprenait la construction d'un cottage du bord de mer sur la plage de sable près de Carmel. Toutefois, la maison ne fut édifiée qu'un an plus tard, lorsque Mme Boomer souhaita un cottage de ce genre dans le désert de l'Arizona. L'idée de »bonnet de soleil« se manifeste de façon flagrante avec les toits à forte inclinaison, qui s'accentuent dès l'arrière du bâtiment et font saillie sur le devant, protégeant ainsi les baies vitrées de l'étage supérieur des rayons directs du soleil pendant l'été. Un balcon qui s'étire à ce dernier étage procure de l'ombre aux fenêtres de l'étage inférieur.

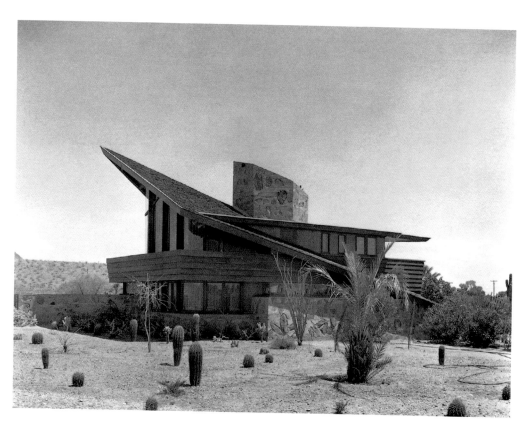

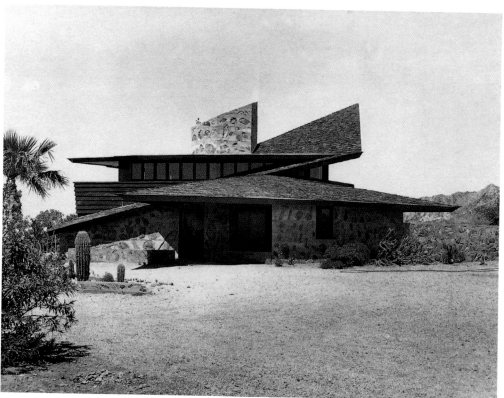

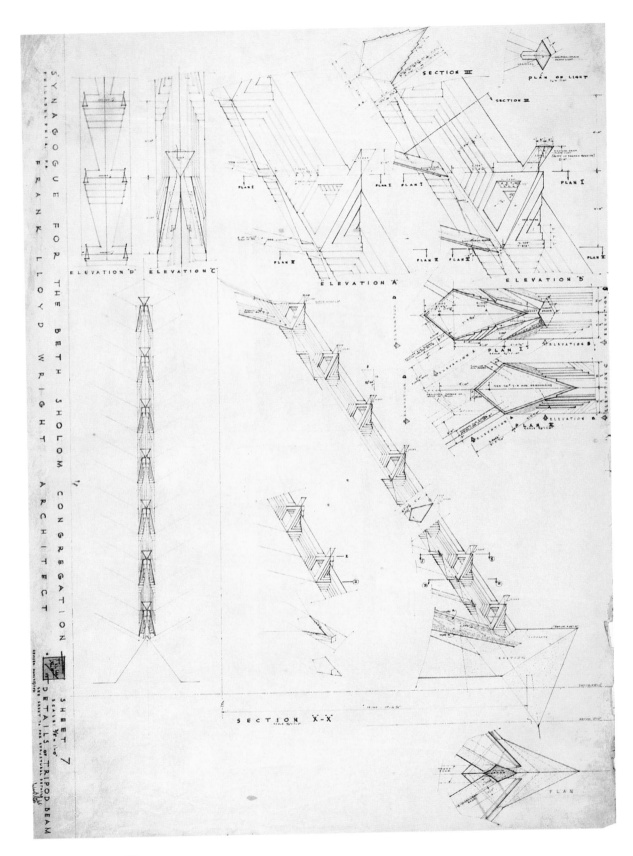

168

Synagogue for the Beth Sholom Congregation, Elkins Park, Pennsylvania, 1954, 1958–1959
Construction details, view, site plan

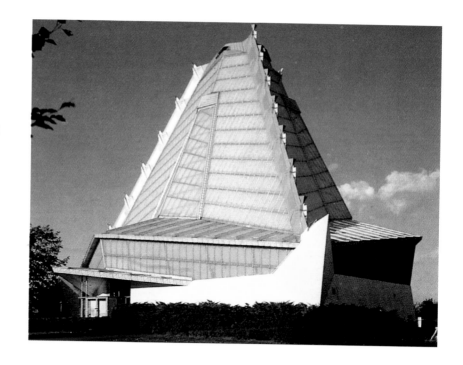

For the Beth Sholom Synagogue, Wright conceived a building that would be the very essence of light: a great translucent form rising out of concrete abutments. When the drawings were received by the Rabbi, he immediately telegraphed Wright, »Sketches arrived safely. All deeply inspired by (their) beauty and majesty. Letter follows.« In Cohens's long letter, written the next day, he further noted, »You have taken the supreme moment in Jewish history and experience – the revelation of God to Israel through Moses at Mt. Sinai and you have translated that moment with all it signifies into a design of beauty and reverence.«

Mit der Beth-Sholom-Synagoge entwarf Wright ein Gebäude, das den reinen Ausdruck des Lichtes vermitteln sollte: Eine große, durchscheinende Form erhebt sich auf Stützpfeilern aus Beton. Als der Rabbi die Zeichnungen erhielt, telegrafierte er umgehend an Wright: »Zeichnungen sicher angekommen. Alle tief beeindruckt von (ihrer) Schönheit und Würde. Brief folgt.« In Cohens langem Brief vom nächsten Tag heißt es: »Sie haben den höchsten Moment in der Geschichte des jüdischen Volkes – die Offenbarung des Herrn durch Moses auf dem Berg Sinai – genommen und diesen Moment in all seiner Bedeutung in einen Entwurf voller Schönheit und Ehrerbietung übertragen.«

Pour la synagogue Beth Sholom, Wright conçut un bâtiment qui était l'essence même de la lumière: une grande forme translucide jaillissant de ses contreforts en béton. Lorsque le rabbin reçut les esquisses, il télégraphia immédiatement une dépêche à Wright: »Croquis bien arrivés. Tous profondément impressionnés par (leur) beauté et majesté. Lettre suit.« Dans sa longue lettre, qu'il rédigea le lendemain, Cohen écrivait: »Vous avez saisi le moment suprême dans l'histoire des Juifs – la révélation de Dieu à Moïse sur le Mont Sinaï – et vouz avez traduit ce moment, avec tout ce qu'il signifie, en un modèle de beauté et de vénération.«

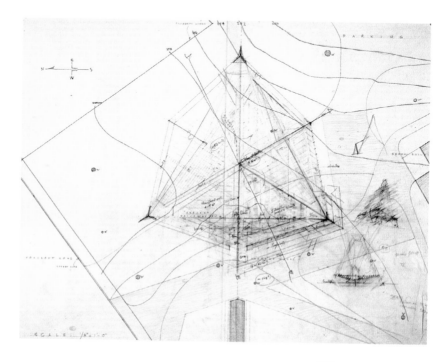

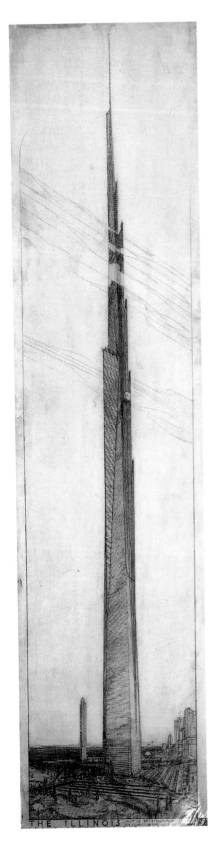

THE ILLINOIS

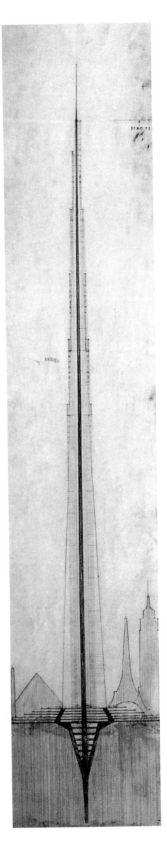

«One Mile High«, High-Rise Building
for Chicago, Illinois, 1956 (project)
Elevation, section and conceptual
drawing

When the proposal to design a TV
broadcasting tower one mile high was
submitted to Wright, he believed it fool-
ish to build such a tower without a
building within it. Thus began the idea
of the Mile High »Illinois« skyscraper.
Many construction factors contributed
to the growth of the design: the tap root
foundation, so successful in both the
Johnson Tower and the Price Tower, the
concrete cantilevered slab also in both
towers which had been built, and the
use of steel suspension cables down the
outer edge of the slab to further stabilize
the structure. Atomic powered
elevators were to rise in glass towers
running on cogs like a vertical train.

Als Wright der Vorschlag unterbreitet
wurde, einen Fernsehsendeturm von einer Meile Höhe zu entwerfen, schien es
ihm völlig unsinnig, einen solchen
Turm ohne nutzbare Gebäudefläche zu
bauen, und dies war der Auslöser für
die Idee des eine Meile hohen Wolkenkratzers »Illinois«. Der Entwurf wurde
wesentlich von konstruktiven Faktoren
mitbestimmt: dem »Pfahlwurzel«-Fun-
dament, das sich sowohl beim Johnson
Tower als auch beim Price Tower be-
währt hatte, ferner von deren freitragenden Betonplatten und der Verwendung
von Stahlkabeln entlang des äußeren
Randes der Platten zur zusätzlichen
Verstärkung. Atomar angetriebene
Fahrstühle sollten wie vertikale Züge
auf Schienen in gläsernen Schächten
emporsteigen.

Lorsqu'on lui proposa de concevoir une
tour de télévision ayant une hauteur
d'un mille, Wright pensa qu'il était ab-
surde de construire une tour pareille qui
soit vide à l'intérieur. C'est ainsi que
naquit l'idée du gratte-ciel »Illinois«,
s'élevant à un mille de hauteur. Plusieurs facteurs de construction ont
contribué à développer ce projet: la
fondation en pivot, qu'il avait employé
avec tant de succès dans les tours Johnson et Price, la dalle de béton en porte-
à-faux, également utilisée dans les deux
tours, et l'emploi de câbles d'acier en
suspension, reliant le bord extérieur de
la dalle afin de renforcer la stabilité de
la construction. Des ascenceurs à cré-
maillère mûs par l'énergie atomique,
devaient s'élever dans des cages de
verre tels des trains verticaux.

170

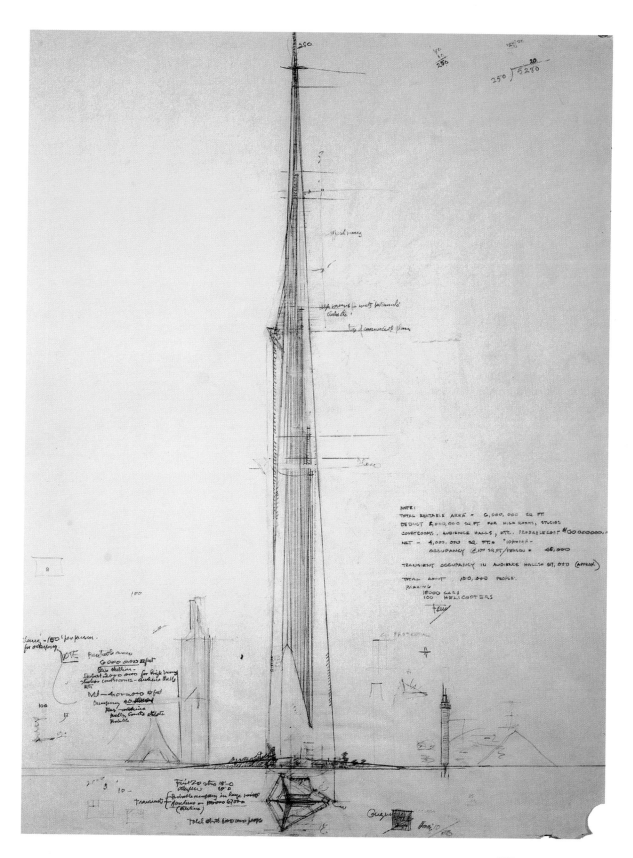

171

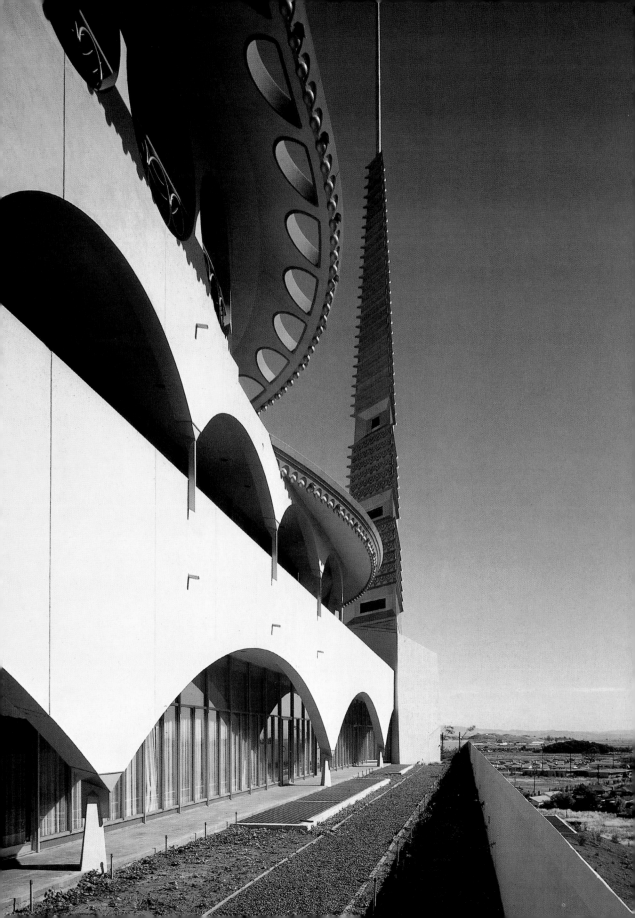

Marin County Civic Center, San Rafael, California, 1957–1966
Views

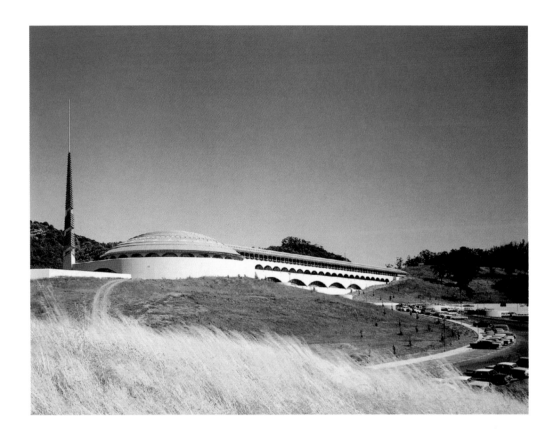

The site of the Marin County Civic Center was a spacious, grassy park, with water lagoon, and three softly-molded hills. The building bridges across the hills with vistas of the park and water. While most government buildings in the United States are imposing, built on a vast scale, with a monumental aspect, the Marin County building is none of these. It puts mankind in a pleasing, human-scale environment exposed to the surrounding landscape. Running down the center of both buildings is an interior garden-court mall, lit by a skylight above. Offices are so planned that a view outside onto the hills is available in one direction, while a view into the skylighted interior mall is had in the other direction. Partitions for the various county offices are movable so as to accommodate the space requirement of each department for any specific year.

Der Standort des Verwaltungszentrums für Marin County war ein weitläufiger Park mit einem flachen See und drei niedrigen Hügeln. Wie eine Brücke verbindet der Komplex die Hügel und bietet Ausblicke auf Park und See. Die meisten Verwaltungsgebäude in den Vereinigten Staaten wirken imposant, ihr Maßstab ist monumental. Nichts davon trifft auf das Marin County Civic Center zu. Es bietet eine angemessene, angenehme, menschliche Umgebung mit vielfältigen Bezügen zur Landschaft. Durch die Mitte beider Hauptgebäude verläuft eine begrünte, durch Glasdächer belichtete Promenade. Die Büros wurden so geplant, daß sie sich sowohl zur Hügellandschaft wie auch zu dieser Innenpromenade öffnen. Die Trennwände der Räume sind verschiebbar, so daß sie flexibel an die jeweiligen Erfordernisse angepaßt werden können.

Le centre civique du Marin Country est situé dans un vaste parc, avec des lagunes et trois petites collines. Le bâtiment forme un pont sur les collines et offre une perspective sur le parc et les lagunes. Le centre civique du Marin County ne présente aucune des caractéristiques de la plupart des bâtiments officiels des Etats-Unis qui sont imposants, construits à vaste échelle et qui ressemblent à des monuments. Il place l'homme dans un cadre plaisant, conçu à son échelle et s'ouvrant sur le paysage environnant. Une cour intérieure de jardins, éclairée par une percée zénithale, traverse le centre des deux bâtiments. Les bureaux sont disposés de telle façon que l'on a d'un côté une vue sur les collines et, de l'autre, une vue sur la cour intérieure. Les parois des différents bureaux sont amovibles de sorte que l'on peut modifier chaque année l'espace nécessaire à chaque service.

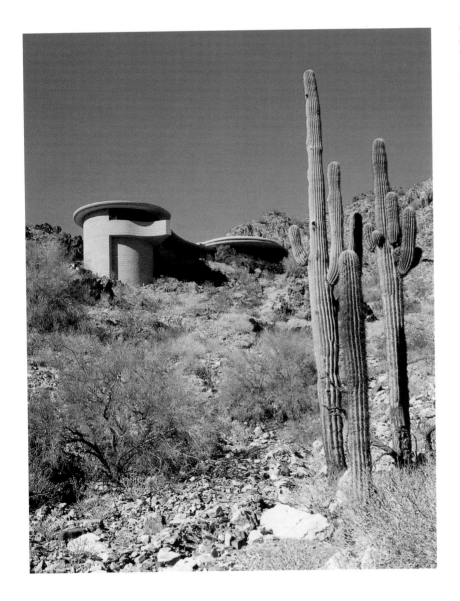

The Lykes house was the last residential
work designed by Frank Lloyd Wright.
The site is a precipitous hillside overlooking Phoenix. The house was care-
fully situated so as not to disturb the
terrain. It appears, in fact, to barely light
upon the desert rocks. A large circular
area for living room, dining room and
work space affords the spectacular view
south over the city and at the same time
is engaged by a larger circle containing
terrace and grass lawn. This spacious
outdoor terrace is walled for privacy,
the southern section pierced with openings to take advantage of the prospect.
The bedroom wings arc out from the
living room, riding upon a crest of boul-
ders.

Das Haus Lykes war das letzte von
Frank Lloyd Wright entworfene Wohnhaus. Der Standort ist ein steiler Berghang, der Phoenix überblickt. Das
Haus wurde besonders sorgfältig plaziert, um die Landschaft nicht zu zerstö-
ren. Tatsächlich scheint es sich nur vor-
sichtig auf den Felsen der Wüste nieder-
gelassen zu haben. Ein großer, runder
Bereich für Wohn-, Eß- und Arbeitszimmer bietet einen grandiosen Ausblick
nach Süden über die Stadt und wird mit
Rasenfläche und Terrasse von einem
weiteren Kreis umfaßt. Diese große
Freifläche ist von einer Mauer umgeben, mit Durchbrüchen, die einen
freien Ausblick geben. Der Schlafzim-
merflügel verläuft vom Wohnzimmer
aus im leichten Bogen auf einem Fel-
senkamm.

La maison Lykes a été le dernier ouvrage d'habitation réalisé par Wright.
L'emplacement est un flanc de côteau à
pic dominant la ville de Phoenix. La
maison a été placée de manière à ne pas
défigurer le paysage. Elle semble en effet se poser avec légèreté sur les rochers
du désert. Un vaste espace circulaire,
qui comporte la salle de séjour, la salle
à manger et un cabinet de travail, s'ouvre au sud sur une vue spectaculaire de
la ville et est contenu dans un large
cercle où s'étend la terrasse. Cette spacieuse terrasse ouverte est entourée de
murs qui préservent l'intimité de ses occupants. Des ouvertures ont été ména-
gées dans la partie sud afin de profiter
de la vue. Les ailes des chambres forment une arcade à partir de la salle de
séjour et sont juchées sur une crête de
rocs.

174

BIOGRAPHY AND EXECUTED WORK

1867 Frank Lloyd Wright born in Richland Center, Wisconsin, on June 8. He is the first child of William Russell Cary Wright and Anna Lloyd Jones Wright.
Frank Lloyd wird am 8. Juni als erstes Kind von William Russell Cary Wright und Anna Lloyd Jones Wright in Richland Center, Wisconsin, geboren.
Le 8 juin, Frank Lloyd naît à Richland Center, Wisconsin. Il est le premier enfant de William Russel Cary Wright et d'Anna Lloyd Jones Wright.

1885 Wright enters the University of Wisconsin at Madison and works for Allan D. Conover, a professor of engineering.
Wright schreibt sich an der Universität von Wisconsin in Madison ein und arbeitet für Allan D. Conover, einen Professor des Ingenieurwesens.
Wright entre à l'Université de Wisconsin, à Madison, et travaille pour Allan D. Conover, professeur à l'école d'ingénieurs.

1887 Wright leaves Madison for Chicago, finding employment first at the office of Joseph Lyman Silsbee and eventually with the architectural firm of Adler and Sullivan.
Wright geht von Madison nach Chicago und arbeitet zunächst im Büro von Joseph Lyman Silsbee, später für das Architektenbüro Adler und Sullivan.
Wright quitte Madison pour aller à Chicago. Il est employé en premier lieu à l'agence de Joseph Lyman Silsbee et travaille plus tard pour l'agence d'architectes Adler et Sullivan.

1889 Wright marries Catherine Lee Tobin.
Wright heiratet Catherine Lee Tobin.
Wright épouse Catherine Lee Tobin.

Frank Lloyd Wright Residence, Oak Park, Illinois

1890 Wright is assigned all residential design handled by Adler and Sullivan.
Wright übernimmt alle Entwürfe für Wohnbauten im Büro Adler und Sullivan.
Wright se charge des plans des maisons d'habitation réalisées par Adler et Sullivan.

House for James Charnley, Ocean Springs, Mississippi
House for W. S. MacHarg, Chicago, Illinois
Cottage and Stable for Louis H. Sullivan, Ocean Springs, Mississippi

1891 Son Frank Lloyd Wright, Jr. born.
Geburt des Sohnes Frank Lloyd Wright jr.
Naissance de son fils Frank Lloyd Wright, Junior.

House for James Charnley, Chicago, Illinois

1892 Wright leaves offices of Adler and Sullivan. Son John Lloyd Wright born.
Wright verläßt das Büro Adler und Sullivan. Geburt des Sohnes John Lloyd Wright.
Wright quitte les bureaux de Adler et Sullivan. Naissance de son fils John Lloyd Wright.

House for George Blossom, Chicago, Illinois
House for W. Irving Clark, La Grange, Illinois
House for Robert Emmond, La Grange, Illinois
House for Thomas Gale, Oak Park, Illinois
House for Dr. Allison Harlan, Chicago, Illinois
House for Warren McArthur, Chicago, Illinois
House for Robert Parker, Oak Park, Illinois
House for Albert Sullivan, Chicago, Illinois
Victoria Hotel Remodelling, with office of Adler and Sullivan, Chicago Heights, Illinois

1893 Wright opens his own practice in Chicago, Illinois.
Wright eröffnet ein eigenes Büro in Chicago, Illinois.
Wright ouvre son propre bureau à Chicago, Illinois.

House for Walter Gale, Oak Park, Illinois
Cottage for Robert Lamp, Madison, Wisconsin
Lake Mendota Boathouse, Madison, Wisconsin
House and Stables for William H. Winslow, River Forest, Illinois
House for Francis Wooley, Oak Park, Illinois
Frank Lloyd Wright Playroom, Oak Park, Illinois

1894 First exhibition of Wright's work is held at the Chicago Architectural Club. Daughter Catherine Lloyd Wright born.
Der Chicago Architectural Club veranstaltet die erste Ausstellung von Wrights Arbeiten. Geburt der Tochter Catherine Lloyd Wright.
Première exposition des travaux de Wright au Chicago Architectural Club. Naissance de sa fille Catherine Lloyd Wright.

House for Frederick Bagley, Hinsdale, Illinois
Baptismal Font for Bagley Company, Chicago, Illinois
House Remodelling for Dr. H. W. Bassett, Oak Park, Illinois
House for Peter Goan, La Grange, Illinois
Four Houses for Robert Roloson, Chicago, Illinois

1895 Son David Samuel Wright born.
Geburt des Sohnes David Samuel Wright.
Naissance de son fils David Samuel Wright.

Francis Apartments for Terre Haute Trust Company, Chicago, Illinois
Francisco Terrace Apartments for Edward C. Waller, Chicago, Illinois
House for Nathan G. Moore, Oak Park, Illinois
Edward C. Waller Apartments, Chicago, Illinois
House for Chauncey Williams, River Forest, Illinois
Frank Lloyd Wright Studio, Oak Park, Illinois
House Remodelling for H. P. Young, Oak Park, Illinois

1896 Wright writes a credo entitled *Work Song*.
Wright schreibt ein Bekenntnis seiner Überzeugungen unter dem Titel *Work Song*.
Wright rédige un crédo intitulé *Work Song*.

House for H. C. Goodrich, Oak Park, Illinois
House for Isidore Heller, Chicago, Illinois
House Remodelling and Stables for Charles E. Roberts, Oak Park, Illinois
»Romeo and Juliet« Windmill Tower for Hillside Home School, Spring Green, Wisconsin

1897 Wright moves his office to Steinway Hall, Chicago.
Wright verlagert seine Büros in die Steinway Hall in Chicago.
Wright transporte son bureau au Steinway Hall, Chicago.

House for George Furbeck, Oak Park, Illinois
Boathouse for Henry Wallis, Lake Delavan, Wisconsin

1898 Daughter Frances Lloyd Wright born.
Geburt der Tochter Frances Lloyd Wright.
Naissance de sa fille Frances Lloyd Wright.

House for Rollin Furbeck, Oak Park, Illinois
River Forest Golf Club, River Forest, Illinois
House for George Smith, Oak Park, Illinois

1899 House for Joseph Husser, Chicago, Illinois
House Remodelling for Edward C. Waller, River Forest, Illinois

1900 House for William Adams, Chicago, Illinois
Garage for George Blossom, Chicago, Illinois
House for Harley Bradley, Kankakee, Illinois
House for Susan Lawrence Dana, Springfield, Illinois
Summer Cottage for Stephen A. Foster, Chicago, Illinois
House for Warren Hickox, Kankakee, Illinois
House Remodelling for E. R. Hills, Oak Park, Illinois
Boathouse for Fred B. Jones, Lake Delavan, Wisconsin
House Remodelling and Garage for Warren McArthur,
Chicago, Illinois
Summer Cottage for E. H. Pitkin, Sapper Island, Desbarats,
Ontario, Canada
Summer Cottage for Henry Wallis, Lake Delavan, Wisconsin

1901 Wright reads his lecture *The Art and Craft of the Machine* at
Hull House in Chicago.
Wright spricht über *The Art and Craft of the Machine* im Hull
House in Chicago.
Wright prononce son texte de conférence *The Art and Craft of
the Machine* à la Hull House de Chicago.

House for E. Arthur Davenport, River Forest, Illinois
House for William Fricke, Oak Park, Illinois
House Remodelling for Dr. A. W. Hebert, Evanston, Illinois
House for F. B. Henderson, Elmhurst, Illinois
House for Fred B. Jones, Lake Delavan, Wisconsin
River Forest Golf Club Additions, River Forest, Illinois
House for Frank Thomas, Oak Park, Illinois
Exhibition Pavilion for Universal Portland Cement Company,
Buffalo, New York
Poultry House, Stables and Gates for Edward C. Waller, River
Forest, Illinois
Gatehouse for Henry Wallis, Lake Delavan, Wisconsin
Stables for T. E. Wilder, Elmhurst, Illinois
House for Ward W. Willits, Highland Park, Illinois

1902 Delavan Yacht Club, Lake Delavan, Wisconsin
Double Cottage for George Gerts, Whitehall, Michigan
Cottage for Walter Gerts, Whitehall, Michigan
House for Arthur Heurtley, Oak Park, Illinois
House Remodelling for Arthur Heurtley, Les Cheneaux Club,
Marquette Island, Michigan
Hillside Home School Rebuilding, Spring Green, Wisconsin
House for Francis W. Little, Peoria, Illinois
House for William E. Martin, Oak Park, Illinois
House for Charles R. Ross, Lake Delavan, Wisconsin
House for George W. Spencer, Lake Delavan, Wisconsin

1903 Son Robert Llewellyn Wright born.
Geburt des Sohnes Robert Llewellyn Wright.
Naissance de son fils Robert Llewellyn Wright.

Abraham Lincoln Center for Jenkin Lloyd Jones, Chicago,
Illinois
House for George Barton, Buffalo, New York
House for Edwin H. Cheney, Oak Park, Illinois
House for W. H. Freeman, Hinsdale, Illinois
Barn, Stables and Gatehouse for Fred B. Jones, Lake Delavan,
Wisconsin
Larkin Company Administration Building, Buffalo, New York
Scoville Park Fountain, Oak Park, Illinois
House for J. J. Walser, Chicago, Illinois

1904 Wright attends the Louisiana Purchase Exposition in Saint
Louis.
Wright besucht die Louisiana Purchase Exposition in Saint
Louis.
Wright assiste à l'exposition-vente Louisiana de Saint Louis.

House for Robert M. Lamp, Madison, Wisconsin
House for Darwin D. Martin, Buffalo, New York
Unity Temple, Oak Park, Illinois

1905 Wright and his wife, Catherine, make their first trip to Japan,
accompanied by Wright's clients Mr. and Mrs. Ward Willits.
Wright begins collecting and dealing in Japanese prints.
Wright und seine Frau Catherine unternehmen in Begleitung
des Ehepaares Willits ihre erste Reise nach Japan. Wright
beginnt mit dem Sammeln und dem Handel mit japanischen
Drucken.
Wright et sa femme Catherine font leur premier voyage au
Japon, accompagnés de M. et Mme Ward Willits, clients de
Wright. Wright commence à collectionner et faire le com-
merce des estampes japonaises.

House for Mary M. W. Adams, Highland Park, Illinois
House for Hiram Baldwin, Kenilworth, Illinois
House for Charles E. Brown, Evanston, Illinois
Real Estate Office for E. A. Cummings, River Forest, Illinois
E–Z Polish Factory for William E. and Darwin D. Martin,
Chicago, Illinois
Three Summer Cottages for Mrs. Thomas Gale, Whitehall,
Michigan
House for T. E. Gilpin, Oak Park, Illinois
House for W. A. Glasner, Glencoe, Illinois
House for Thomas P. Hardy, Racine, Wisconsin
House for William R. Heath, Buffalo, New York
House for A. P. Johnson, Lake Delavan, Wisconsin
Lawrence Memorial Library, Dana House, Springfield,
Illinois
Gardener's Cottage for Darwin D. Martin, Buffalo, New York
River Forest Tennis Club, River Forest, Illinois
Rookery Building, Interior Remodelling, Chicago, Illinois
Bank for Frank L. Smith, Dwight, Illinois

1906 Wright exhibits his collection of Hiroshige prints at the Art
Institute of Chicago.
Wright stellt seine Sammlung von Hiroshige-Drucken im Art
Institute in Chicago aus.
Wright expose sa collection d'estampes Hiroshige au Art
Institute of Chicago.

House Remodelling for P. A. Beachy, Oak Park, Illinois
Garage Additions for George Blossom, Chicago, Illinois
House for K. C. DeRhodes, South Bend, Indiana
House for Grace Fuller, Glencoe, Illinois
House for A. W. Gridley, Batavia, Illinois
House for P. D. Hoyt, Geneva, Illinois
House for George Madison Millard, Highland Park, Illinois
House for Frederick Nicholas, Flossmoor, Illinois
Pettit Mortuary Chapel, Belvidere, Illinois
River Forest Tennis Club Rebuilding, River Forest, Illinois
House for Frederick C. Robie, Chicago, Illinois
House Remodelling for C. Thaxter Shaw, Montreal, Canada

1907 House for Avery Coonley, Riverside, Illinois
House Remodelling for Col. George Fabyan, Geneva, Illinois
Fox River Country Club Remodelling, Geneva, Illinois
House for Stephen M. M. Hunt, La Grange, Illinois
Larkin Company Exhibition Pavillion, Jamestown, Virginia
Emma Martin House Additions to the Fricke House, Oak
Park, Illinois
Pebbles and Balch Remodelled Shop, Oak Park, Illinois
»Tanyderi«, House for Andrew Porter, Hillside, Spring
Green, Wisconsin
House for F. F. Tomek, Riverside, Illinois
House for Barton J. Westcott, Springfield, Ohio

1908 German philosopher Kuno Francke meets with Wright in Oak
Park; the Wasmuth portfolio would be the result of this meet-
ing.
Wright trifft den deutschen Philosophen Kuno Francke in Oak
Park; aus diesem Treffen geht das Wasmuth-Portfolio hervor.

Le philosophe allemand Kuno Francke rencontre Wright à Oak Park; le carton à dessins Wasmuth serait le résultat de cette rencontre.

House for E. E. Boynton, Rochester, New York
Browne's Bookstore, Chicago, Illinois
Como Orchards Summer Colony, Darby, Montana
House for Walter V. Davidson, Buffalo, New York
House for Robert W. Evans, Chicago, Illinois
House for Eugene A. Gilmore, Madison, Wisconsin
House for L. K. Horner, Chicago, Illinois
House for Meyer May, Grand Rapids, Michigan
House for Isabel Roberts, River Forest, Illinois
House for Dr. G. C. Stockman, Mason City, Iowa

1909 Wright leaves his practice and family for Europe, accompanied by Mamah Borthwick Cheney.
Wright läßt Büro und Familie zurück, um in Begleitung von Mamah Borthwick Cheney nach Europa zu reisen.
Wright abandonne sa clientèle et sa famille pour aller en Europe avec Mamah Borthwick Cheney.

House for Frank J. Baker, Wilmette, Illinois
Bitter Root Inn, near Darby, Montana
City National Bank and Hotel, Mason City, Iowa
Robert Clark House Additions to the Little House, Peoria, Illinois
House Remodelling for Dr. W. H. Copeland, scheme 2, Oak Park, Illinois
House for Mrs. Thomas Gale, Oak Park, Illinois
House for Kibben Ingalls, River Forest, Illinois
House for Oscar M. Steffens, Chicago, Illinois
House for George Stewart, Montecito, California
Stohr Arcade and Shops, Chicago, Illinois
Thurber's Art Gallery, Fine Arts Building, Chicago, Illinois
Bathing Pavilion for Edward C. Waller, Charlevoix, Michigan

1910 Wright travels to Berlin and then to Fiesole. In Fiesole, Wright, son Lloyd, and others prepare the illustrations for *Ausgeführte Bauten und Entwürfe*, published that year in Berlin by Ernst Wasmuth.
Wright reist nach Berlin und anschließend nach Fiesole. Dort arbeitet er mit seinem Sohn Lloyd und anderen an den Illustrationen für das Buch *Ausgeführte Bauten und Entwürfe*, das im gleichen Jahr von Ernst Wasmuth in Berlin herausgegeben wird.
Wright se rend à Berlin, puis à Fiesole. C'est là que son fils Lloyd ainsi que d'autres préparent les illustrations du livre *Ausgeführte Bauten und Entwürfe* publié cette année à Berlin par Ernst Wasmuth.

House for J. H. Amberg, Grand Rapids, Michigan
Blythe-Markeley Law Office, City National Bank Building, Mason City, Iowa
House for E. P. Irving, Decatur, Illinois
Universal Portland Cement Company Exhibition Pavilion, Madison Square Garden, New York
House for Reverend J. R. Ziegler, Frankfort, Kentucky

1911 Wright begins building a new home and studio near Spring Green, Wisconsin. The complex is called Taliesin.
Wright beginnt mit dem Bau eines neuen Wohnhauses und Studios in der Nähe von Spring Green, Wisconsin. Die Anlage wird Taliesin genannt.
Wright commence la construction d'une nouvelle maison et d'un atelier près de Spring Green, Wisconsin. Le complexe reçoit le nom de Taliesin.

House for Herbert Angster, Lake Bluff, Illinois
Banff Park Pavilion, Banff National Park, Alberta, Canada

Playhouse, Gardener's Cottage and Stables for Avery Coonley, Riverside, Illinois
Lake Geneva Inn, Lake Geneva, Wisconsin
Taliesin I, Spring Green, Wisconsin
Taliesin Hydro House, Spring Green, Wisconsin
Oak Park Home and Studio Remodelling for Frank Lloyd Wright, Oak Park, Illinois

1912 Wright publishes *The Japanese Print: An Interpretation*.
Wright veröffentlicht das Buch *The Japanese Print: An Interpretation*.
Wright publie *The Japanese Print: An Interpretation*.

House for William B. Greene, Aurora, Illinois
»Northome«, House for Francis W. Little, Wayzata, Minnesota
Park Ridge Country Club Remodelling, Park Ridge, Illinois

1913 Wright visits Japan to secure the commission for the Imperial Hotel and to acquire Japanese prints for American clients.
Wright reist nach Japan, um den Auftrag für das Imperial Hotel zu vereinbaren und japanische Drucke für amerikanische Kunden zu erwerben.
Wright retourne au Japon pour assurer la commande de l'Hôtel Impérial et acquérir des estampes japonaises pour des clients américains.

House for Harry S. Adams, Oak Park, Illinois
Midway Gardens, Chicago, Illinois

1914 Julian Carlston kills Mamah Cheney and six others, then sets fire to Taliesin. Wright meets Miriam Noel.
Julian Carlston ermordet Mamah Cheney und sechs andere Personen und steckt anschließend Taliesin in Brand.
Julian Carlston tue Mamah Cheney et six autres personnes, puis incendie les bâtiments de Taliesin. Wright rencontre Miriam Noel.

1915 Wright opens an office in Tokyo.
Wright eröffnet ein Büro in Tokio.
Wright ouvre un bureau à Tokyo.

House for Emil Bach, Chicago, Illinois
House for Sherman Booth, Glencoe, Illinois
House for E. D. Brigham, Glencoe, Illinois
A. D. German Warehouse, Richland Center, Wisconsin
Imperial Hotel, Tokyo, Japan
Ravine Bluffs Bridge, Glencoe, Illinois
Ravine Bluffs Housing, Glencoe, Illinois

1916 House for Henry J. Allen, Wichita, Kansas
House for Joseph Bagley, Grand Beach, Michigan
House for Frederick C. Bogk, Milwaukee, Wisconsin
House for W. S. Carr, Grand Beach, Michigan
Imperial Hotel Annexe, Tokyo, Japan
Duplex Apartments for Arthur Munkwitz, Milwaukee, Wisconsin
Duplex Apartments for Arthur L. Richards, Milwaukee, Wisconsin
Small House for the Richards Company, Milwaukee, Wisconsin
House for Ernest Vosburgh, Grand Beach, Michigan

1917 American Homes (ARCS), Milwaukee, Wisconsin
»Hollyhock House« for Aline Barnsdall, Olive Hill, Los Angeles, California
House for Aisaku Hayashi, Tokyo, Japan
House for Stephen M. B. Hunt, Oshkosh, Wisconsin

1918 Wright goes to Peiping, China. He visits the monuments and art treasures as a guest of the writer Ku Hung Ming.
Wright reist nach Peiping in China. Dort besucht er Bauten und Kunstschätze als Gast des Schriftstellers Ku Hung Mings.
Wright va à Peiping en Chine. Il visite les monuments et les trésors artistiques et réside chez L'écrivain Ku Hung Ming.

House for Arinobu Fukuhara, Hakone, Japan
House for Tazaemon Yamamura, Ashiya, Japan

1920 »Residence A« and »Residence B« for Aline Barnsdall, Olive Hill, Los Angeles, California
Rebuilding of the Taliesin Hydro House, Spring Green, Wisconsin

1921 Jiyu Gakuen School, Tokyo, Japan
»Little Dipper« Kindergarten for Aline Barnsdall, Olive Hill, Los Angeles, California

1922 Wright opens an office in Los Angeles. Wright and Catherine are divorced.
Wright eröffnet ein Büro in Los Angeles. Scheidung von Catherine.
Wright ouvre un bureau à Los Angeles. Wright et Catherine divorcent.

1923 Kanto earthquake demolishes much of Tokyo. The Imperial Hotel survives. Wright publishes *Experimenting with Human Lives* concerning the earthquake and the Imperial Hotel. He marries Miriam Noel.
Das Erdbeben Kanto zerstört große Teile Tokios. Das Imperial Hotel bleibt unbeschädigt. Wright veröffentlicht das Buch *Experimenting with Human Lives* über das Erdbeben und das Imperial Hotel. Er heiratet Miriam Noel.
Le séisme Kanto démolit la majeure partie de Tokyo. L'Hôtel Impérial résiste aux secousses. Wright publie *Experimenting with Human Lives* qui concerne le tremblement de terre et l'Hôtel Impérial. Il épouse Miriam Noel.

House for Charles Ennis, Los Angeles, California
House for Samuel Freeman, Los Angeles, California
»La Miniatura«, House for Alice Millard, Pasadena, California
House Rebuilding for Nathan G. Moore, Oak Park, Illinois
House for John Storer, Los Angeles, California

1924 Wright meets Olgivanna Lazovich Hinzenburg.
Wright lernt Olgivanna Lazovich Hinzenburg kennen.
Wright rencontre Olgivanna Lazovich Hinzenburg.

1925 Second major fire occurs at Taliesin. Daughter Iovanna born to Frank Lloyd Wright and Olgivanna Hinzenburg.
Taliesin brennt zum zweiten Mal. Geburt von Jovanna, Tochter von Wright und Olgivanna Hinzenburg.
Deuxième incendie important à Taliesin. Naissance de Iovanna, fille de Wright et de Olgivanna Hinzenburg.

Taliesin III, Spring Green, Wisconsin

1926 The bank of Wisconsin takes title to Taliesin, due to Wright's indebtedness. Wright and Hinzenburg are arrested near Minneapolis for allegedly violating the Mann Act.
Die Bank von Wisconsin übernimmt Taliesin aufgrund Wrights Verschuldung. Wright und Hinzenburg werden in der Nähe von Minneapolis wegen angeblich unsittlichen Verhaltens festgenommen.
En raison de ses dettes, la banque acquiert un titre de propriété sur Taliesin. Wright et Hinzenburg sont arrêtés près de Minneapolis pour un prétendu outrage aux mœurs.

1927 Wright begins a series of articles under the heading *In the Cause of Architecture*, subsequently published in *The Architectural Record*. Wright divorces Miriam Noel Wright.
Wright schreibt eine Serie von Aufsätzen unter dem Titel *In the Cause of Architecture*, die monatlich in der Zeitschrift *The Architectural Record* veröffentlicht werden. Scheidung von Miriam Noel Wright.
Wright commence une série d'articles intitulée *In the Cause of Architecture*, publiée tous les mois dans la revue *The Architectural Record*. Wright et Miriam Noel divorcent.

»Greycliff«, House for Darwin D. Martin, Derby, New York
Ras-el-Bar, Vacation Cabins by the Sea, Damiette, Egypt

1928 Wright marries Olgivanna Hinzenburg.
Wright heiratet Olgivanna Hinzenburg.
Wright épouse Olgivanna Hinzenburg.

Arizona Biltmore Hotel, Phoenix, Arizona
»Ocotillo«, Frank Lloyd Wright Desert Compound and Studio, near Chandler, Arizona

1929 Work continues on projects for Chandler, but following the stock-market crash on October 29, these projects come to a halt.
Die Arbeit am Chandler-Projekt wird zunächst fortgesetzt, dann jedoch nach dem Börsenkrach am 29. Oktober abgebrochen.
Les travaux se poursuivent pour les projets de Chandler, puis sont interrompus lors du krach de la Bourse en 29 octobre.

Camp Cabins for the Chandler Land Improvement Co., Chandler, Arizona
House for Richard Lloyd Jones, Tulsa, Oklahoma

1930 Wright delivers the Kahn Lectures at Princeton University and publishes them under the title *Modern Architecture*.
Wright hält die Kahn-Vorlesungen an der Universität von Princeton und veröffentlicht sie unter dem Titel *Modern Architecture*.
Wright prononce une conférence sur les textes de Kahn à l'Université de Princeton et publie ces textes sous le titre de *Modern Architecture*.

1931 Exhibition of Wright's life work travels to New York City, Amsterdam, Berlin, Frankfurt, Brussels, Milwaukee, Eugene and Chicago.
Eine Ausstellung über das Lebenwerk Wrights ist in New York, Amsterdam, Berlin, Frankfurt, Brüssel, Milwaukee, Eugene und Chicago zu sehen.
L'exposition itinérante, présentant ses travaux réalisés jusqu'ici, se rend à New Work, Amsterdam, Berlin, Francfort, Bruxelles, Milwaukee, Eugene et à Chicago.

1932 The Wrights found the Taliesin Fellowship and convert the Hillside Home School buildings into the Taliesin Fellowship Complex. Wright publishes *An Autobiography* and *The Disappearing City*. Exhibition of Wright's work included in *The International Style* at The Museum of Modern Art, New York City.
Die Wrights gründen die Taliesin-Gemeinschaft und wandeln die Gebäude der Hillside Home School zur Gemeinschaftsanlage um. Wright veröffentlicht *An Autobiography* und *The Disappearing City*. Seine Arbeiten werden in die Ausstellung *The International Style* im Museum of Modern Art in New York aufgenommen.
Les Wright fondent la Communauté Taliesin et transforment l'école privée de Hillside, en Complexe de la Communauté.
Wright publie *An Autobiography* et *The Disappearing City*.
L'exposition des travaux de Wright est comprise dans *The International Style* au Museum of Modern Art, New York.

Taliesin Fellowship Complex, Hillside, Spring Green, Wisconsin

1933 Hillside Playhouse, Taliesin, Spring Green, Wisconsin
House for Malcolm Willey, Minneapolis, Minnesota

1934 Wright and apprentices begin construction of a scale model of Broadacre City. The first issue of *Taliesin*, a magazine founded by Wright is published by the Taliesin Press.
Gemeinsam mit Lehrlingen beginnt Wright, ein maßstäbliches Modell von Broadacre City zu bauen. Die erste Ausgabe des von Wright gegründeten Magazins *Taliesin* erscheint bei Taliesin Press.
Wright et ses élèves entreprennent la construction d'un modèle réduit de la Cité Broadacre. Le premier numéro de *Taliesin*, revue créée par Wright, est publié par les éditions Taliesin.

1935 The completed model of Broadacre City is exhibited at the Industrial Arts Exposition at the Rockefeller Center, New York.
Das Modell von Broadacre City wird bei der Industrial Arts Exhibition im Rockefeller Center in New York ausgestellt.
La maquette de la Cité Broadacre tout entière est présentée à l'exposition des arts industriels au Rockefeller Center à New York.

»Fallingwater«, House for Edgar J. Kaufmann, Bear Run, Pennsylvania

1936 »Honeycomb House« for Paul R. and Jean Hanna, Stanford, California
House for Herbert Jacobs, Westmoreland, Madison, Wisconsin
S. C. Johnson and Son Co. Administration Building, Racine, Wisconsin
»Deertrack«, House for Mrs. Abby Beecher Roberts, Marquette, Michigan

1937 Wright and author Baker Brownell write and publish *Architecture and Modern Life*.
Gemeinsam mit dem Autor Baker Brownell schreibt und veröffentlicht Wright *Architecture and Modern Life*.
Wright et l'auteur Baker Brownell écrivent et publient *Architecture and Modern Life*.

»Wingspread«, House for Herbert F. Johnson, Wind Point, Wisconsin
Office for Edgar J. Kaufmann, Kaufmann's Department Store, Pittsburg, Pennsylvania
House for Ben Rebhuhn, Great Neck Estates, New York
Taliesin West, Scottsdale, Arizona
Gift Booth for Frances Wright

1938 Wright designs the January issue of *Architectural Forum*, which is dedicated to his work and appears on the cover of *Time* magazine.
Wright gestaltet die Januar-Ausgabe der Zeitschrift *Architectural Forum*, die seiner Arbeit gewidmet ist. Wrights Bild erscheint auf dem Titel des Magazins *Time*.
Wright entreprend la réalisation graphique du numéro de janvier de *Architectural Forum* qui est consacré à son travail. Wright apparaît sur la couverture du *Time*.

House for L. N. Bell, Los Angeles, California (Project), executed for Joe Feldmann, Berkeley, California, 1976
Florida Southern College Master Plan for Dr. Ludd M. Spivey, Lakeland, Florida
Anne Pfeiffer Chapel, Florida Southern College, Lakeland, Florida

House for Ralph Jester, Palos Verdes, California (Project), executed for Arthur E. and Bruce Brooks Pfeiffer, Taliesin West, Scottsdale, Arizona, 1971
Guest House for Edgar J. Kaufmann, Bear Run, Pennsylvania
House for Charles L. Manson, Wausau, Wisconsin
Midway Barns and Farm Buildings, Taliesin, Spring Green, Wisconsin
House for John C. Pew, Madison, Wisconsin
Sun Top Homes for Otto Mallery and the Todd Company, Ardmore, Pennsylvania

1939 Wright is invited to London to deliver a series of lectures at The Sulgrave Manor Board. They are published as *An Organic Architecture*.
Wright wird nach London eingeladen, um eine Reihe von Vorträgen am Sulgrave Manor Board zu halten. Die Vorträge werden unter dem Titel *An Organic Architecture* veröffentlicht.
Wright est invité à Londres pour une série de conférences au Sulgrave Manor Board. Ces textes sont publiés sous le titre *An Organic Architecture*.

House for Andrew F. H. Armstrong, Ogden Dunes, Indiana
House for Sidney Bazett, Hillsborough, California
House for Joseph Euchtman, Baltimore, Maryland
House for Lloyd Lewis, Libertyville, Illinois
House for Rose and Gertrude Pauson, Phoenix, Arizona
House for Loren Pope, Falls Church, Virginia
House for Stanley Rosenbaum, Florence, Alabama
House for Bernard Schwartz, Two Rivers, Wisconsin
House for Clarence Sondern, Kansas City, Missouri
»Auldbrass«, House and Adjuncts for Leigh Stevens, Yemassee, South Carolina
House for George Sturges, Brentwood Heights, Los Angeles
House for Katherine Winckler and Alma Goetsch, Okemos, Michigan

1940 *The Work of Frank Lloyd Wright*, a major retrospective exhibition is held at The Museum of Modern Art, New York.
Das Museum of Modern Art in New York veranstaltet die große Retrospektive *The Work of Frank Lloyd Wright*.
Une importante exposition rétrospective *The Work of Frank Lloyd Wright* a lieu au Museum of Modern Art de New York.

House for Gregor Affleck, Bloomfield Hills, Michigan
House for Theodore Baird, Amherst, Massachusetts
House for James Christie, Bernardsville, New Jersey
Community Church, Kansas City, Missouri
Seminar Buildings, Florida Southern College, Lakeland, Florida
Gatehouse and Retreat for Arch Oboler, Malibu, California

1941 Wright and Frederick Gutheim publish *On Architecture*.
Gemeinsam mit Frederick Gutheim veröffentlicht Wright das Buch *On Architecture*.
Wright et Frederick Gutheim publient *On Architecture*.

Roux Library, Florida Southern College, Lakeland, Florida
House for Roy Petersen, Racine, Wisconsin (Project), executed for Haddock, Ann Arbor, Michigan, 1979
House for Stuart Richardson, Glen Ridge, New Jersey
»Snowflake«, House for Carlton D. Wall, Detroit, Michigan

1942 Industrial Arts Building, Florida Southern College, Lakeland, Florida

1943 Solomon R. Guggenheim Museum, New York, New York
Farm Unit for Lloyd Lewis, Libertyville, Illinois

1944 Hillside Theatre Foyer, Spring Green, Wisconsin
»Solar Hemicycle«, House for Herbert Jacobs, Middleton, Wisconsin
S. C. Johnson and Son Co. Research Tower, Racine, Wisconsin
Midway Barns, Farm Building at Taliesin, Spring Green, Wisconsin

1945 Wright publishes *When Democracy Builds*.
Wright veröffentlicht sein Buch *When Democracy Builds*.
Wright publie *When Democracy Builds*.

Administration Building, Florida Southern College, Lakeland, Florida
Lodge for Arnold Friedman, Pecos, New Mexico
Solomon R. Guggenheim Museum, revised scheme, New York, New York
House for Lowell Walter, Cedar Rock, Quasqueton, Iowa

1946 House for Albert Adelman, Fox Point, Wisconsin
House for Amy Alpaugh, Northport, Michigan
Esplanades, Florida Southern College, Lakeland, Florida
House for Douglas Grant, Cedar Rapids, Iowa
House for Chauncey Griggs, Tacoma, Washington
Additions to House for Paul R. and Jean Hanna, Stanford, California
Home Building Revision, Taliesin, Spring Green, Wisconsin
House for Dr. Alvin Miller, Charles City, Iowa
House for Herman T. Mossberg, South Bend, Indiana
House for Melvyn Maxwell Smith, Bloomfield Hills, Michigan

1947 House for Carroll Alsop, Oskaloosa, Iowa
House for Dr. A. H. Bulbulian, Rochester, Minnesota
Dairy and Machine Shed, Midway Barns, Taliesin, Spring Green, Wisconsin
Galesburg Country Homes, Galesburg, Michigan
Additions to Guest House for Edgar J. Kaufmann, Bear Run, Pennsylvania
Parkwyn Village Housing, Master Plan, Kalamazoo, Michigan
Unitarian Church, Shorewood Hills, Wisconsin
Usonia II Housing, Master Plan, Pleasantville, New York

1948 Additions to Sondern House for Arnold Adler, Kansas City, Missouri
House for Erling Brauner, Okemos, Michigan
House for Maynard Buehler, Orinda, California
House for Samuel Eppstein, Galesburg, Michigan
Water Dome, Florida Southern College, Lakeland, Florida
House for Sol Friedman, Usonia II, Pleasantville, New York
House for Jack Lamberson, Oskaloosa, Iowa
House for Robert Levin, Kalamazoo, Michigan
House for Curtis Meyer, Galesburg, Michigan
Gift Shop for V. C. Morris, San Francisco, California
House for Eric Pratt, Galesburg, Michigan
Additions to House for Stanley Rosenbaum, Florence, Alabama
Boathouse and River Pavilion for Lowell Walter, Quasqueton, Iowa
House for David Weisblatt, Galesburg, Michigan
House for Charles T. Weltzheimer, Oberlin, Ohio
Sun Cottage for Iovanna Lloyd Wright, Taliesin West, Scottsdale, Arizona

1949 House for Howard Anthony, Benton Harbor, Michigan
House for Eric Brown, Kalamazoo, Michigan
Cabaret Theatre, Taliesin West, Scottsdale, Arizona
House for James Edwards, Okemos, Michigan
House for Willis Hughes, Jackson, Mississippi

House for Kenneth Laurent, Rockford, Illinois
House for Ward McCartney, Kalamazoo, Michigan
House for Henry J. Neils, Minneapolis, Minnesota
House for Edward Serlin, Usonia II, Pleasantville, New York
House for Mrs. Clinton Walker, Carmel, California

1950 House for Robert Berger, San Anselmo, California
House for Raymond Carlson, Phoenix, Arizona
House for John O. Carr, Glenview, Illinois
House for Dr. Richard Davis, Marion, Indiana
House for S. P. Elam, Austin, Minnesota
House for John A. Gillin, Dallas, Texas
House for Dr. Ina Harper, St. Joseph, Michigan
House for John Haynes, Fort Wayne, Indiana
House for Thomas E. Keys, Rochester, Minnesota
House for Arthur Mathews, Atherton, California
House for Robert Muirhead, Plato Center, Illinois
House for William Palmer, Ann Arbor, Michigan
House for Wilbur Pearce, Bradbury, California
House for Don Schaberg, Okemos, Michigan
House for Seymour Shavin, Chattanooga, Tennessee
House for Richard Smith, Jefferson, Wisconsin
Southwest Christian Seminary for Peyton Canary, Glendale, Arizona (Project), executed for the First Christian Church, Phoenix, Arizona, 1973
House for Karl A. Staley, North Madison, Ohio
House for J. A. Sweeton, Cherry Hill, New Jersey
House for Robert Winn, Kalamazoo, Michigan
House for David Wright, Phoenix, Arizona
House for Isadore J. Zimmerman, Manchester, New Hampshire

1951 Wright and his apprentices design and construct an exhibition of Wright's work entitled *Sixty Years of Living Architecture*. The show opens at the Palazzo Strozzi in Florence. Wright opens West Coast office in San Francisco with Aaron Green, Associate.
Gemeinsam mit seinen Schülern entwirft und baut Wright eine Ausstellung zu seiner Arbeit mit dem Titel *Sixty Years of Living Architecture*, die im Palazzo Strozzi in Florenz eröffnet wird. In San Francisco eröffnet er zusammen mit seinem Partner Aaron Green eine Dependance.
Wright et ses élèves conçoivent et réalisent une exposition des travaux de Wright intitulée *Sixty Years of Living Architecture*, qui est organisée au Palazzo Strozzi à Florence. Wright ouvre avec son associé Aaron Green un bureau sur la Côte ouest, à San Francisco.

House for Benjamin Adelman, Phoenix, Arizona
House for Gabrielle Austin, Greenville, South Carolina
Summer Cottage for A. K. Chahroudi, Lake Mahopac, New York
House for W. L. Fuller, Pass Christian, Mississippi
House for Charles F. Glore, Lake Forest, Illinois
S. C. Johnson and Son Co., Additions, Racine, Wisconsin
House for Patrick Kinney, Lancaster, Wisconsin
House for Russell Kraus, Kirkwood, Missouri
House for Roland Reisley, Usonia II, Pleasantville, New York
House for Dr. Nathan Rubin, Canton, Ohio

1952 A fire partly destroys Wright's Hillside Home School buildings in Spring Green.
Ein Feuer zerstört einen Teil der Gebäude der Hillside Home School in Spring Green.
Un incendie détruit une partie des bâtiments de L'école privée de Hillside à Spring Green.

Anderton Court Shops, Beverly Hills, California
House for Quentin Blair, Cody, Wyoming
House for Ray Brandes, Issaquah, Washington
Hillside Theatre, Spring Green, Wisconsin

House for George Lewis, Tallahassee, Florida
House for R. W. Lindholm, Cloquet, Minnesota
House for Luis Marden, McLean, Virginia
House for Louis Penfield, Willoughby Hills, Ohio
House for Arthur Pieper, Paradise Valley, Arizona
Price Tower for the H. C. Price Company, Bartlesville, Oklahoma
House for Frank Sander, Stamford, Connecticut
Studio-Residence for Archie Teater, Bliss, Idaho

1953 Wright publishes *The Future of Architecture* and *In the Cause of Architecture*.
Er veröffentlicht *The Future of Architecture* und *In the Cause of Architecture*.
Wright publie *The Future of Architecture* et *In the Cause of Architecture*.

Cottage for Jorgine Boomer, Phoenix, Arizona
House for Andrew B. Cooke, Virginia Beach, Virginia
House for John Dobkins, Canton, Ohio
Music Building, Florida Southern College, Lakeland, Florida
Science and Cosmography Building, Florida Southern College, Lakeland, Florida
House for Lewis Goddard, Plymouth, Michigan
House for Harold Price, Jr., Bartlesville, Oklahoma
Riverview Terrace Restaurant, Spring Green, Wisconsin
»Sixty Years of Living Architecture« Exhibition Buildings, Los Angeles, California and New York, New York
House for William Thaxton, Houston, Texas
House for Robert Llewellyn Wright, Bethesda, Maryland

1954 Wright publishes *The Natural House*.
Wright veröffentlicht das Buch *The Natural House*.
Wright publie *The Natural House*.

House for E. Clarke Arnold, Columbus, Wisconsin
House for Bachman and Wilson, Millstone, New Jersey
Beth Sholom Synagogue, Elkins Park, Pennsylvania
House for Cedric Boulter, Cincinnati, Ohio
House for John E. Christian, West Lafayette, Indiana
House for Ellis Feiman, Canton, Ohio
Danforth Chapel, Florida Southern College, Lakeland, Florida
House for Louis B. Frederick, Barrington Hill, Illinois
House for Dr. Maurice Greenberg, Dousman, Wisconsin
House for I. N. Hagan, Chalkhill, Pennsylvania
Jaguar Showroom for Max Hoffman, New York, New York
House for Willard Keland, Racine, Wisconsin
»Grandma House« for Harold Price, Paradise Valley, Arizona
House for Gerald Tonkens, Cincinnati, Ohio
House for W. B. Tracy, Normandy Park, Washington
Guest House for David Wright, Phoenix, Arizona
Hotel Plaza Apartment Remodelling for Frank Lloyd Wright, New York, New York

1955 Dallas Theatre Center for Paul Baker, Dallas, Texas
House for Randall Fawcett, Los Banos, California
Solomon R. Guggenheim Museum, revised scheme, New York, New York
House for Max Hoffman, Rye, New York
House for Dr. Toufic Kalil, Manchester, New Hampshire
Kundert Medical Clinic, San Luis Obispo, California
House for Don Lovness, Stillwater, Minnesota
House for T. A. Pappas, St. Louis, Missouri
House for John Rayward, New Canaan, Connecticut
Remodelling of the Isabel Roberts House for Warren Scott, River Forest, Illinois
House for Robert Sunday, Marshalltown, Iowa
House for Dr. Dorothy Turkel, Detroit, Michigan

1956 Mayor Richard Daley of Chicago declares October 17 »Frank Lloyd Wright Day«.
Der Bürgermeister von Chicago, Richard Daley, erklärt den 17. Oktober zum »Frank-Lloyd-Wright-Tag«.
Le maire de Chicago, Richard Daley, proclame le 17 octobre le »Jour de Frank Lloyd Wright«.

Annunciation Greek Orthodox Church, Wauwatosa, Wisconsin
House for William Boswell, Cincinnati, Ohio
House for Frank Bott, Kansas City, Missouri
House for Allen Friedman, Bannockburn, Illinois
Solomon R. Guggenheim Museum, final revised scheme, New York, New York
Additions to House for Paul R. and Jean Hanna, Stanford, California
Lindholm Service Station, Cloquet, Minnesota
Clinic for Dr. Kenneth Meyers, Dayton, Ohio
Music Pavilion, Taliesin West, Scottsdale, Arizona
Remodelling of Frank Lloyd Wright's Oak Park Home and Studio for Clyde Nooker, Oak Park, Illinois
House for Dudley Spencer, Brandywine Head, Delaware
House for Dr. Paul Trier, Des Moines, Iowa
Wyoming Valley School, Wyoming Valley, near Spring Green, Wisconsin

1957 Wright is invited to Baghdad, Iraq, to design an opera house, cultural center, museum, university, and postal-telegraph building. Wright publishes *A Testament*.
Wright wird nach Bagdad eingeladen, um ein Opernhaus, ein Kulturzentrum, ein Museum, eine Universität und ein Telegrafenamt zu entwerfen. Wrights Buch *A Testament* erscheint.
Wright est invité à Bagdad, en Irak, afin de concevoir un opéra, un centre culturel, un musée, une université et un bâtiment des postes. Wright publie *A Testament*.

Clinic for Herman Fasbender, Hastings, Minnesota
House for C. E. Gordon, Aurora, Oregon
House for Sterling Kinney, Amarillo, Texas
Marin County Civic Center, San Rafael, California
Rayward Playhouse for Victoria and Jennifer Rayward, New Canaan, Connecticut
House for Carl Schultz, St. Joseph, Michigan
House for Dr. Robert Walton, Modesto, California
House for Duey Wright, Wausau, Wisconsin

1958 Wright publishes *The Living City*.
Wright veröffentlicht *The Living City*.
Wright publie *The Living City*.

House for Dr. George Ablin, Bakersfield, California
Juvenile Cultural Study Center, Building A, University of Wichita, Wichita, Kansas
Lockridge Medical Clinic, Whitefish, Montana
House for Paul Olfelt, St. Louis Park, Minnesota
Cottage for Seth C. Petersen, Lake Delton, Wisconsin
Cottage for Seth C. Petersen, Stillwater, Minnesota
Pilgrim Congregational Church, Redding, California
Additions to House for John Rayward, New Canaan, Connecticut
House for Don Stromquist, Bountiful, Utah

1959 Wright dies April 9.
Wright stirbt am 9. April.
Wright décède le 9 avril.

Grady Gammage Memorial Auditorium, Arizona State University, Tempe, Arizona
House for Norman Lykes, Phoenix, Arizona

CREDITS

All drawings and many of the vintage photographs included in this publication were kindly provided by the Frank Lloyd Wright Foundation in Scottsdale, Arizona.
Other illustrations come from the following institutions and photographers:

The Art Institute of Chicago, Chicago, Illinois: 16, 44, 54, 81

Bibliothek der Landesgewerbeanstalt, Nürnberg: 14, 17

Buffalo and Erie County Historical Society, Buffalo, New York: 60 o.

The Domino's Center for Architecture & Design, Ann Arbor, Michigan: 70, 71, 72/73, 76, 77

Esto/Ezra Stoller, Mamaroneck, New York: 84 o., 98, 99, 100, 114, 115, 124, 125, 128, 131, 135, 147, 148, 149, 150, 154, 155 o., 156, 157 o., 158, 172, 173
Esto/Wayne Andrews: 167 o.

Peter Gössel, Nürnberg: 53

David Heald copyright 1993 The Solomon R. Guggenheim Foundation, New York: front cover

Hedrich Blessing, Chicago, Illinois: 2, 78/79 o., 117

Christopher Little, New York, New York: 118, 119, 122, 123

Norman McGrath, New York, New York: 86, 87

The Metropolitan Museum of Art, New York, New York: 58, 60 u., 83

RETORIA, Yukio Futagawa & Associated Photographers, Tokyo, Japan: 8, 40, 45 o., 46/47, 51, 55, 62/63, 97, 112/113 o., 133, 138/139, 143, 162, 169 o., 174

Julius Shulman, Los Angeles, California: 104, 105, 152, 160, 161

USIS, Embassy of the United States of America, Bonn: 30, 36

Jeff Koons

1955 born in York (PA); lives and works in New York (NY), USA

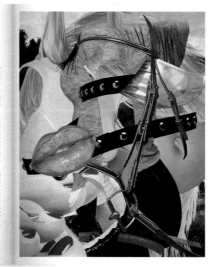

Jeff Koons can rightly be called the one of the most spectacular art-world icons of recent decades. As a self-made man, who used to finance his complex projects in New York by playing the stock market, he has become the promoter par excellence of his own provocative work. From an early age, Koons was attracted by America's folk art and Surrealism. Later, he combined these influences with the strategies of pop-art. His glamorous sculptures were inspired by the world of advertising, cheap kitsch and everyday objects. Not dull to flinch, in his 1991 *Made in Heaven* series of appearing in flagrante with his then-wife, the Italian porn star Ilona Staller, also known as "Cicciolina". What some saw as sabotage of the art business, others regarded as an expression of the optimism that pervaded during the economic boom of the 1980s. Despite all the scandals, Koons continued to be a great muralist, whose declared aim was to exploit the accessibility and popularity of his work to bring art to the masses. During the 1980s not a great deal was heard of Koons. But in autumn 1989 he returned to the scene with *Easyfun*, a series of large-format paintings and columns which shaped like the heads of cartoon animals. The *Easyfun* paintings are impressive and exuberant collages of advertising images and references to popular culture, like the body of breakfast cereal swirling around in a waterfall of milk in *Cut Out*. Here he sails pieces out of certain motifs and underlays them with outlandish images to create an eerie, surreal, psychedelic effect. Koons himself has defined *Easyfun*'s esoteric but calculated imagery as "baroque".

[German text paragraph]

[French text paragraph]

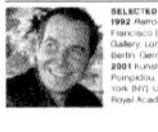

SELECTED EXHIBITIONS •
1992 Retrospective, San Francisco Museum of Modern Art, San Francisco (CA), USA 1993 A Survey 1981–1994, Aarhus (CFA), Gallery, London, UK 2000 *Easyfun—Ethereal*, Deutsche Guggenheim, Berlin, Germany
2001 Kunsthaus Bregenz, Au-Weil-Le spectacle Dance Georges Pompidou, Paris, France Pop and War Museum of Modern Art, New York (NY), USA Apocalypse: Beauty and Horror in Contemporary Art, Royal Academy of Arts, London, UK Greek Ster Serpentine

SELECTED BIBLIOGRAPHY •
1992 Jeff Koons, Cologne 2000 Jeff Koons, *Easyfun—Ethereal*, Deutsche Guggenheim, Berlin *Hypermoral* Hahnemühle Verlag Basel 1999–2000, Iron Liberator Dali Art Jeff Koons, Kunsthaus Zürich, Zürich 2001 Jeff Koons, Kunsthaus Bregenz, Au-Weil-Le spectacle Centre Georges Pompidou, Paris

Gallery/Konrad & Mart Museum, London, UK

Featured Art Newspaper information on Jeff Koons

Representation
Gagosian Gallery
555 West 24th Street
USA – New York, NY 10111
tel: +1 212 741-1111
fax: +1 212 741-9611
www.gagosian.com

Galerie Max Hetzler
Zimmerstraße 90/91
D – 10117 Berlin
tel: +49 (0)30 229-2437
fax: +49 (0)30 229-2417
www.maxhetzler.com

Sonnabend Gallery
532 West, 22nd Street
USA – New York, NY 10111
tel: +1 212 627-1018
fax: +1 212 627-0489

Collections
Baltimore Museum of Art, USA
capcMusee d' Art Contemporain, Bordeaux, France
Des Moines Art Center, USA
Deutsche Guggenheim Berlin, Germany
Groninger Museum, Groningen, The Netherlands
Guggenheim Museum, Bilbao, Spain
Hirschhorn Museum and Sculpture Garden, Washington D.C., USA
Kunstmuseum Wolfsburg, Germany
Metropolitan Museum, Tokyo, Japan
Milwaukee Art Museum, USA
Museum Boijmans Van Beuningen, Rotterdam, The Netherlands
Museum Ludwig, Cologne, Germany
Museum of Contemporary Art, Chicago, USA
Nationalgalerie im Hamburger Bahnhof, Museum für Gegenwart, Berlin, Germany
San Francisco Museum of Modern Art, USA
Staatsgalerie Stuttgart, Germany
Stedelijk Museum, Amsterdam, The Netherlands
Tate Gallery, London, UK
The Museum of Contemporary Art, Los Angeles, USA
The Museum of Modern Art, New York, USA
The National Gallery, Washington D.C., USA
Whitney Museum of American Art, New York, USA
Wright State University Art Museum, Dayton, USA

Price Range
$10,000 (multiples); $150,000 – $3,000,000 (other works); several million for monumental sculpture

Auction Sales
Price: $5,100,000
Michael Jackson and Bubbles, 1988
porcelain ceramic blend, num. 3/3, 107 x 179 x 83 cm
Date Sold: 15-May-01
Auction House: Sotheby's, New York

Price: $2,600,000
Woman in tub, 1988
porcelain, num. 1/3, 62 x 91 x 69 cm
Date Sold: 17-May-01
Auction House: Christie's, Rockefeller NY

Price: $1,700,000
Ushering in banality
polychromed wood, num. 2 of 3, 96 x 157 x 76 cm
Date Sold: 14-Nov-01
Auction House: Sotheby's, New York

Price: $1,650,000
Pink Panther, 1988
porcelain, num. 3/3, 104 x 52 x 48 cm
Date Sold: 16-Nov-99
Auction House: Christie's, New York

Price: $1,550,000
Woman in tub, 1988
Porcelain, num. 3/3, 157 x 23 x 175 cm
Date Sold: 16-May-00
Auction House: Christie's, Rockefeller NY

Franz Ackermann	Tacita Dean	Damien Hirst	Aernout Mik	Elizabeth Peyton	Thomas Struth
Doug Aitken	Thomas Demand	Carsten Höller	Jonathan Monk	Paul Pfeiffer	Superflex
Darren Almond	Rineke Dijkstra	Jonathan Horowitz	Mariko Mori	Daniel Pflumm	Fiona Tan
Pawel Althamer	Mark Dion	Gary Hume	Sarah Morris	Richard Phillips	Vibeke Tandberg
Kai Althoff	Peter Doig	Pierre Huyghe	Vik Muniz	Paola Pivi	Wolfgang Tillmans
Francis Alÿs	Keith Edmier	Christian Jankowski	Muntean/Rosenblum	Peter Pommerer	Rirkrit Tiravanija
Ghada Amer	Olafur Eliasson	Mike Kelley	Takashi Murakami	Neo Rauch	Grazia Toderi
Miriam Bäckström	Elmgreen & Dragset	Rachel Khedoori	Yoshitomo Nara	Navin Rawanchaikul	Luc Tuymans
Matthew Barney	Tracey Emin	Karen Kilimnik	Mike Nelson	Tobias Rehberger	Piotr Uklański
John Bock	Ayşe Erkmen	Bodys Isek Kingelez	Shirin Neshat	Jason Rhoades	Kara Walker
Cosima von Bonin	Malachi Farrell	Martin Kippenberger	Ernesto Neto	Daniel Richter	Jeff Wall
Monica Bonvicini	Sylvie Fleury	Jeff Koons	Rivane Neuenschwander	de Rijke/de Rooij	Franz West
Candice Breitz	Ceal Floyer	Udomsak Krisanamis		Pipilotti Rist	Pae White
Olaf Breuning	Tom Friedman	Elke Krystufek	Olaf Nicolai	Ugo Rondinone	T. J. Wilcox
Glenn Brown	Ellen Gallagher	Oleg Kulik	Manuel Ocampo	Thomas Ruff	Johannes Wohnseifer
Daniele Buetti	Kendell Geers	Jim Lambie	Albert Oehlen	Gregor Schneider	Richard Wright
Angela Bulloch	Liam Gillick	Zoe Leonard	Chris Ofili	Cindy Sherman	Cerith Wyn Evans
Janet Cardiff	Dominique Gonzalez-	Atelier van Lieshout	Henrik Olesen	David Shrigley	Andrea Zittel
Merlin Carpenter	Foerster	Won Ju Lim	Gabriel Orozco	Santiago Sierra	Heimo Zobernig
Maurizio Cattelan	Felix Gonzalez-Torres	Sharon Lockhart	Laura Owens	Dirk Skreber	
Jake & Dinos Chapman	Douglas Gordon	Sarah Lucas	Jorge Pardo	Andreas Slominski	
Martin Creed	Andreas Gursky	Michel Majerus	Philippe Parreno	Yutaka Sone	
John Currin	Fabrice Gygi	Paul McCarthy	Manfred Pernice	Eliezer Sonnenschein	
Björn Dahlem	Thomas Hirschhorn	Jonathan Meese	Dan Peterman	Simon Starling	

Martin Creed

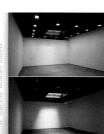
Rineke Dijkstra

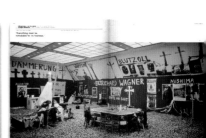

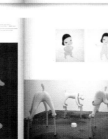
Keith Edmier

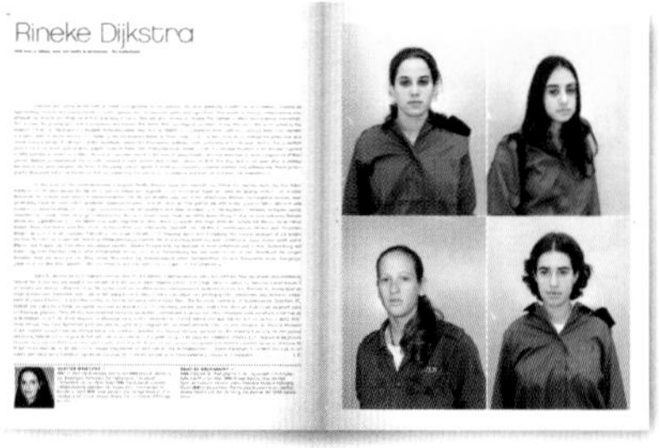

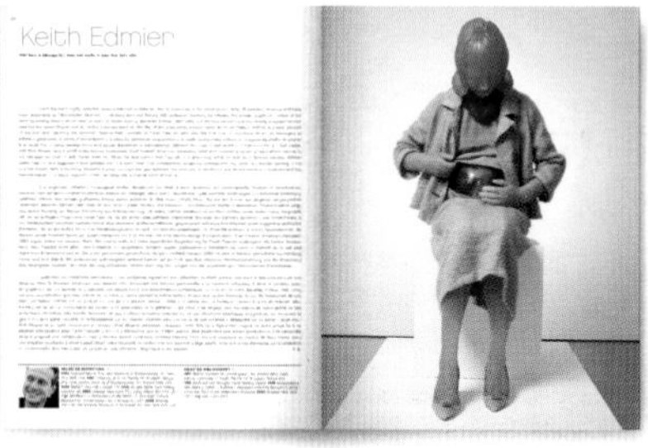

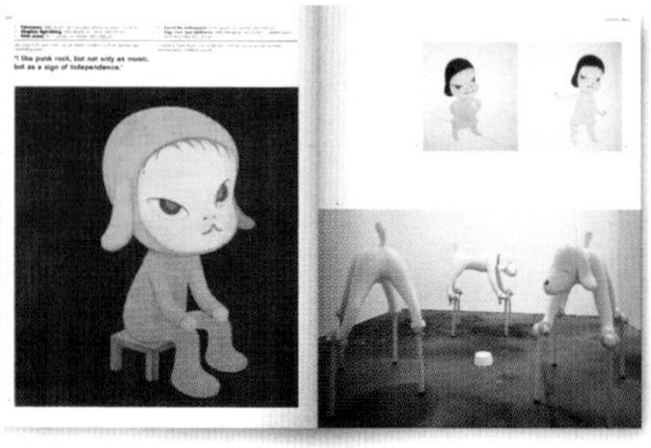

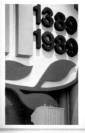

Who, what, when, where, and how much $$$

Contemporary art in a nutshell

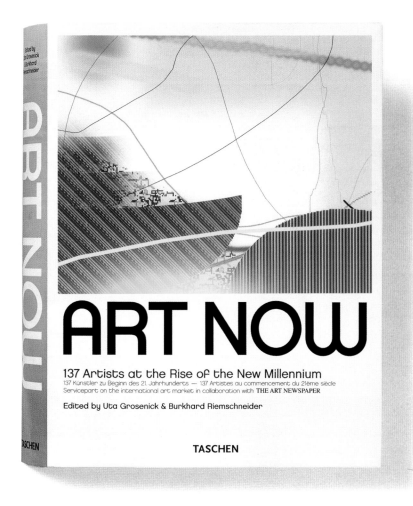

ART NOW

137 Artists at the Rise of the New Millennium
137 Künstler zu Beginn des 21. Jahrhunderts — 137 Artistes au commencement du 21ème siècle
Servicepart on the international art market in collaboration with THE ART NEWSPAPER

Edited by Uta Grosenick & Burkhard Riemschneider

TASCHEN

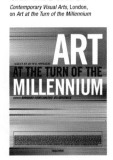

Dear Taschen,
I love your book *Art at the Turn of the Millennium* but it's been a few years now and the art scene changes so fast these days. How about an updated and expanded version? I would like to learn not only who are the hottest artists working today, but also how to work the art scene like a pro, and how to shop for art without looking like a novice. Could you make a new book like this, just for me?
Thanks,
Harry L.

Dear Harry,
We've been working hard on your request and think you'll be pleased with the result. Enclosed is the spanking-new *Art Now*, in which you'll find the most recent work and updated biographical information for our revised selection of today's 150 most influential artists. *Art Now* also includes a completely new section—a sort of "service guide"—produced in collaboration with *The Art Newspaper* which lists museums, restaurants, and hotels we recommend you check out while you're cruising the global art scene, and even gives the scoop on how much one can expect to pay for a Damien Hirst or a Sharon Lockhart and whom to contact if you decide to buy. We also let you know useful details like how many prints Wolfgang Tillmans made for a certain edition and what sorts of sums big players like Koons, Sherman,

and Struth bring in at auction. **Think of it as an indispensable reference book, travel guide, and art market directory all rolled into one**.
We hope you like it, and thanks for writing!
Love, TASCHEN

P.S. This book actually turned out quite good, so we've decided to publish it. We hope you don't mind.

Art Now Ed. Burkhard Riemschneider / Uta Grosenick
English/German/French edition / Japanese/English/French edition /
Italian/Spanish/Portuguese edition / Flexi-cover, format: 19.6 x 24.9 cm
(7.6 x 9.8 in.), 640 pp. / US$ 40 / £ 20 / € 32 / ¥ 4.500

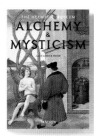

Alchemy & Mysticism
The Hermetic Museum / Alexander Roob / Flexi-cover,
Klotz, 712 pp. / US$ 30 / £ 17 / € 24 / ¥ 3.800

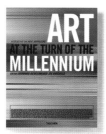

Art at the Turn of the Millennium
Ed. Burkhard Riemschneider, Uta Grosenick / Flexi-cover,
576 pp. / US$ 40 / £ 20 / € 32 / ¥ 4.500

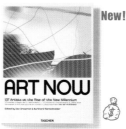

New!

Art Now
Ed. Burkhard Riemschneider, Uta Grosenick / Flexi-cover,
640 pp. / US$ 40 / £ 20 / € 32 / ¥ 4.500

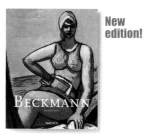

New edition!

Beckmann
Reinhard Spieler / Flexi-cover, 200 pp. /
US$ 15 / £ 13 / € 16 / ¥ 3.000

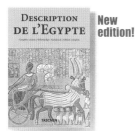

New edition!

Description de l'Egypte
Gilles Néret / Hardcover, Klotz, 1008 pp. /
US$ 19.99 / £ 9.99 / € 12.99 / ¥ 2.500

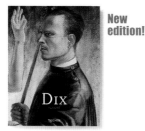

New edition!

Dix
Eva Karcher / Flexi-cover, 216 pp. /
US$ 15 / £ 13 / € 16 / ¥ 3.000

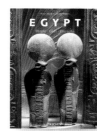

New edition!

Egypt
Rose-Marie & Rainer Hagen / Flexi-cover, 240 pp. /
US$ 15 / £ 13 / € 16 / ¥ 3.000

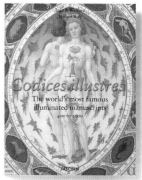

Codices illustres. The world's most famous illuminated manuscripts
Ed. Ingo F. Walther / Hardcover with vellum jacket, 504 pp. /
US$ 60 / £ 40 / € 60 / ¥ 6.500

"The one book you want if you are interested in illuminated manuscripts —and once you open it, you will be. [An] exceptionally handsome book.... Run, don't walk."
—*The Wall Street Journal*, New York

Timetunnel to the 15th century:

1493's must-have history book and city guide

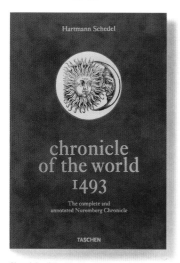

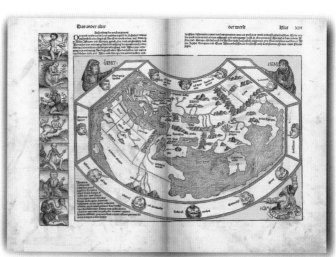

Chronicle of the World—1493
Hartmann Schedel
Stephan Füssel / Padded cover, 688 pp. /
US$ 60 / £ 40 / € 60 / ¥ 6.500

"... ist Schedels 'Weltchronik' gewiß das den heutigen Leser faszinierendste Buch vor 1500. Daß es nun wohlfeil unters Volk kommt (frühere Faksimile-Drucke kosteten noch um die 2000 Euro), ist eine bildungsgeschichtliche Sensation." —*Die Presse*, Wien

"... schon das Gefühl, die ... 3,5 kg schwere Neuausgabe der Schedel'schen Weltchronik im weichen braunen Samteinband in Händen zu halten, ist die wahre Freude —und die steigt beim Blättern in dem ehrwürdigen Zeugnis früher Druckkunst sogar noch an. Natürlich hat der TASCHEN-Verlag für sein Faksimile der berühmten 'Nürnberger Chronik' ... eine besonders schön kolorierte Vorlage gewählt. Freuen wir uns über den überaus hochwertigen und preiswerten Nachdruck!" —*Nordbayerischer Kurier*, Bayreuth

"An extraordinary facsimile at a remarkably reasonable price."
—*United Press International*, USA

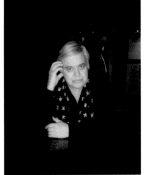

H.R. Giger, Zurich, 2000

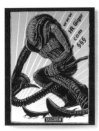

www HR Giger com
HR Giger / Hardcover, 240 pp. /
US$ 30 / £ 17 / € 20 / ¥ 3.800

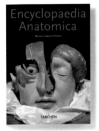

Encyclopaedia Anatomica
Museo La Specola, Florence / M. von Düring, M. Poggesi,
G. Didi-Huberman / Flexi-cover, Klotz, 704 pp. /
US$ 30 / £ 17 / € 24 / ¥ 3.800

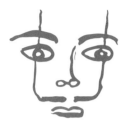

Art—all titles

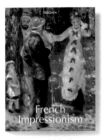

French Impressionism
Peter H. Feist, Ed. Ingo F. Walther / Hardcover, 440 pp. /
US$ 40 / £ 25 / € 32 / ¥ 5.000

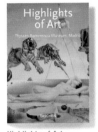

Highlights of Art
Thyssen-Bornemisza Museum, Madrid / Teresa Pérez-Jofre
Flexi-cover, Klotz, 768 pp. / US$ 30 / £ 17 / € 24 / ¥ 3.800

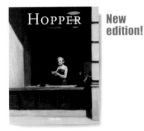

New edition!

Hopper
Ivo Kranzfelder / Flexi-cover, 200 pp. /
US$ 15 / £ 13 / € 16 / ¥ 3.000

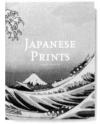

New edition!

Japanese Prints
Gabriele Fahr-Becker / Flexi-cover, 200 pp. /
US$ 15 / £ 13 / € 16 / ¥ 3.000

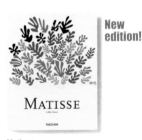

New edition!

Matisse
Gilles Néret / Flexi-cover, 256 pp. /
US$ 15 / £ 13 / € 16 / ¥ 3.000

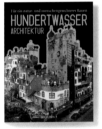

Hundertwasser Architecture
Ed. Angelika Taschen / Hardcover, 320 pp. /
US$ 40 / £ 25 / € 32 / ¥ 5.000

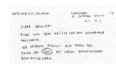

"Dear Philippi, thank you for the regards
and for the dummy. I'm working hard.
Now I'm already at number 400, with a lot of
fantastic little stories for the image captions."
—fax from Hundertwasser to TASCHEN vice
editor-in-chief Simone Philippi, 1998

Hundertwasser sent over 3,500 faxes during the
preparation of the book

Hundertwasser
–his complete works

**This edition, the last book created by
Friedensreich Hundertwasser, includes:**

* Two volumes in a slip case designed by Hundertwasser,
  lavishly printed in ten colors on rounded, black-edged pages
* Hundertwasser's original layout design
* 1.792 pages and over 2.000 illustrations, documenting
  Hundertwasser's life and œuvre from 1928 to 2000, with many
  personal notes and comments by the artist
* An original 24 x 20 cm color etching (9.4 x 7.9 in.),
  specially created for this edition, numbered and marked
  with the Hundertwasser estate stamp
* Limited edition of worldwide 10.000 copies
* US$ 750 / £ 500 / € 750 / ¥ 90.000

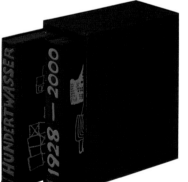

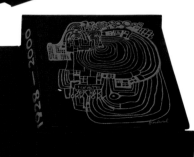

**Subscription price
until November 1, 2002:
£ 350 / € 500**

**Outside Europe until
January 1, 2002:
US$ 500 / ¥ 60.000**

The Lucky Seven: classic reference books, new size – small price!

"An extraordinary bargain"

—*The Sunday Times*, London

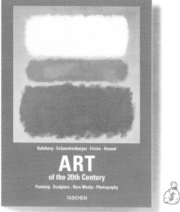

Art of the 20th Century
K. Ruhrberg, M. Schneckenburger, C. Fricke, K. Honnef /
Ed. Ingo F. Walther / Flexi-cover, 840 pp. /
US$ 40 / £ 20 / € 32 / ¥ 4.500

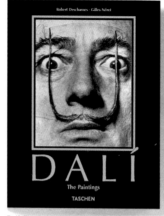

Dalí. The Paintings
Robert Descharnes, Gilles Néret / Flexi-cover, 780 pp. /
US$ 40 / £ 20 / € 32 / ¥ 4.500

"And while the end of the 20th century might not give us much occasion for celebration, in celebrating this book we can all agree." —*Süddeutsche Zeitung*, Munich, on *Art of the 20th Century*

"Bound to become the standard reference work."
—*Le Figaro*, Paris, on *Dalí*

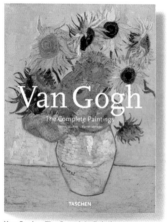

Van Gogh – The Complete Paintings
Rainer Metzger, Ed. Ingo F. Walther / Flexi-cover, 740 pp. /
US$ 40 / £ 20 / € 32 / ¥ 4.500

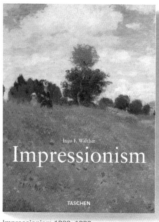

New edition!

Impressionism 1860–1920
Ed. Ingo F. Walther / Flexi-cover, 712 pp. /
US$ 40 / £ 20 / € 32 / ¥ 4.500

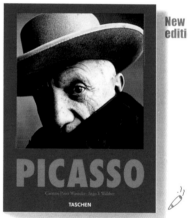

New editi

Picasso
Carsten-Peter Warncke / Ed. Ingo F. Walther / Flexi-cover, 740 pp. /
US$ 40 / £ 20 / € 32 / ¥ 4.500

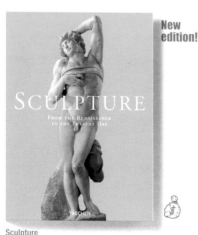

New edition!

Sculpture
Georges Duby / Hardcover, 1.184 pp. /
US$ 30 / £ 17 / € 25 / ¥ 3.000

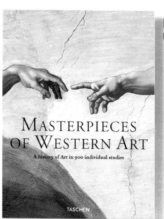

New edition!

Masterpieces of Western Art
Ed. Ingo F. Walther / Flexi-cover, 768 pp. /
US$ 40 / £ 20 / € 32 / ¥ 4.500

"... the definitive introduction to the scope and range of Picasso's work."
—*The Times*, London, on *Picasso*

"... nine expert writers present over 900 pictures analyses ranging from Giotto to Jean-Michel Basquiat, born 1960.
The period from Gothic to the present is divided into ten chapters with detailed introductions, directed at advanced museum-goers but also painless reading for lay readers ...
536 potted biographies in the appendix make a reference work of this fine compendium." —*art*, Hamburg, on *Masterpieces of Western Art*

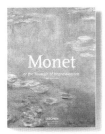

Monet or the Triumph of Impressionism
Daniel Wildenstein / Ed. Gilles Néret / Hardcover, 480 pp. /
US$ 40 / £ 25 / € 32 / ¥ 6.500

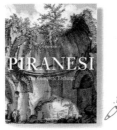

Piranesi. The Complete Etchings
Luigi Ficacci / Flexi-cover, 800 pp. /
US$ 40 / £ 20 / € 32 / ¥ 4.500

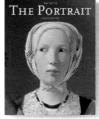

New edition!

The Portrait
Norbert Schneider / Flexi-cover, 192 pp. /
US$ 15 / £ 13 / € 16 / ¥ 3.000

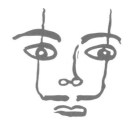

Art—all titles

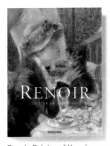

Renoir. Painter of Happiness
Gilles Néret / Hardcover, 440 pp. /
US$ 40 / £ 25 / € 32 / ¥ 5.000

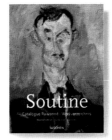

Soutine – Catalogue Raisonné
M. Tuchman, E. Dunow, K. Perls / Ed. Ingo F. Walther /
Hardcover, 780 pp. / US$ 50 / £ 30 / € 32 / ¥ 6.500

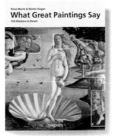

What Great Paintings Say
Rose-Marie & Rainer Hagen / Hardcover, 500 pp. /
US$ 40 / £ 20 / € 32 / ¥ 5.000

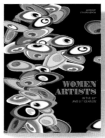

Women Artists
Ed. Uta Grosenick / Flexi-cover, 576 pp. /
US$ 40 / £ 20 / € 32 / ¥ 4.500

"... Ce superbe ouvrage présente les artistes les plus marquantes du XX et du XXI siècle par le biais de leurs œuvres, souvent surprenantes. A découvrir."
—*Le Vif / L'express*, Bruxelles

"Perhaps this year's most unusual book"
—*Town & Country*, USA, on *Cabinet of Natural Curiosities*

"A vast and beguiling tome... Any one of the reproductions... could be framed as a picture in its own right." —*The Times*, London, on *Cabinet of Natural Curiosities*

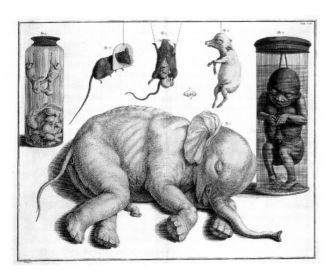

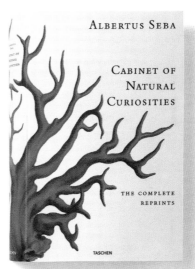

New price: January 1, 2003: US$ 200 / £ 135 / € 200 / ¥ 25.000

"This is an extraordinary and beautiful book, stuffed with information. TASCHEN has reproduced the entire set of plates—449 in all— from a hand-coloured Dutch edition. The price is high, but the alternative is to save up for a plate or two and chase round the auction rooms (...). There's no question that people will want it. While it sat on my desk at *New Scientist*, everyone who spotted it offered to give it a home."
—*The New Scientist*, London, on *Cabinet of Natural Curiosities*

Albertus Seba. Cabinet of Natural Curiosities
Irmgard Müsch, Jes Rust, Rainer Willmann / Hardcover, 588 pp. /
US$ 150 / £ 100 / € 150 / ¥ 20.000

"This is a massive book. It is also, probably, one of the most beautiful you are ever likely to see... Fortean Times verdict: Academic Publishing at its glorious best. 10 out of 10."
—*Fortean Times*, London, on *Cabinet of Natural Curiosities*